Ted Schwartz is the author or co-author of approximately 70 books which fall into a range of categories as diverse as true crime, business, popular psychology, biography and history. He lives in Cleveland, Ohio.

by the same author

True Crime

Deadly Whispers
False Arrest
The Hillside Srangler

WHEN THE DEVIL COMES TO VISIT

Ted Schwartz

ARROW

Published by Arrow Books in 1995

1 3 5 7 9 10 8 6 4 2

© Ted Schwartz 1995

The right of Ted Schwartz has been asserted
under the Copyright, Designs and Patents
Act, 1988 to be identified as the author of this
work

First published in the United Kingdom by
Arrow Books Limited
20 Vauxhall Bridge Road, London SW1V 2SA

Random House Australia (Pty) Limited
20 Alfred Street, Milsons Point, Sydney,
New South Wales 2061, Australia

Random House New Zealand Limited
18 Poland Road, Glenfield,
Auckland 10, New Zealand

Random House South Africa (Pty) Limited
PO Box 337, Bergvlei 2012, South Africa

Random House UK Limited
Reg. No. 954009

A CIP catalogue record for this book is
available from the British Library

Papers used by Random House UK Limited
are natural, recyclable products made from
wood grown in sustainable forests. The manufacturing processes conform to the environ-
mental regulations of the country of origin.

ISBN 0 09 932851 8

Printed and bound in Great Britain by
BPC Paperbacks Ltd, a member of
The British Printing Company Ltd.

CHAPTER 1

In the last half of the twentieth century, Los Angeles has led the nation in defining pop culture. The clothing Hollywood designers create for film stars to wear on the screen frequently begins fashion fads with greater speed and more intense loyalty than the most ingenious and widely publicized Parisian couturiers. Car designers seek suggestions and test concept vehicles in Los Angeles, knowing that if one is popular there, eventually it will be popular throughout the nation. Even murder has a unique West Coast style – The Hillside Strangler, The Green River Slayer, The Sunset Slasher, The Night Stalker, and numerous other demons of the night have gained recognition as much for where they committed their crimes as the ways in which they did them.

It is not that serial murder is unique to Los Angeles or the western United States. Most large cities have been plagued by men and, occasionally, women who poison, garrotte, shoot, slash, and otherwise murder over and over again. Such serial killers are unable or unwilling to stop what they do. The death of others becomes a part of their lifestyle. The regular taking of a life is as important and relaxing for them as the average person's routine poker game, bowling league, softball game, or jazzercise class. And they are as likely to pursue their obsession on the East Coast, the Midwest, the Rockies, the Plains, or anywhere else they are living.

But there is something about post-World War II California that seems to attract the most ingenious of the nation's serial killers. In fact, though serial killers have plagued the world for centuries, it was not until Harvey Glatman came up with the novel idea of using personal ads and legitimate modeling agencies to locate his victims that law enforcement began to understand what happens when the devil comes to town.

Harvey Glatman was a quiet man, self-employed, a repairman of television sets. It was 1950, and even in Los Angeles, California, the new technology was not in very many homes. What sets existed were large, cumbersome, expensive, and usually had to be repaired in the owner's house or apartment. Service work of this nature required an outgoing personality and the skill necessary to leave a satisfied customer. Repair shops often succeeded by word of mouth, and Harvey's business was very prosperous.

Approximately six years after Glatman's business became a success, he decided that he needed a hobby from which he could also make money. That was when he turned to photography, investing in cameras, lights, a tripod, and other expensive tools of the profession. He owned enough equipment to operate a small studio, and eventually converted one of the rooms of his home into just such a venture.

During the same period when Harvey turned to photography, there were extensive opportunities for free-lancers to make modest sums of money selling cover and inside illustration photographs to what were called 'pulp' magazines. Printed on low quality (pulp) paper, the publications ranged from working class male oriented magazines (Blue Book For Men, True, etc.) to confession magazines (True Story, Modern Romances, True Confessions) to true crime publications (Confidential Detective, Real Detective, True Detective, Headquarters Detective). Their target audience was the 'low brow' reader, the individual who had no more than a high school education yet loved short stories.

Both fiction and non-fiction pulps were aimed primarily towards a male audience. All of these used two types of illustrations – posed photographs (a happy couple, a pretty girl, a 'crime' in progress) and pen and ink drawings. The latter might show women in tattered clothes chained inside a cave, an American GI single-handedly about to save them from their sadistic SS guards. The photographs purchased for little money from new professionals ranged from color images for the outside – a pretty girl smiling on the cover of the confessions, or a 'crime in progress' for the detective magazines – to an occasional black-and-white inside photo of a nicely dressed couple embracing romantically or that same couple engaged in criminal activity. Since several publishers produced both types of magazines, photographers learned to hire a pair of models for a session that would produce images for both.

The models who worked for the pulps were invariably unknowns, reflecting the low pay for such work. Yet the idea of being a cover girl, or the subject of an article illustration, was so appealing that there were always more young women willing to pose than photographers seeking their services. They all saw such work as an important stepping stone to a full time career. The fact that few of them succeeded in reaching their dreams meant little. Just as there were always far more 'wannabe' actresses in Hollywood than roles in the movies, everyone focused on the one or two exceptions whose stories became legends.

For example, a girl named Norma Jean Baker posed for 'cheesecake' pictures (low cut blouses, short shorts, and an emphasis on her legs) used in some of the pulp magazines of the late 1940s. While she did not appear on confession and crime magazines, she was used in popular pulp magazines that combined pretty girl images with jokes. One of the avid readers was billionaire Howard Hughes who wanted to date her after seeing her picture in the cartoon and joke magazine he loved. She eventually changed her name and became known to the world as Marilyn Monroe.

Most young models knew that Norma Jean/Marilyn was the exception. But they willingly did whatever the photographers asked in the hope that they, too, would be another exception whose story could become the next great legend of pulp magazine modeling.

The other reason young women were so willing to pose for the pulps was because there were not many other ways to break into modeling in the Los Angeles of the 1950s. There were fashion and runway models working for department stores and clothing manufacturers. There were models for undergarments, though these jobs were usually in manufacturing centers such as New York, and the work was not respected. And there were jobs posing for the pictures in pulp magazines.

In Los Angeles, where Harvey Glatman was establishing himself as a photographer, the greatest amount of freelance work for aspiring models came from the pulps. Since the pay was also low for the photographer, young women trying to enter the field did not think it strange when Harvey Glatman, a man with a makeshift studio and limited experience, claimed to be working for some of the true detective magazines.

Harvey Glatman had acquired a minor reputation as a serious photographer when, on August 1, 1957, he approached 19-year-old Judy Dull about posing for pulp magazine covers. Photography was expensive in those years, and studio costs could be prohibitive. Rental studios equipped with seamless paper backdrops, changing rooms for the models, and either floodlights or electronic flash units were available by the hour. Agencies specializing in beginning models found the bulk of their clients from among the men who used such rental studios. And when both the young women and the photographers gained some experience, many of them continued working together to produce catalog advertising, newspaper ads, and the like.

Since Glatman had both rented studios and hired agency models in the past, he was considered legitimate. No one realized that he fantasized an even deadlier scenario than was portrayed on the covers of the detective magazines. And no one suspected that, with Judy Dull, an inexperienced model, he was about to act it out.

Judy Dull never hesitated about letting Harvey Glatman tie her up. He was successful enough to no longer have to rent studio space. He was posing her in the studio he had built in his home, and only the more prosperous among the new photographers she had heard about were able to do that. The next step was to rent a larger facility in the downtown area where he would specialize in commercial photography, and if she was lucky, he could be her ticket to success.

Judy was relaxed as Harvey Glatman secured her wrists together behind her back, then had her sit while he bound her ankles. Even when he took a cloth and tied it around her mouth to gag her, she did not object. The camera was there. The lights were ready. She was physically helpless for the photographs he was about to take, but she still thought she was in control of the rest of her life.

And then she saw the gun . . .

Ken Bianchi had a different style. Tall, handsome, outgoing and personable, he had a variety of jobs, from driving an ambulance, to working in an office, to training to become a security guard.

Ken had known an emotionally difficult life, his father dying when he was nine, and his first wife leaving him after an affair with a cousin for whom he worked in Rochester, New York. He was 'too romantic,' she said by way of explanation when he finally talked with her after returning from his job to an empty home. Without alerting him that there was trouble with their relationship, she had stripped their apartment of all belongings and filed for divorce.

The only happiness Ken knew was with Kelly Boyd, a woman he met in Los Angeles, then followed to her home state of Washington. They had a son together, but he was shattered when she, too, left him. This time there was no other man. She felt he was too immature for her. She resented the fact that he seemed to be stealing from his employer, a discount department store chain. And she wanted some distance, to see if not being with the son he loved would shock him into becoming the type of man she could respect.

Ken seemed to handle the pain well. He made friends easily. He threw himself into work, taking overtime assignments. But in private, the pressures of relationship problems became too great. A dozen female victims, ranging in age from 13 to 28, were scattered about the Los Angeles hillsides. And in Bellingham, the last two victims met their deaths before Ken was finally arrested for serial murders.

Ken Bianchi's murder spree began almost exactly 20 years after that of Harvey Glatman. The change in the United States during that period was extraordinary. Glatman was despised, and while newspapers delighted in showing the bondage photos he took before murdering the three women who were known to have been his victims, the public responded with revulsion. His execution in 1958 was swift and without public protest. He had raped and strangled, as Bianchi would do a generation later, and death was determined to be the only proper sentence.

The reaction to Bianchi was dramatically different. When I first arranged to interview the serial killer in his jail cell, I had trouble getting an appointment. His normal visiting hours were filled with a steady stream of women admirers, including a bright, beautiful woman who worked for the Playboy organization. Some claimed to be curious. Some claimed he was innocent. Some declared undying love for him. And one, Veronica Lynn Compton, whose story is told later in this book, was willing to commit a look-alike murder to ensure his release. Eventually one of his fans married him.

Yet Ken Bianchi raped and killed an estimated 17 females. He said that when you kill a 'cunt,' you make the world a better place.

Bianchi was also offered a hundred thousand dollars for his story and those of his mother and girlfriend. Norman Mailer was said to have been approached by a packager to write the book. A movie of the week would be made, and allegedly Bianchi's family would be allowed to have influence concerning the screenplay. It was the type of celebrity contract normally reserved for movie stars, rock singers, and popular politicans. To his credit he turned it down, he, Kelly, and Ken's mother telling their stories without remuneration. But the fact that the offer was made, that the money would have been paid had the family agreed, was a remarkable change in public attitudes.

In the twenty years between Glatman and Bianchi, serial murder had become a means to fame. And today, Charles Manson is writing popular music from jail. John Wayne Gacy was a sought after prison artist whose clown pictures are a constant reminder of his avocation during the time he killed 33 men and boys. And movies about such psychopaths remain a staple of prime time television.

Part of the fascination with serial killers is the fact that they are the ultimate bogey men. Usually male, frequently intelligent, and almost always likeable individuals, they could be anyone's neighbor, anyone's friend, anyone's beloved husband, brother, son, or father. They may belong to fraternal organizations. They may routinely pray in churches or synagogues. They may be active in the local parent-teacher organization at their children's school. When confronted with reality after the arrest of a serial killer, co-workers and neighbors frequently say, 'But he was so nice.' And the truth is that he was pleasant to everyone except his victims.

Americans want their monsters to be 18 feet tall and fire breathing. They want to see an outer expression of the inner capacity for violence. They want to be able to cross the street, leave the neighborhood, or change their job so neither they nor their families are at risk. They want anything except to have to worry about a possible dark side to the nice guy next door, in the classroom, or in the office. Since serial killers are so much like everyone else except for their drive to violence, we protect ourselves from the fear of the unknown by turning them into celebrities. We know movie stars are average people with above average talent and luck, but we never expect to personally encounter one. Perhaps we attended high school with someone who now is a regular on television, whose picture is in *People* and the *National Enquirer*. But high school was long ago and we feel that their lives will never again interact with ours.

The same is true with serial killers. We glamorize their existence because, if they are as famous as movie stars, we feel assured that we will never directly encounter one. The world of the celebrity is not our world. We will only be terrified from afar.

Yet with serial killers, unlike movie stars, life is not

so simple. That is why there is so much terror combined with so much seemingly irrational appeal when the 'devil' comes to town.

Americans are rather sexist about their serial killers. There are women who feel compelled to murder over and over again, yet they are rarely labeled serial killers. Perhaps this is because women tend to be more subtle. Men often prolong the agony with bondage and torture, or take great delight in angrily mutilating the corpse. Women are more direct, such as the retirement home owner who used poison to gently end the lives of guest after guest. Yet because Americans don't wish to see such deadly compulsions in their women, they call the women 'poisoners' or 'multiple murderers.' Any term other than what they are – females who are serial killers. Yet the truth is that some of the most brilliant killers in history have been women.

In the United States, for example, serial killer Amy Archer Gilligan is politely called a greedy poisoner. Yet the truth is that she was a compulsive murderer who could not stop regardless of any other rewards she might gain from the deaths of her clients. She was the proprietor of the Archer Home For The Elderly And Indigent (some sources call it the Archer Home For Elderly People) in Windsor, Connecticut, a business founded with her first husband, James H. Archer, in 1907.

The concept of the home was a simple one. Most of the residents had no family, though whether or not there were living relatives was never a concern. They were all old, but their health was so good that they had no idea how much life was left to them. They were worried about finances, worried about quality care. As a result, they were happy to pay a one time fee of as much as $1,500 in order to receive lifetime room, board, and nursing if necessary. The payment assured them

9

peace of mind. Their ages were such that no one would be suspicious when they died.

Archer's husband was among the first to go, Amy killing him in 1910. She remarried in 1913, but that husband, Michael Gilligan, lasted only a few months. Then, on May 30, 1914, Amy made her only mistake. Resident Franklin R. Andrews, a man in excellent health, took ill following his evening meal, dying within hours. The doctor was summoned, but he found a robust individual whose only problem had been gastric ulcers, not something that could cause sudden death. The corpse was of a man too healthy to have died from natural causes.

Amy, it was learned, had purchased a massive quantity of arsenic from a local pharmacist. The pharmacist would later claim he thought she needed to poison rats, though the amount was such that the worst city rodent plagues could have been stopped with the amount he innocently sold her. This poison was used to take the lives of her boarders.

The exact number of victims was uncertain. Amy was watched closely for two years prior to her arrest. It was noted that from 1907, when the home was opened, until 1910, only 12 boarders died. From 1911 to 1916, at least 48 deaths could be attributed to Amy. There was only circumstantial evidence to convict Amy in 1917, though that evidence was considered overwhelming. However, because she maintained the position that she was a churchgoer, a nurse, and loving caregiver, she won a retrial in June, 1919. It was only at that time that she confessed to her crimes, and was imprisoned for life.

Amy Archer was merely following in the tradition of many European serial killers when she chose to poison her victims. For example, arsenic had been the favorite poison used by Marie de Brinvilliers of Paris, France, who began her killing spree in 1664 when she was 34 years old. Like so many of the European murderers of the seventeenth century, the time of a great many female serial killers, she was a woman of immense wealth.

Marie was born Marie Madeleine d'Aubray in Paris on July 22, 1630. Her father, Antoine Dreux d'Aubray, was the Civil Lieutenant of Paris. When she married in 1651, she and her husband, the very wealthy Antoine Gobelin de Brinvilliers, had an annual income of $250,000.

Marie and her husband enjoyed all the pleasures money could buy, including lovers, jewels, clothes, servants, and the chance to gamble. She was a small woman, thin and beautiful, who was often described as having expressive blue eyes. She also was an amateur chemist who delighted in creating her own poisons. Starting with an arsenic base, she would mix whatever seemed likely to enhance its killing power. Then she would take her latest creation to the Hotel Dieu, the Paris hospital for the poor and downtrodden. There she would bring them food, wine, and her latest samples of poison to make certain they worked. Between 50 and 100 people died at her hands, though no one suspected her of such murder.

Once perfected, the poisons were used to kill friends, family members, and others for whom she had a disliking. For example, in 1659 she took Gaudin de Sainte-Croix as her lover. He was a respected, married cavalry officer, and their mutual adultery was discovered by her father who had Sainte-Croix thrown into the Bastille on March 19, 1663. Marie vowed revenge, and from January through September 10, 1666, Marie carefully administered 27 separate doses of poison to her father. The quantity was small enough so that there would never be adequate traces for autopsy detection. It was large enough so that his health steadily declined.

After her father's death, Marie discovered that his will favored her two brothers, so she immediately poisoned them. Then she decided to marry her lover who, by then, was released from the Bastille. The facts of what happened next are uncertain. It is believed that Marie let Sainte-Croix know she was poisoning her husband. It is also believed that Sainte-Croix had no interest in marrying his sex partner, and managed to slip Marie's husband the antidote for the poison. Whatever the case, the husband lived and Sainte-Croix died in July, 1672.

During this period, Marie's personal assistant, Jean Hamelin (known as La Chaussée), was investigated for the poisoning of Marie's family. He was arrested and tortured, confessing Marie's actions before he died. She then fled to a convent in Liège where she thought she was safe from the law. However, an officer disguised himself as a visiting abbé, visiting her, then asking her to go outside for a walk. Feeling safe with a man of the cloth, she stepped outside the convent walls, immediately losing all legal protection. She was immediately arrested, then allowed to write her confession before she was executed four years, almost to the day, after her lover's death.

While lacking the financial resources of Marie, a contemporary of hers, Catherine Deshayes of Paris, greatly exceeded even her murderous abilities. Deshayes had greater motivation, though, for she and her husband, Antoine Monvoisin, were trying to recover from a failed business.

Catherine Deshayes, who was born at some time in the 1640s, came from humble origins. Fortunately for her ambitions, the social prestige of one's family was not the best way to be accepted by society's elite. What mattered was one's financial success, and new money was as acceptable as wealth that had been inherited over several generations. A poor woman who could succeed in business would have access to the rich and famous of the day.

Antoine Monvoisin was a small businessman who tried to support his new wife by selling cheap jewelry in the Paris square. When that failed, Catherine suggested he open a shop, thinking a permanent location might attract more customers. Unfortunately he was even less successful with that business, and the couple was facing poverty.

Catherine Deshayes decided that, if they were to eat, she would have to do whatever was necessary to bring income to the family. She had an interest in the occult and opened a business providing potions and advice to the gullible and the cut-throat. She told fortunes, made prophecies, and soon became popular with the aristocracy. When she added the sideline of arranging abortions, high born women, often pregnant by the wrong man, were anxious to use her services.

It is not known when Deshayes first discovered her compulsion to kill. What is known is when she arranged her first murder. Marguerite Leferon, one of her customers, confided that she was bored with her husband, a judge, who was 'insufficient' in bed. Money changed hands, a potion was provided, and the judge died on September 8, 1669.

Delighted with her new widowhood, Leferon discretely spread the word concerning Deshayes' special help with problem lovers and spouses. Soon she had acquired a regal clientele and wealth beyond her wildest dreams. The Duke of Buckingham, the Duchesse de Vivonne, the Duchesse de Bouillon, the Duc of Luxembourg, and others graced her shop.

Deshayes did not like, however, being a vicarious purveyor of death when she could enjoy the first hand pleasure of the kill. As with most serial killers, she discovered a compulsion within her that was not satisfied with merely supplying the means for murder. Since she already had a reputation for her occult activities, it was not difficult to find a few fanatics who would join her for black masses.

These black masses were excuses for murder. Sometimes pregnant women were kidnapped, their babies delivered, and the babies' throats slashed while lying on their mothers' still breathing bodies. At other times she would buy babies for bread. Starving peasants often sold their children to the wealthy, gaining food for their own survival and ensuring a better future for their children. Some of the starving peasants may have known the children would be killed, but if they did, nothing was said. Whatever the case, all the infants were slaughtered.

The number of deaths kept mounting, and eventually her activities were discovered by the authorities. On December 27, 1679, there was a knock at Catherine's door. By then she had murdered a minimum of 2,500 adults and children, either directly or through her business. She was wealthy and respected by all except King Louis XIV who arranged her arrest. There was no question of her guilt, and on February 22, 1680, after being allowed to get drunk, she was tied to a stake and burned to death.

In an intriguing footnote, the arrest preceded by a day an appointment that obviously could not be kept. This was with the Marquise de Montespan, King Louis' favorite mistress. She had grown bored with her lover and had planned to break off the relationship with poison. Had the king delayed the arrest by as little as 24 hours, he could have been another of her victims.

The most gruesome of seventeenth-century female serial killers was also its first, having been born in 1560 and not coming to trial until 1611. This was Elizabeth Bathory, a Hungarian, whose story was probably the original source for the legend of Dracula.

Elizabeth Bathory came from a family of nobility and

insanity. Her mother, Anna, was sister to the King of Poland. Her father, Gyorgy, was a soldier. They were so prominent that when she married Ferencz Nadasdy on May 8, 1575, she retained the Bathory name to preserve its status. What went unspoken though whispered by all who knew was that the Bathory family, though elevated, was comprised of sadists who tortured their servants, Satan worshippers, open practitioners of incest, lesbians, drunks, and murderers.

Elizabeth and Ferencz moved into the Castle Csejthe in northwest Hungary. It was a large structure, and because Ferencz frequently had to travel, Elizabeth Bathory had the castle redesigned for her comfort. Among other changes, she installed a torture chamber so she could indulge her more violent whims.

Elizabeth had difficulties getting pregnant, not giving birth until she was 25, ten years after she married. Her mother-in-law ridiculed her, and the two women were constantly at odds. To make life more difficult, she also suffered from epilepsy, having occasional seizures and severe headaches.

At first Elizabeth's servants helped her indulge in hedonistic pleasures meant to ease her emotional pain. They helped Elizabeth change her clothing and jewelry five or six times a day. They made cosmetics to adorn her face, then carefully applied them to her skin as she studied herself in the mirror.

The mistress/servant relationship turned hostile when Elizabeth could no longer stand her mother-in-law's nagging. Instead of being satisfied with the servants indulging her every whim, she began hitting them and sticking pins in their flesh. Some she smeared with honey, then restrained them in places where they would be covered with ants and bees.

The servants feared fighting back, and a few decided to help Elizabeth find an alternative for her torturous rage. They began seeking young peasant girls who could be brought into the castle with the promise of a job, or drugged and kidnapped when all else failed.

Elizabeth became bloodthirsty in ways amost beyond imagination. Her husband discovered what she was doing but did not stop her hobby (He died in either 1600 or 1604, the date being in question). He had begun taking mistresses and did not want to be thwarted. Besides, he thought some of her actions were fun and occasionally joined her.

The tortures were numerous. The peasant girls were jabbed with needles, knives, and red hot pokers. They were also whipped, and pins were inserted in numerous sensitive areas of their bodies. She did everything she could imagine would cause intense agony without proving fatal.

Ultimately there were to be no witnesses. When it was time to kill the torture victims, some were taken outside into the snow, restrained, and covered with cold water until they froze. Another favorite trick was to use a cylindrical cage she invented. There were sharp iron spikes protruding from the back, then a platform in front where the victim could stand safely. The victim would get on the platform, being careful to not move back far enough to be stabbed. Then the cage would be raised off the ground to ensure that jumping would be fatal. Finally hot pokers were used to prod the victim back into the spikes. If the victim was lucky, death would be instantaneous. Usually the victim would move about enough to suffer a series of wounds and burns before dying.

The tortures increased in intensity. One victim had a strip of flesh removed, then was forced to grill and eat it before being killed.

Eventually the peasants learned to protect their daughters. They became witnesses after the fact to what had been going on because the corpses were burned, sending up tell-tale smoke, left to rot in areas where the foul odor was unmistakable, or thrown over the castle walls at night, to be found the next day. Forewarned, the peasants hid their daughters or refused to cooperate with the servants when they came looking for new castle 'employees.' As a result, Elizabeth's servants had to find other victims, eventually selecting higher type women with connections to King Matthias. Suddenly the secret horrors of the castle became public knowledge. He arranged for Bathory's nearest neighbor, Count Thurzo, to stage a night raid on the castle and Elizabeth was caught in the act of murder.

The trial took place in 1611, Elizabeth being held accountable for only 80 murders. Half a dozen of her servants were separately tried, all of them convicted and executed. But rapid death was considered the wrong punishment for Bathory. Instead, she was walled in her apartment, the only connection with the outside being a series of slits, some for ventilation, and some for passing through food. She was to never again speak with another human being, nor was she provided with anything to pass the time.

It was August 21, 1614, when the guards decided that plates of food visible through the slits had been untouched for too many days. They broke through the wall and found her corpse. It was not known when she died.

The historic serial killers were gruesome, seemingly far deadlier than the contemporary men and occasional women who are compelled to murder again and again. Yet history has recorded the serial killers of Europe as horrifying deviants, people whose very existence seem to be rare exceptions when studying the lives and deaths of our ancestors. No one ever glorified Elizabeth Bathory and the others. No one ever made them the subject of movies of the week, comic books, and trading cards as has been done with contemporary serial killers.

17

No one ever interviewed them as a means of popular entertainment. No one ever expressed joy in loving them.

It can be argued that serial killing has become the most popular form of non-sports entertainment in America at the end of the twentieth century. News reporters and editors love to have a serial killer loose in their communities. Natural disasters are big, dramatic, and end within seconds (an earthquake), minutes (major storms), or hours (major fires and floods). Teams of writers and photographers blanket the area where the event occurred, recording the havoc, then documenting the aftermath. There are the tearful families who have lost their homes and possessions, the joyous reunions of parents and children separated by the crisis, and the hope filled stories of community rebuilding. But the major drama, the disaster that makes for an exciting visual opportunity, does not last.

Serial killers provide excitement for what may be weeks or months of coverage. Each newly discovered corpse, each special task force, each exclusive interview with the horrified family and friends of the victims brings new opportunities to dominate the ratings. Special reports saturate the nightly news. Newspapers provide weekly recaps of the mounting terror in the community. Even advertising increases as self-defense schools, weapons dealers, and other businesses capitalize on the fear that grips the city.

Small town reporters fantasize that their reports will lead them to jobs on big city newspapers, radio and television stations. Big city reporters await the Pulitzer Prize, a local broadcast Emmy, or some similar reward.

Law enforcement officers are equally enticed. Uniformed patrol officers try to solve serial killings in order to jump start their careers as homicide detectives. Homicide detectives, early in such cases, see a solution as the key to promotion and bonuses. And both the police chief and other top law enforcement personnel often see a quick resolution as their ticket to a run for political office.

Sometimes the cases become a game. Some members of Mensa, the organization for people with genius level IQs, have carefully studied the identity of the murderer known as Zodiac, identifying by name the person they feel is the killer. Yet until a friend of one of the members turned over the documents to law enforcement, few, if any, who saw the material, had apparently thought to turn the "game" into reality by supplying the details to investigators. (At this writing it is believed by the professionals that the person named is either the killer or someone who fits accurately enough to need to be eliminated as a suspect.)

And sometimes a cottage industry is created by the serial killer and/or those who are around him. Jeffrey Dahmer, Milwaukee, Wisconsin's most unusual gourmand (he murdered and ate dark skinned males), has a father who earned a reported $150,000 advance for writing a book about his son, and a defense counsel who is selling Jeffrey's possessions in order to pay bills.

The world of the serial killer is broader and more fascinating than the men and women who are driven to commit murder over and over again. And it is this world that will be explored in the following chapters.

CHAPTER 2

The Harvey Glatman case introduced the idea of serial killing to law enforcement officers. There had been serial murderers in the United States in the past, many of them reported on the pages of such lurid tabloids as *The Police Gazette*. But the Glatman case was the first time that law enforcement took a serious look at a man who felt compelled to kill over and over again. The way Glatman selected his victims and committed his crimes was so unusual that police for the first time realized they needed a new way to stop such killers.

Los Angeles homicide detective Pierce Brooks was the man who handled the investigation of what, at first, seemed to be unrelated murder cases. The deaths occurred in different locations at a time when there seemed no reason for the various police jurisdictions to share information. As a result of Brooks's work, not only was Glatman arrested, the concept of profiling serial killers was first developed.

Harvey Murray Glatman had no intention of making history when he was a boy growing up in Denver, Colorado. He was skinny, bright, and wore thick glasses. Today he would be considered a 'nerd.' Back then, in the 1930s and early 1940s, he was the brunt of jokes by both boys and girls. The only person who seemed to matter in his life was his mother, an elderly widow who both dominated and indulged him. She had no sense of proportion with her son, and when her unwillingness to say no to his actions led him to get into trouble with other children or at school, she tried to protect him from any consequences. He both resented the woman and used her as a buffer against the social maturity needed to get along in adult society.

As a teenager, Glatman led a secret fantasy life involving issues of sex, violence, and control. He liked playing with rope, learning knots that would restrain and nooses that could kill. His sexual fantasies involved both bondage and violence. He either never tried to develop a normal dating relationship with a girl or was turned down each time he approached someone in his high school. Whatever the case, at 17 he took a realistic looking toy revolver, got in a car, and drove to Boulder, Colorado, determined to lose his virginity by force if necessary.

Harvey's sexual coming of age could not have occurred at a worse time. The year was 1945, and with the wars in both Europe and Asia winding down, boys who had been soldiers were returning home to the girls they left behind. A skinny kid like Harvey, too young to have been drafted or enlist, was looked upon with disdain. He was just another local kid, not a man who has seen the world. The Denver girls ignored him as they ignored most other boys in his class, a fact he did not notice nor would he have cared about if he did. He wanted to have sex, and he was certain that in Boulder he could achieve his desires. Not only would he be a stranger who could create whatever history he wanted for himself if it would impress the girl, he also had the gun if necessary.

Glatman followed first one and then another teenaged girl, hoping to get someone alone. Eventually he located a girl who was walking along an otherwise deserted side street. He stopped his car, pointed his gun, and ordered her to take off her clothes. Instead of freezing in terror and obeying his command, the girl screamed, ran, and got the police. Glatman was arrested soon afterwards.

Glatman's mother paid for his bail. The girl had been untouched, the gun had been a toy, and the bail was low. Had he gone to court, he probably would have been given probation. But Harvey had no intention of ending up in court and his mother seemed to feel that losing the bail money was a small price to pay for protecting her son. As soon as he was released, he immediately left the state, moving to New York City to live.

Harvey had been occasionally snatching purses when he lived in Denver. He was good enough to never be identified or caught, and he decided to try a variation of that career in New York. Instead of running up and grabbing someone's handbag, he switched to robbery, using a gun and becoming as excited by the fear in his victims' eyes as he was by the money he was taking.

The money he could earn from robbing was unpredictable, so Harvey took up burglary, a business where he had no skill whatever. He was quickly discovered while breaking and entering, arrested, and sentenced to five years in Sing Sing (Ossining, New York).

Glatman was a model prisoner, not surprising since his only violent tendencies were towards women. The prison was all male, and with an intelligence measured at 130, just a few points below what was considered genius level, he learned how to adjust his behavior to stay friendly with both prisoners and guards. He also began to receive counseling, something that continued after his release.

Glatman's mother tried to help in every way she could. Her son wanted to move to Los Angeles, so she paid for his trip. He wanted to learn a trade, so she paid for him to study television repair. He wanted to go into business for himself, and again his mother had money for the shop.

The only problem that Glatman did not discuss during his visits with a psychiatrist was his frustration with being a virgin as he approached his thirtieth birthday. He had tried to be intimate with girls, but when one was willing, he was always impotent at the last moment.

As would eventually be found typical of serial killers, Glatman blamed the women for his troubles. They were too demanding. They had no desire to please a man. They wanted everything for themselves, ignoring the man once their pleasures were met.

The answer, in Glatman's mind, was to find the woman who would be his perfect partner. In his fantasy, such a woman was only interested in his having a good time, no matter what was involved. His word would be law. She would do to him or let him do to her whatever brought him pleasure. And she would act this way from pure lust for him, acquiescing in being completely passive, her enjoyment coming from his total pleasure.

The more Glatman fantasized, the more he worked out the encounter they would have together. In his fevered imagination, the woman would be beautiful, friendly, and yielding. She would want him to render her helpless. Her pleasure would begin as he tied her hands and feet, then gagged her mouth to silence her. She would be unable to say anything, only muffled sounds of pleasure escaping the cloth that would seal her lips. Her excitement would come from his touch. His excitement would come from her desiring anything he wanted to do to her, always at his own pace, always helpless so that he was in control.

There was a rational side to Glatman's thinking. He knew from past failures that there were limits to what he could ask a date or a prostitute to do for him. The date might turn him down. The prostitute might also set parameters, though even if she didn't, the fact that he would have to pay her meant that, ultimately, she was controlling him. He knew he had to trick the women, and to do so he used a method so original that no one thought they might be in danger until it was too late. Glatman became a freelance photographer who sought models, in part, through personal advertising.

Today the use of personal ads to meet others is common. Most of the people who place them are legitimate, though enough horror stories have occurred so that special protocols have been developed by the people who counsel women on how to avoid rape. They suggest that the first dates should be held in neutral locations, such as coffee shops, movie theaters, nightclubs, and concerts. Each person should arrive and leave alone, neither giving the other a home address until the couple is comfortable together. Only then should they travel in the same car.

But stories of violence between strangers meeting through the personal columns did not exist in 1957 when Glatman finally felt driven to kill again and again. In fact, personal columns were a novelty back then, the newest idea in classified advertising.

Careful to hide his identity, and determined that the woman would obey him, Glatman bought himself a real gun and took the name Johnny Glynn, magazine photographer. He primarily sought the women trying to enter modeling through the pulp publications. They would be most willing to go along with anything he requested, eager for any work they fantasized would be a stepping stone in their 'career.'

Glatman probably did not plan to kill when he first began using the personal ads. Perhaps he lacked the courage. Perhaps he wanted to see how much cooperation he would get before he had to use violence. And perhaps his interest in photography was such that he truly wanted to improve his talents when he first began. Whatever the case, several women were photographed in public studios, the photography sessions being normal for the times.

Glatman, like most of the advanced amateur and aspiring professional photographers in Los Angeles in the 1950s, used public photo studios. These were locations of varying sizes fully equipped with seamless background paper, flood lights or electronic flash units, a dressing area, and other amenities needed to photograph models or products. They could be rented by the hour or by the day. Sometimes they had processing facilities, and a few could provide assistants if desired for more elaborate projects.

Photographers who could not yet justify the overhead of a full time studio would rent space when they had an assignment. There they would shoot portraits, fashion, and even products for department store catalogues and other accounts. The cost of the studio would be billed to the client. A few, like Glatman, used the smaller spaces solely to photograph models. Sometimes they paid. Sometimes they used someone as new as they were themselves, exchanging a portfolio of posed photographs for the model's time and skill. The photographer learned to be more effective, and the model had pictures to show other photographers interested in hiring her.

Glatman used different identities when hiring models and renting the studios. The agencies that provided models willing to pose at public studios, as well as the young women who answered such personal ads, did not have any way to check. So long as the photographer paid the agreed price and the session was genuine, no one cared. The agencies were not covers for prostitution, the models rarely posed partially dressed or nude, and there was no disgrace in using the rental spaces. However, because Glatman was consistent in his use of aliases, he unwittingly left a paper trail if anyone put together enough clues to follow them.

The first woman Glatman was known to have approached after he decided to rape a model was typical of the Hollywood 'wannabes.' Her name was Lynn Lykles, a young woman who arrived from Florida and was taking photography modeling jobs as a way of earning money until she could be 'discovered' by the studios or the major advertising agencies. She shared her apartment with two other young women, Betty Carver and Judy Dull, the latter a married woman with a 14-month-old baby.

Judy was an unusual young woman for her day. She was only 19, having married right out of high school a husband who had a good job as a pressman for the *Los Angeles Times*. Robert Dull was hard working and had every reason to assume that his wife had traditional values of the day. He expected her to be a housewife, raising the children while he supported the family.

Judy had other plans. She wanted to be a mother, but she did not want to be a housewife. She was pretty, aggressive, and decided that she was going to try and gain success in modeling no matter what her husband wanted. When he made it clear that she would have to choose between following her dream and him, she shocked him by moving out.

Judy quickly found success in the lowest level of the magazine modeling business – artistically posed nudes and 'cheesecake' posing. Glamour photography was quite popular at the time, photographers using carefully placed lights to sculpt the model in the manner of one of the Old Masters. One type of lighting recommended for this work was even named after the artist Rembrandt.

Cheesecake was different, usually involving a low cut blouse and the showing of bare legs. Tabloid newspapers such as the *New York Daily News* ran at least one such posed picture, usually of an actress or new model, each day.

Fashion models posing for department store ads, clothing designers, and manufacturers never allowed themselves to be photographed in cheesecake poses. They also refused to pose in undergarments or most lingerie.

Judy Dull fantasized that she was gaining experience and building a portfolio of photographs she could use to get jobs in the Los Angeles garment district or from department stores. She had no idea that the models who succeeded never admitted the work they did for money when first starting in the business.

The pay per hour was low and the models seldom benefitted from the resale of their pictures. But even a model like Judy Dull, who was popular, could earn a higher income than from the office jobs available to women. And so the women who posed most frequently convinced themselves that they were successful, that they would get better and better jobs for even more money. They also raised the few successes in the pulp magazine and glamour photo businesses, such as Marilyn Monroe, to the level of almost mythological heroines.

Glatman's original contact had been made through the personal column, an important clue towards understanding the case. Glatman's personal ads said that he was looking for women interested in modeling. No professionals needed to apply. He wanted attractive young women with no experience. Those interested could contact him through the paper, a fact that added to his anonymity.

The women who responded to the ads were a mix of amateurs and professionals new to the business. Glatman telephoned each of them, convincing them that he was legitimate, setting a price for the work they would perform.

Glatman arrived at the apartment Lynn Lykles shared with her two roommates when both she and

Judy Dull were out. Only the third roommate, Betty Carver was home, and she decided to let him come inside.

Glatman, posing as Johnny Glynn, dressed in a manner so casual as to be almost disreputable. But this was the era of the Beatnik, the Bohemians who looked upon a somewhat slovenly or counter-culture appearance as being 'hip.' Many photographers adopted such an image, thinking it made them appear more creative. Though Betty Carver may have had reservations about Glatman, he talked knowledgeably about the business and seemed legitimate. She let him inside and showed him the various portfolios and pictures available.

There were photographs of Lynn Lykles, but when he saw the pictures of Judy Dull, a beautiful, curvaceous blond, he wanted to possess and destroy her. She was the one he would 'hire.' She was the one he would use for the magazines.

Betty Carver asked for 'Johnny Glynn's' telephone number, but this was in the days before answering machines. He explained that he was usually away from the studio, on assignment. He did not have a receptionist, and he was not using an answering service, neither situation unusual for new professionals. He said it would be easier if he called Judy for an appointment, especially since, with three roommates, someone was likely to always be around to answer her telephone. Again, given the times and the circumstances, there was no reason for anyone to be suspicious.

It was August 1 when Johnny Glynn reached Judy Dull by telephone. The three roommates were having breakfast, and though Betty's comments about the photographer's appearance were not complimentary, he seemed genuine. Judy decided to model for Glatman/Glynn.

Then 'Johnny' said something that made her relax entirely. His studio was not available that day. He had been in her apartment. He had seen how Judy could be photographed at home. Would she mind if he brought his equipment there?

Suddenly all concern vanished. No one with evil intentions was going to be willing to work in her own home where her roommates were likely to be present. Such a person would not want to be seen.

Judy's trust continued when 'Glynn' showed up and told her he had been able to arrange to borrow a friend's studio for the afternoon. He was unconcerned about her hourly fee, and he happily provided Betty the telephone number of the studio. Judy had other appointments that day, and this would ensure that everything could be worked out satisfactorily. 'Glynn' agreed to pay for two hours of work, and Judy grabbed her suitcase with the various cheesecake costumes and make-up.

The borrowed studio was actually Glatman's apartment. It was on the second story of an ageing building on Melrose, not very far from Judy Dull's place at 1302 Sweetzer Avenue. Although the premises were not very attractive, they were not unusual. Low budget photographers frequently converted apartments to studio space, either living in the place where they worked or selecting apartments whose space cost less than in commercial buildings. Again, there was no reason for Judy to be suspicious when she entered the darkened living room, the window blinds shut, a tripod mounted camera, lights, and other equipment set up on the floor.

Although Judy Dull had posed nude, there was to be no nudity for the day's work. Instead, she was to change from her dress into a skirt and sweater. These were more form fitting and showed more leg, typical of the cheesecake and related assignments of the day.

The pictures were not to be cheesecake, though. After Judy returned to the studio area, 'Glynn' picked up several lengths of white sash cord he had specifically cut for the purpose. He explained that his assignment was to shoot a detective magazine cover. As was typical, she would be an innocent kidnap victim, bound, gagged, and terrified of the man who had captured her.

Later Glatman would talk about how Judy believed what he was saying. She warned him to keep the ropes fairly loose so there would be no lingering marks on her skin when she went to her next assignment. He agreed, then made certain the knots were tight enough so she could not work loose. At first she did not think he was trying to hurt her since he seemed to take no pleasure in how she was bound. But he also did not bother loosening the rope when she reminded him of her other work that day.

Despite her anger about his unwillingness to listen to her, Judy felt safe the way he posed her. Her wrists were tied behind her back, but both her ankles and her knees were also secured with rope. He could not rape her in that way, and when he began working the controls of the camera, she probably decided he was just a creep for whom she would never work again.

Finally Glatman began taking pictures, and there was no difference between what he was doing and what she had been through with other photographers. Except for being helpless.

The existence of the photographs would become important in the years ahead. As the actions of serial killers would be documented, it was found that they all kept souvenirs of their victims. The souvenir might be a shoe, a piece of jewelry, or some other item that reminded him of the person killed. The smartest of the killers got rid of the souvenir within hours of the killing. The others kept them for months or years, sometimes hidden at home, other times in plain sight. Occasionally the souvenir – usually a piece of jewelry, an expensive, new looking scarf, or some similar item – would be given to a spouse or lover who thought it was purchased new as a gift.

Glatman was no different, but as would prove to be the case with several other serial killers over the years, the souvenir he wanted was a photograph. Some serial killers liked to take pictures of their victims' corpse. Glatman wanted his pictures to reflect the helplessness of his living victims, and in turn, his power. But Judy could not know this, and the familiar click of the shutter, the brightness of the lights, and the studio-like surroundings were comforting. She was another pulp magazine model, and having her picture on the cover of *True Detective* or one of its rivals would make a useful addition to her portfolio.

As Glatman later confessed, he then told Judy that he wanted some additional photos that made her look as though she had been raped before being bound. He unbuttoned her sweater, then pulled down her bra, exposing her breasts. No popular market magazine in the country could be sold on the newsstands with such an image on the cover. As he reached for her skirt, which he pulled from her legs, she knew she was in trouble. There was no questioning where the photo session was heading, and she began screaming despite the gag in her mouth.

Judy was pushed to the ground, her back arched with her hands bound behind her. She was wearing only panties as he fondled her, trying to get an erection before he freed her enough for intercourse.

She screamed again, the sounds muffled and distorted, her fear of him and lack of desire for what he was doing evident even to a man trying to live out his fantasies. Glatman knew she was serious about resisting, gaining no pleasure from his touch. She was like so many other women he had dated, saying no to him, not playing the game that he wanted. He could not handle the rejection. He was no longer able to stay sexually aroused.

Glatman brought out his gun, telling Judy Dull of his past. He made it clear that he had been to jail, that he would hurt her if she kept resisting. Then he removed her gag so she could speak.

Probably there was no way that Judy Dull could escape with her life. However, what she did next assured her death, though she apparently did not realize that at the time. She explained that she would cooperate with him fully so long as he put away the gun.

As Glatman later related the incident, Judy said she was in a custody battle with her husband for the daughter they both wanted. Robert Dull felt that modeling was immoral, and he was using that argument to have her declared unfit, again a typical situation of the times. She claimed that if she filed a police report about what Glatman had done, it would only be additional evidence against her. She had to cooperate. She just didn't want him to leave her tied up, and she didn't want him always pointing the gun.

To Judy, the reasoning was probably meant to get herself in a position to flee. She also may have believed that if she cooperated, the worst that would happen would be a rape. It was later learned from friends that she loved her child intensely and would probably willingly endure physical violence if that was the only way to be able to keep the child.

The trouble was that Glatman was highly intelligent. He knew that Judy was not yielding to him. She was trying to manipulate the circumstances so she could get away. In his mind, she was actually trying to control him. She wanted him to put away the gun and release her from the bonds. Then she would be more comfortable. Then she might be able to escape.

Glatman refused. He was in control, not Judy. He

would keep her helplessly tied if he so chose. She had to know who was boss.

Glatman put the gun in his pocket and kept the gag from her mouth, but those were the only concessions he made to Judy's wishes. He wasn't about to release her. He liked her helplessness, liked the way her bra and open sweater were so askew, she might as well have been almost naked. He picked her up, showing how strong he was, and carried her into the hallway. Then he left her on the floor while he went to the kitchen to eat, watching her roll back and forth in a desperate attempt to free her hands and feet. He had known that she was tied too well to get loose. Now she knew it as well, and her helplessness at his hands increased his sexual arousal.

The desperate woman managed to bump her nose enough for it to begin bleeding. Harvey grabbed a pillowcase when he saw the blood, pressing it against her nose to stop the flow. Then he carefully set aside the pillowcase to keep as yet another souvenir.

Finally Glatman freed Judy Dull, photographing her nude. Then, since it was probably his first time with a woman, he lost his virginity. The terror she had endured served as adequate foreplay. Judy's agreeing to cooperate after he untied her kept him firmly in control. The situation was perfect in his mind. He could at last sustain an erection.

There was a second rape, then Judy was told to get dressed. She maintained that she dared not report anything to the police because of the custody battle. He told her that he understood, that he would let her go without further harm. However, he wanted to drive her out to a rural area where she could catch a bus into town. She would be able to safely return, but only after a long enough time for him to be able to make his own get-away.

Glatman was lying. He knew he could not let her go

33

free. She had seen his face. She knew where he lived. He had used a false name, but the apartment would be traced directly back to him. His reasoning made sense given the nature of his crimes and his fear of going to jail. What he did not want to admit was that the full sexual pleasure of their 'date' would not be his until he strangled her to death.

Oddly, he later talked of being uncomfortable lying to his victim. He liked Judy, liked the time they had spent together. He had taken the time between rapes to sit with her and watch television as they might have done on a real date. The fact that she was again helplessly tied, that her mouth was gagged so there could be no further protests, never intruded on his fantasy.

Glatman drove Judy towards Palm Springs, then turned off on the route that would ultimately lead to Phoenix. There was little traffic and it was easy to find a deserted area between the highway and the Southern Pacific Railroad tracks where he could finish with his victim.

Some time around midnight, Glatman walked Judy to an area where he could spread a blanket both for her comfort and to use as a background for his last photographs. Her wrists were tied behind her because he did not trust her statement that she would cooperate. The camera equipment, including flash bulbs, had been transported in the trunk of his battered black Dodge sedan.

Glatman told Judy that he wanted a few final images before freeing her. He bound her arms and ankles as she lay face down on the blanket, making certain she could not free herself no matter how violently she struggled. Then, instead of taking more pictures as she expected, he quickly looped a length of cord from her ankles to her neck. Then he kneeled on her back and pulled the rope taut, strangling her as her screams grew ever fainter.

34

Still lying to himself about his compulsion, Glatman apologized to Judy's corpse for the unfortunate necessity of killing her. He explained his reasoning, told her about the mistake of letting her into his home. He untied her, keeping the ropes and her shoes as souvenirs. Then he scooped a shallow grave in the sandy earth, rolling her body into the hole.

Judy Ann Dull was missed immediately. During the time when she was being raped, the legitimate photographers for whom she worked called her apartment to find out why she wasn't keeping her other appointments.

Betty nervously called the telephone number of Glynn's studio, discovering that it was phony. She called the sheriff, as did Robert Dull when he learned his wife was missing. However, no Johnny Glynn, photographer, could be located in the telephone book, and no address checked out. His description of his appearance was imprecise enough so that he could not be identified even if he had been spotted somewhere.

The demons that drive serial killers vary with the individual. Some need to kill daily. Some weekly. Some go in spurts, often with ever increasing frequency. But Glatman felt no pressure. He had simply acted out a 'delightful' sexual fantasy, lost his virginity, and gained some souvenirs

The next time, neither Harvey Glatman nor 'Johnny Glynn' was on the prowl. Instead, a plumber named 'George Williams,' a new member of a 'lonely hearts club,' an early version of a contemporary dating service, was going to spend some time with Shirley Ann Bridgeford.

Shirley was both hurting and lonely. Just 24, she had been divorced after giving birth to two children. She lived with her mother, which she found intolerable.

During the previous year she had been engaged to a man who abruptly broke off the relationship. There had been no warning, and after the initial shock, she joined the same lonely hearts club as 'George Williams.' The cost was $10 in order to meet eligible bachelors in her community of Sun Valley. Her date with 'George' was set for March 8, 1958, and she hoped it would lead to something positive in her life.

Glatman/Williams was desperate. He had satisfied his sexual fantasies with Judy Dull. He had lost his virginity. But during the previous seven months a new pressure had developed within him, a need to kill another woman.

Harvey knew, at least with hindsight after his arrest, that he could not stop killing. The time spent living a quiet, normal existence had been agony. He could not last for such a long period between murders again.

Glatman/Williams told Shirley they were going square dancing and Shirley dressed appropriately. However, he was in his usual casual attire when he picked her up and did not make a good first impression. But that was the risk with a lonely hearts club. Besides, there would be other dates, other men, all guaranteed by the membership fee. Sometimes the first new relationship was successful. Sometimes it was the tenth. Lonely hearts clubs were considered safe ways to meet a variety of people, and frequently the relationships became long-lasting ones.

Glatman's excuse for being dressed as he was had to do with the weather that night. It was warm, clear, and with an almost full moon that assured being able to enjoy the scenery along the coast road leading to San Diego. He told her he believed such a beautiful evening should not be wasted indoors. They should go for a ride together, and she agreed.

Glatman drove a hundred miles south of Los Angeles, pulling off just before Oceanside. He drove briefly towards the isolated mountain region, then stopped the car. He put his arm around her and began kissing her. He was intensely sexually aroused, but he still had enough control so she suspected nothing. Obviously some women who joined lonely hearts clubs were desperate enough to 'go all the way' on the first date, but she was not one of them. She expected a good night kiss, but 'necking' was not appropriate. She told him he was moving too fast, that she could not tolerate such behavior.

Glatman agreed, apologizing. He said that he was hungry and perhaps they should find a drive-in where they could eat before returning north. There would be bright lights, car hops, and Shirley had to admit that she was hungry. The night might prove pleasant after all.

Glatman was still convinced he could have his way with Shirley. He drove with one hand on the steering wheel and the other hand fondling her body as she angrily fought off his advances.

Outraged, he stopped the car, took out his gun, and forced her into the back seat. He thought she would be so frightened that she would do what he wanted. Instead, Glatman ultimately had to tear Shirley's clothes from her body. She was not about to let him have sex with her if she could help it, even if he did have a gun.

This time resistance strengthened Glatman's resolve. Instead of losing his erection, the knowledge that he would soon overpower and murder her enabled him to strip, then rape her. When he was finished, he tied her wrists behind her back and drove her to Butterfield Stage Road in the area that has since been named Anza Borrego Desert State Park. Totally empty at that hour of the morning, he was able to set the stage for yet another photography session and murder.

First Glatman spread out the blanket he had brought,

the same one he had used when he killed Judy Dull. Then he removed the camera gear he had in his car, setting up the flash so there would be plenty of light. Finally he walked Shirley to the blanket, tying her feet, gagging her, and positioning her for his souvenir photos. Once finished, he removed her gag, listening to her pleas to let her live for the sake of her two children as he looped the ankle rope around her neck. Once again his victim was strangled, this time her red panties and labels from her clothes being added to his souvenir collection. And once more a shallow grave was dug for the corpse.

The Los Angeles Police Department was called when Shirley did not return from her date. The lonely hearts club was contacted for the address on the application form, but neither the address nor the name 'George Williams' proved accurate. It was obvious something was seriously wrong.

The investigating officer, a detective named Pierce Brooks, contacted the Los Angeles County Sheriff's office to learn about other missing persons cases. Judy Ann Dull's name came up, though there was nothing linking the two cases. Brooks had a suspicion that they were somehow connected, though, and eventually began scouring the newspaper personal advertisements in surrounding communities, checking them against missing person and murder reports. It was an approach not previously used, one that eventually would become routine in such matters when computers were affordable. But while computers were in use in 1958, they were too massive and expensive for law enforcement.

As would prove the case with other serial killers, once Glatman committed his second murder, the third followed quickly. This time it was a 'Frank Johnson' who contacted a modeling service on West Pico Boulevard. It was July 22, slightly over four months after his previous murder.

Exactly what happened next is uncertain. Some of the information came from the crime scene investigation. The rest came from Glatman. Even the profession of the victim, Ruth Rita Mercado, a 24-year-old former striptease dancer who had moved to California from Florida, was in doubt. Using the name Angela Rojas, she officially worked as a nude model for amateur photographers.

The nude modeling business had several variations, and often the choice was that of the young women who posed. Nude modeling was considered a safe alternative to prostitution. Sometimes the photographer took pictures and nothing more. In fact, a few of the facilities where the women worked supplied Polaroid cameras, then still fairly new and expensive. The woman would take any pose the man requested, but he could not touch her. At other times the man was allowed to masturbate while the model posed. Cameras were also available, and some men brought their own. But few took pictures, and fewer, still, kept them. The vicarious sex thrill was what was desired.

Obviously many of the women were propositioned, and some also engaged in prostitution, with or without the knowledge and/or approval of the 'modeling agency.' These were more expensive and far less reputable than the agencies that supplied models for pulp magazine photographers, glamour photographers, and the like.

From what Glatman later said, Ruth Rita/Angela Rojas seemed to 'enjoy' some of the sexual aspects of what they did together. It is possible that she was a prostitute, in which case she would not have been a stranger to violence from one of the 'Johns'. A few men felt that when they paid the women, they were being permitted to use those women any way they desired, including with violence. They knew that the women would not report them, especially if they paid well, and the prostitutes came to accept beatings, cuttings, and the like as a hazard of the job. It is also possible that she understood the danger she was in and thought that by cooperating completely, he would let her go.

Angela Rojas made an appointment to meet Frank Johnson, but she did not like the look of him when he came to get her. She told him she was ill, that she could not keep their appointment. However, by then, Glatman knew where she lived.

The next night Glatman stopped by Ruth Rita's home to try and catch her by surprise. She was not home, so he went to a bar to brood and plan his next move. After drinking several beers, he decided to return to her home. This time she was in, opening the door before she realized Glatman was the Frank Johnson she had rejected the previous day.

Glatman made no pretense of what he wanted. He was carrying lengths of rope, rubber gloves, and cloth to gag her. His cameras were in his car. When Ruth Rita answered the door in tight capri pants and a sweater that clung to her well endowed chest, Glatman forced his way inside. He took her upstairs to her bedroom, tying her hands and feet, gagging her, then exploring the house for souvenirs. He returned to the bedroom, threatened her, then untied her and raped her.

Desperate to get rid of her assailant, Ruth Rita told Glatman that her boyfriend would be coming soon. Realizing he had to get out of there, he said they were going for a drive and a picnic. She had sandwiches in her refrigerator and a container of drinking water. These were packed along with two bottles of brandy she kept in her liquor cabinet that she suggested bringing along.

No one knows Ruth Rita's motives. Perhaps she planned to get him drunk. Perhaps she thought he would pay her well for cooperating with all his fantasies.

When he finally confessed, there was a surreal quality to Glatman's story of the hours preceding his third murder. The two drove to the same general area where he had murdered and buried Shirley Ann Bridgeford. He chose a location that was out in the open, yet so isolated that there was only the slightest chance that anyone else would ever come near. He spread his blanket under the moonlight, brought out his camera equipment, the food, the water, and the brandy. Then the couple partied until dark the evening of the 24th.

As Glatman related, and the pictures proved, the day combined eating and drinking with photography sessions and rape. He tied and gagged Ruth Rita in a variety of ways, usually while naked, taking pictures each time. They also had sex four or five times, as he remembered the experience.

Ruth Rita was always unresisting during sex, feeding Glatman's fantasy so that he was able to sustain an erection. He was convinced that she was as aroused by the activities as he was, that his repeated rapes reflected her desire for him. He said that he told her that she was a 'pretty good sport,' and he liked her so much that he thought about not killing her. They could become friends and lovers, seeing each other on a regular basis. She would cook for him or they would go to restaurants. They would play bondage games, and he would rape her because she enjoyed the experience so much. The only problem with the fantasy was that the evening's activities had left him as unsatisfied as his previous kidnappings and rapes. An orgasm was a prelude to murder, not an end in itself.

Disappointed that the pleasure was about to come to an end, Glatman told Ruth Rita that he wanted one more set of pictures. They got in his car, drove a few more miles, and found another spot. He took the blanket, the rope, camera, flash, and other items of what had become his murder kit. Then, with his victim fully

41

dressed, he tied her hands behind her back, tied her feet, gagged her, and laid her on the blanket for flash pictures. Having finished with the photos, he strangled her as he had the others.

It was only when gathering souvenirs from her body that 'Frank Johnson' realized that Angela Rojas had also been lying about her name. He found her identification indicating that she was really Ruth Rita. This he took with him, along with her watch, her white slip, and her nylon stockings. They, along with the photographs, would be prized additions to his collection.

This time Glatman had a long lead time before the police were called. Due to the nature of Ruth Rita's work and lifestyle, no one found her disappearance unusual. It was more than two weeks before law enforcement became involved.

The next victim was slated for October, again the time between deaths diminishing as it would with other serial killers. 'Frank Johnson,' like 'Johnny Glynn,' had been photographing models at a public studio. One of the models, Diane, was a young woman of 20 who planned to partially retire from the nude modeling business. She did part-time work through the agency that had booked her in the past, but being semi-retired, she could choose her photographers. She never liked Johnson/Glatman, but she believed him to be serious when he wanted to hire her to pose for calendar art.

On October 27, after yet another contact by Glatman, Diane suggested that he talk with a friend named Lorraine Vigil. She had relocated from San Francisco, was a model, and was in enough need of money to be willing to work for clients Diane rejected.

Glatman changed his pattern for Lorraine Vigil. He scheduled his appointment for 10 p.m., not an unusual hour for the women who worked as nude models. Men involved with photography on a part time basis often rented studio space for hours when they were done with their day jobs and, in some instances, family obligations. Lorraine put on make-up and an evening gown, though it was unclear whether the outfit was requested by Glatman or one she thought appropriate for the job. She would be paid $15 for the work, which was expected to last about an hour, in addition to the driving time to and from the studio.

Instead of coming to Lorraine's door, Glatman just sounded his car horn, making her come to the Dodge. She was angry, considering him rude, but she needed the money and had no reason to question his motives. Unlike the other victims, she had every reason to believe in Glatman's legitimacy. Her friend, Diane, had posed for him without problems. Lorraine knew she did not have to like the men who employed her. What mattered was the money and the fact that Glatman had paid promptly in the past.

The first change Lorraine encountered was in the shooting arrangement. She thought Glatman would shoot her in the same studio where he had worked with Diane. Instead, he told her they were going to drive to Anaheim, to a different studio.

Glatman paid Lorraine $10 of her money, telling her he would pay the rest when the shoot was over. Somewhat comforted by that action, they drove south on the Santa Ana Freeway, heading towards Anaheim. But when Glatman did not take the proper turn-off, continuing on to Tustin Avenue, a more rural area, she panicked.

This time Glatman was unlucky. He chose an area where other cars passed by with some frequency. And when he pulled his gun, threatening to shoot her in the breast if she did not let him tie her up, she fought. First she begged him not to bind her wrists. Then, moments later, when a car's headlights came upon them, she screamed, striking the windows with her fists, trying to get the attention of the passing driver.

Another car followed and she did the same. However, neither of the drivers noticed her, or if they did, they chose not to stop. Glatman grabbed Lorraine, a physically small woman he thought he could easily overpower. He covered her mouth with his hand, telling her that he was angry, that he should kill her, not just tie her up. Lorraine was convinced that she was fighting for her life. She grabbed the gun, and in the struggle, the weapon went off, the bullet grazing her thigh.

The sound of the bullet seemed to shock Glatman. He hesitated, providing the break Lorraine needed to reach for the driver side door, open it, and push him back. The two landed beside the car, Lorraine grabbing the gun, pointing it at Glatman, and trying to shoot him. The weapon was an automatic, a type that was susceptible to jamming. Each time she fired, the mechanism failed. However, before either of them could do anything else, Highway Patrolman Tom Mulligan arrived on his motorcycle. He saw the struggle, pulled his revolver, and arrested Glatman for what he thought was attempted rape. Only after the arrest, when Glatman's apartment was searched, were the souvenir photographs and other personal items found. His walls were covered with enlargements of his previous victims, and other items were found in the closet.

There was no question of Glatman's guilt. He was also identified in a line-up by the friends of the victims who had seen him. He confessed, pleaded guilty, and asked the public defender assigned to his defense to let him die. He wanted to go to the gas chamber, and the judge agreed. He was executed on August 18, 1959, though not before providing an extensive confession to Pierce Brooks. To the end, Glatman maintained the falsehood that the murders were solely the result of his anger over the women trying to control him. Had they not gone too far, there would have been no problems.

It was the Glatman case that led Pierce Brooks to try to link all departments in California so that they could pool crime information. He sought a way to reveal similarities in murders committed in both the same and different jurisdictions. He wanted to document the method used to kill the person, to locate the victim, or other factors that could lead to a possible narrowing of suspects or even an early arrest. However, it would be years before that was possible, and by then a somewhat similar case was creating terror, fascination, and 'groupies' in Los Angeles.

'There is a distinction between love and madness.' – Veronica Compton, writing about her relationship with Ken Bianchi, the Hillside Strangler, after his arrest.

Ken Bianchi was a nice guy, That's the one trait about him that everyone who knew him could agree on. Tall, handsome, respectful, he was the kind of young man every parent wants to see escort his or her daughter to the high school prom.

Ken's childhood had always been troubled. His biological mother was going through difficult times of her own. She was in and out of the juvenile court system before she was 14, extremely nervous, and a chain cigarette smoker. Eventually she became pregnant by a 24-year-old man, marrying a different youth, a soldier stationed at Fort Dix, New Jersey, who separated from his wife not long after the marriage. This was all right with her because, by then she was interested in a Buffalo, New York, man who, at 43, was approximately 26 years older.

By the time the Monroe County, New York, Children's Court became involved with the teenager, the adoption report for the baby she would deliver described her as 'a pathetic creature of limited intelligence . . .'

There is some question as to whether the assessment was accurate, the woman having changed when she matured. But at the time, her situation was one where the baby needed to be placed for adoption. The biological mother was considered unfit.

Ken Bianchi's birth was normal, but when he was immediately placed in a foster home, the first foster mother was seen as uncaring. She reportedly passed him from neighbor to neighbor, not willing to devote herself to his care. A few weeks later, a new foster care arrangement was made.

Frances Buono and Nicholas Bianchi had been married on December 27, 1941, and both had hoped to have a family immediately. Their frequent love making failed to result in pregnancy, and when Frances went to see the doctor, she discovered that she had a serious health problem. A hysterectomy was needed to save her, but the operation ended her ability to conceive.

The Bianchis were emotionally devastated. Friends and neighbors saw them as the type of couple who need to parent, who were gentle, kind, and had much to offer. They were encouraged to adopt, and when they became aware of the infant Ken and his situation, they arranged to make him their son. His biological father was an Italian Catholic much like themselves, though almost half their age. They had everything to offer the child and permission was granted for the Bianchis to take in Ken. According to the adoption report on the Bianchis, the family lived in a rather unattractive area of Rochester, New York, but had managed to fix up their suite:

'The apartment consists of four rooms which are freshly redecorated. Mrs. Bianchi states that she did the redecorating herself. She has individual taste in her choice of paper but has shown good artistic sense even though most people would not prefer paper with a Chinese design in the living room. The home depicts good housekeeping and women's ability to make a cheerful environment out of something which could otherwise be very drab.

Kenneth has his own bedroom which is equipped with a child's maple furniture. The room is cheerful and colorful with cut out pictures and toys arranged around the wall so as to attract the child's attention.'

The realities of the childhood have never been certain. Medical records show that from his birth in 1951, Mrs. Bianchi frequently took him to the doctor. He had asthma for a while, then was plagued with problems ranging from *petit mal* seizures, possibly related to an elementary school playground injury, to urinating and dribbling in his pants.

Throughout childhood, Ken was noted to have psychological complaints that always went untreated. For example, in December of 1958, a report from Rochester General Hospital discussed his various ailments. It also stated: 'Dr. Townsend said that although there were physical findings for this boy, he also had many emotional problems. He proved to be "a little minx" on the floor. Everything went fine during the day except during visiting hours when his mother was there and then everything was wrong, especially for his mother's benefit. He would have one complaint after another and Mrs. Bianchi would take these up with any available nurse or doctor who happened to be handy. Having this child hospitalized proved to be a trying experience and Dr. Townsend wondered if his social or home environment could be considered at all adequate.'

The Greece (a suburb of Rochester) School District also found Bianchi to be a troubled child. Following a parent–teacher conference on December 16, 1958, the note was made in his file: 'Mrs. Bianchi in. She is very nervous person, easily upset. As a result, Ken is also nervous and wets his pants. Check his health record. Mother needs to be calmed down.'

No one knows if early intervention could have helped Ken Bianchi. What is important is that there was a paper trail of a troubled childhood beginning with the lack of bonding with any adult following birth. And never is there a record of anyone trying to help the child or the family.

The family faced a series of short term setbacks, including the Bianchis losing their home. They had tried to buy a place beyond their means. Oddly, one result was that Ken's mother had to go to work, and social work reports indicate that Ken did better with his mother's absence. More important, during this time his father was also happier, apparently feeling less financial pressure. Yet the record of disturbance continued.

On March 13, 1959, Strong Memorial Hospital of the University of Rochester had this note in Ken's file: 'The impression is gained that this mother is herself a seriously disturbed person, and her discussion about the handling of the child by various medical men indicates some apparent paranoid trends. It is apparent that she has been strongly controlling toward this boy, keeping him out of school very frequently, particularly in the last several months, because of her fear that he would develop a sore throat and begin to wet.'

In 1962, with Ken in the fifth grade at Holy Family School, he was taken to the DePaul Clinic in Rochester. This time the note was even more telling. Under a heading, 'Child's Problems,' a note read:

'The boy drips urine in his pants, doesn't make friends very easily and has twitches. The other children make fun of him and mother is extremely angry at the school because they do not stop the other children. The mother sounded as if she were very overprotective of this boy. When the boy fell on the playground in kinder-garten early in the school year, she kept the boy home the total year.'

Studies of serial killers indicate that it may be unfair to try and place too much blame on early childhood. For example, Dr Ron Markman, a man who is both an attorney and a psychiatrist, has extensively studied men and women who commit violent crimes. He has shown that all serial killers have childhood experiences of play-ing with matches, torturing animals, and wetting their beds an inordinate amount of time. Yet there are any number of troubled youths who exhibited the same behaviors and went on to lead normal, productive adult lives.

No one knows what made Ken different. Certainly repressed rage was recognized early on. For example, when Ken was approximately 11 years old, the DePaul Clinic staff made yet another note in his record:

'Dr. Dowling reported that Kennedy is a deeply hos-tile boy who has extremely dependent needs which his mother fulfills. He depends upon his mother for his very survival and expends a great deal of energy keeping his hostility under control and under cover. He is very eager for other relationships and uses a great deal of denial in handling his own feelings. For example, he says that his mother and father are the best parents in the world.

'He is [a] very lonely boy who wants to move away from mother. He is very constricted however, and feels [sic] being hurt if he should move away from her. Mother seems to allow him only one friend in the house. There seems some basic confusion around his own identity. He tries very hard to placate his mother, but she always seems to be dissatisfied. To sum up, Dr. Dowling said that he is a severely repressed boy who is very anxious and very lonely. He felt that the only outlet whereby he could somehow get back at his mother was through his psychosomatic complaints. Dr. Dowling felt that without this defense of the use of his somatic complaints he might very well be a severely disturbed boy.'

The reports continued, sometimes with a terrifying hint of the kind of man Bianchi was to become. On January 30, 1963, a clinic note said, 'His fun is putting on scary plays with his boyfriends in which he is the monster.'

There was also a subtler note in the report. 'He said that the children sometimes blame him for doing things that he hadn't done and the teacher believes it so he gets blamed.'

It was also during this time, as Ken reached puberty, that he became close to his father. Nicholas Bianchi had to spend many hours working to provide for the family. As a result, he seemed to become both a positive fantasy figure and a genuine friend. Ken had grown to a height where his clothing was the same size as his adoptive father's, and the two men proudly bought identical dress shoes together.

Ken and his father went on a fishing trip together, Ken taking both a pair of ageing sneakers and, proudly, his new dress shoes. He kept the new shoes separate so they would not get muddy, then forgot that he had brought them and returned without them. A few days later, before the shoes could be retrieved, Ken's father died unexpectedly. The corpse was found in a telephone booth, though who he was calling was unknown. He had been suffering from exhaustion from the overwork and lack of sleep, and the cause of death was probably a heart attack.

The trauma was compounded in two ways for Ken. First, no one seemed to reach out to him to help him through the crisis. Each day he'd go up to the attic, sitting in the dark, crying and talking with his dead father. If any of the family tried to comfort him, he spurned them.

Among the theories about Bianchi is the idea that he was a multiple personality. His mind had dissociated into several different distinct personalities, each meant to handle an aspect of his life, and each generally unaware of the actions of the others. It was felt that his early years were filled with abnormal emotional abuse along with physical traumas that may have been perceived by Bianchi as sexual in nature. For example, his mother's constant concern about his penis dribbling urine led to tests that included catheterization when he was only a few years old. Awake, without anesthetic, a sterile tube was inserted through his penis into the bladder. It is a normal procedure for some problems related to urination, yet for a small child, it could easily have felt like the equivalent of male rape. Certainly it involved a sexual organ used in a function very much out of his control.

To understand multiple personality, the extreme form of what is known as hysteric dissociation, you have to first understand the difference between 'positive' and negative abuse. Positive abuse is not good for a child, but it usually will not cause extreme harm. With positive abuse the victim may carry great anger into adulthood. The person may also have low self-esteem and/ or a tendency to abuse his or her children in the same manner as he or she experienced as a child.

Negative abuse is the result of inconsistent violence. For example, suppose a child spills his milk and is beaten severely for his clumsiness. He is yelled at and told he can't do anything right. If this happens every time the child spills milk, he may feel incompetent. He may feel as though he is incapable of doing even the simplest of tasks without making mistakes. And he may have relationships only with women who reinforce his low self-image (the same is true of emotionally or physically battered girls who grow up to marry abusive men, at least for their first serious relationship).

By contrast, suppose the child spills milk one day and is beaten half to death for the clumsiness. Then, the next day, milk is again spilled. This time, though, the child is hugged, kissed, and told that accidents happen, that there is no serious problem. A fresh glass of milk is provided, along with a cookie for a treat.

The child does not know how to behave. There is no consistency with the punishment. One day an action is terrible. The next time the same situation arises, the reaction is radically different. If this happens often enough, and if there is a sexual component to the punishment or reward, or a separate sexual trauma during this period, the reaction can be extreme. Some children literally go insane from the inability to cope. Other children fail to thrive emotionally and physically. They often have disease resistance so low that a cold ultimately turns into pneumonia, and the pneumonia or some other problem proves fatal. There is no other reason for the death. It happens because the child does not wish to go on living and the child's body obliges.

The third experience is the creation of an alter-personality. Often this evolves from the normal imaginative play of all children. Many boys and girls have a fantasy friend with whom they speak. This is normal, and the first defense mechanism might be to blame that fantasy person – 'I didn't spill the milk. Harry spilled the milk when he was flying over the kitchen table.' But the difference with the child who becomes a multiple personality is that the fantasy child becomes 'real,' leading its own life, its actions usually unknown by the child who created the 'person.'

For example, several years ago Dr Ralph Allison, one of the psychiatrists who would ultimately come to examine Ken Bianchi, had a patient named Christina Peters. Her father, a psychopath who died in prison, kidnapped her from her mother when she was five years old. Before releasing her, he raped his daughter.

Christina was overwhelmed by the trauma of being raped by her father. She immediately created three alter-personalities to cope with the rape. The first was a violent persona whose sole purpose was to stop the rape. However, even an enraged five year old is still too weak to overcome an adult male attacking her. Yet until she entered therapy almost 30 years later, that personality was violent towards husbands, lovers, and anyone else with whom she had a volatile relationship. This personality submerged into the mind, leaving the way clear for a second personality, created to endure all pain. And since the original personality was psychologically submerged, a third alter-ego was created to handle normal daily routine. Thus there were four core personalities, the original and three alters, all created to cope with overwhelming physical trauma from which it was impossible to flee.

Eventually several of the psychiatrists investigating Ken Bianchi felt that he was a multiple personality. The children in his school who blamed him for doing things that were bad were accurate witnesses, though instead of Ken doing it, the actions were those of the violent personality Steve. And it was Steve who would become a serial killer.

Whatever the accuracy of all this, Ken Bianchi grew to adulthood an extremely disturbed man with suppressed rage and denial about his childhood. After reading the reports from the DePaul Clinic following his eventual arrest, he told Dr Jack Watkins: 'You could have talked till you were blue in the face, about my mother, you could have talked till you were blue in the face, try to discredit her. And I would have fought tooth and nail, thumb screw, I mean I – I would have disagreed with whatever you had to say about her. Because I've always had a respect and a – and deep love for her. But now looking at one report when I was 11 years old and seeing that I had problems, some more serious than others, which could develop into serious problems. Maybe they wouldn't, who knows? But it leaves a question there that I probably should have had help, more professional help.'

The rage is believed to have first manifested itself in Rochester, New York, following Bianchi's marriage. It was 1971, shortly after graduation from Gates-Chile High School, that Ken married Laura. The relationship was typical of too young marriages. Ken was lonely, mistaking companionship and sexual pleasure for love. And neither he nor his bride understood the stress of a relationship started while still in the midst of adolescence.

Ken had enjoyed his share of girls in high school. Although the sexual revolution of the 1960s was affecting some of his classmates' older siblings, the school was as conservative as a generation earlier. The girls who attended were one of two types. Some had reputations as 'round heels,' enjoying sex with almost any boy they dated. Whether or not they were truly promiscuous, the other students thought they were, and no one dated them with thoughts of the future. The other type, like Laura, was classed as a 'virgin.' These were the girls with whom you might indulge in 'heavy petting,' but with whom you knew sex went only with marriage or, if lucky, an engagement.

With hindsight, there seemed to be several problems with Ken's marriage. First, both were more attached to their mothers than was healthy for the relationship each wanted from the other. Each seemed to use his or her mother as arbiter and for advice, talking daily to their respective Moms instead of discussing things with each other.

The second problem came with radically different expectations. Ken wanted a perfect family. He was going to be the Dad, going to work, earning money, and coming home to his wife and however many children they had. She was going to be the Mom, staying at home, cooking, cleaning, and nurturing the children until they all went to school. He wanted the family of a 1950s television situation comedy – *Father Knows Best*; *Make Room for Daddy*; *Ozzie and Harriet*. She wanted to party and have fun. She was willing to commit to marriage, but only if she could continue acting her age, limiting her responsibilities. Family could come later.

Frequent arguments, a reluctance to solve problems without family help, and the stress of two different views of what married life should be caused the marriage to flounder after just eight months. There were also allegations that Laura was having an affair with the man for whom Ken worked.

Ken tried to keep the relationship together through a romantic courtship. He wrote Laura poetry and sent her flowers. But nothing worked. As one friend of the couple later commented, 'He seemed to live in a fantasy world about the marriage. It was like he thought he could avoid talking about his problems, go about his business and everything would magically be okay.'

One night, four months short of his first anniversary, Ken came home to an empty apartment. While he was at work, Laura had stripped the apartment of furniture and personal possessions, then filed for an annulment. Ken, she said, was too romantic. He was enraged and emotionally devastated at the same time. He felt he was one of those people who goes through life being dumped on by others. He did not consider his own personal responsibility for the problems.

Ken began trying to change. He took the Air Force qualifying test, discovering that he would be eligible to enter the electronics field. However, the test seemed merely to be a way to prove his abilities, for he had no serious interest in enlisting.

He tried Monroe Community College in Rochester, for a while, studying such subjects as police science, which interested him, and political science. But he did not like the fact that his grades were usually high Cs. He thought he should be doing better even though he was having trouble concentrating, so he finally dropped out.

There were also civilian jobs, such as becoming a bar bouncer. However, when he had to strike a customer who was drunk and out of control, the fact that hurting the man had been necessary to protect his employer troubled him. He hated hurting anyone and soon decided to enter one of the helping professions. That was when he became an ambulance driver, studying advanced first aid and considering careers either with the police or as a paramedic. But the police weren't hiring right then, and there was no paramedic training available in the community.

As life seemed to be going nowhere, Ken was having further problems with women. He was handsome, friendly, and able to pickup the women both at work and in bars. Among them was Eve who apparently thought she was more special to Ken than she actually was. As Bianchi later explained:

'She and I were going out. Nothing hot and heavy. Just going out, and she discovered . . . she ran into another girl I was going out with and . . . there was nothing wrong with it in my book, but apparently she really took offense to it.

'There was a knock on my door one night, and I opened my door and here comes this ball of fire, Eve. I had an antique mug collection and I had antiques all over my apartment. I was living alone in the town of Greece, just outside Rochester. And she went through my apartment like a tornado. Whatever she could grab her hands onto she did, and just winged everything at me. I lost all kinds of mugs. And she finally picked up a small wrench and she winged it at me and that hit me in the head.

'Then what happened, I just jumped for her and grabbed her and threw her down. And the police came because of the disturbance and they asked me if I wanted to press charges on her because there had been a couple eyewitnesses that had come into the hallway. She just tore my apartment apart. Crazy.'

How tormented was Bianchi at that point? No one is certain. He was enraged by the way he had been treated by his wife, his employer, Eve, and others in his life. He had a cousin, Angelo Buono, living in Hollywood. He could drive across country and start a new life, even though it meant leaving his mother. But the rage . . . the rage . . .

Harvey Glatman was driven to murder through his fantasies. He confused tricking a woman into being bound and gagged with consensual kinky foreplay. And when he raped, he was convinced the woman was enjoying the experience as much as he was.

Ken Bianchi, or his violent alter-personality, Steve, had a murder kit similar to Glatman's. He had developed the kit after experimenting with ways to murder his earliest known victims. Sometimes he used handcuffs, tape, and even plastic bags tied together to strangle his victims. But once he mastered the art of murder, he found that simplicity was best. He explained, 'There was Ace bandages . . . that rope, rubbers . . . condoms . . . that's it. They were inside a yellow bag.' The Ace bandages were effective as gags. The rope was cut into lengths that could be used for binding the hands and feet, as well as for comfortably holding while strangling. However, as he learned when he first began killing in Los Angeles, sex was not an interest when he approached his victims. Glatman was

57

a rapist who murdered. He wanted a 'meaningful relationship' with a woman, even if it only lasted a few hours and he had to bind and rape her to have it. Bianchi was a murderer who raped. Sexual arousal occurred only when his victims were helpless and knew they were about to be murdered.

The difference was most evident with one victim Bianchi later discussed with horror. She was one of the 'nice' victims according to the press coverage at the time. Most serial killers are drawn to prostitutes as victims when they make a conscious choice about the type of woman to kill. This is because they are comfortable entering a car with a stranger. They are also not likely to leave a trail anyone can follow when they are killed. Glatman used a variety of names, but he still left a paper trail because of the way he obtained his victims. Prostitutes are not even likely to be missed if they are not back at their posts within a set period of time since the man may have offered them enough money to spend the night.

Ken Bianchi and his cousin, Angelo Buono, were much the same during their killing spree in Los Angeles. Their first victim, Yolanda Washington, was a prostitute with whom they had sex before strangling her with her own clothing, then dumping her on a hillside – the 'killer' became known as the Hillside Stranger. However, their victims also included an art student, an actress, and others from mainstream society. It was one of the 'respectable' victims who caused Bianchi trouble.

Although the police had the information, the full story was never released to the press, to protect the family. As Bianchi told of the experience, and investigators confirmed, the victim was 'arrested' by Bianchi and his cousin who were posing as Metro Squad undercover police officers. They claimed that the victim was violating the curfew laws, handcuffed her, and placed her in the back seat of a dark sedan.

Oddly, posing as an undercover police officer was not an unusual situation in Los Angeles in the late 1970s. During the course of the Hillside Strangler investigations, it was discovered that there were police buffs so serious that they outfitted their cars with equipment to fit their fantasies. They would choose dark sedans of a type often adapted for police work. They would have scanners installed to listen to police calls. They would add high powered search lights that plugged into their cigarette lighters. And they would obtain a portable strobe light with magnetic base that could be attached to the dashboard or placed on the roofs of their cars in a manner similar to undercover officers. Some went so far as to have a siren installed, to buy handcuffs, a realistic looking toy badge or generic security officer's badge they placed in leather identification wallets, and other items meant to enhance their fantasy. Some of them liked to be voyeurs at crime scenes. Others liked to use their light and/or siren to stop motorists they thought were driving improperly, 'letting them off with a warning' since there was no way they could issue real tickets for traffic violations.

Ken Bianchi and Angelo Buono did not go that far. They had obtained a special window decal used by city officials in Glendale and similar to ones found on unmarked cars of the Metro Squad. The latter was a special unit of the Los Angeles Police Department that included Special Weapons And Tactics. During this period, *unmarked* cars used by most police departments were not like present day *undercover* cars which are frequently vehicles seized from drug dealers and others owing large sums of money for fines. Undercover cars are meant to look like any other vehicle on the road. The unmarked cars had decals, special license plates, and/or visible two way radio antennas that made them readily spottable. If the victim had any reason to question the 'arrest' by the two men, the decal would make her think the car was genuine.

There was a consistency to the way the victims were murdered. During one of his confessions, Bianchi explained how he and his cousin worked in Los Angeles:

'In regards to the killings, there was never any socializing. It was just go over and let's go out tonight and try to pick somebody up and he'd say, Okay, and he'd go get his stuff and change his shirt and out we'd go.'

The restraint varied when the girl was first picked up. Both handcuffs and rope were used, though handcuffs were usually taken for the initial pick-up because of the impression that the men were police officers. The handcuffed victims were usually silent until they realized they were not being taken to a police station, at which time, if frightened, they could be gagged. By leaving their mouths free at first, they could drive through the street without any passer-by suspecting a kidnapping was taking place.

The Los Angeles killings almost all took place in Angelo's house. 'Always in the spare bedroom. Always on the floor.'

'I was – I was doing an awful lot of thinking, trying to feel – trying to get a feel for what exactly was going on – what the reasons were for everything taking place basically – what the motivation was – or the emotions that were being felt. I've always felt a great anger – I mean, a really intense, horrifying, just cut-loose anger . . . It seems to me I've – I've put the reasons for the killings and what took place prior to and during . . . as falling into three categories. One category is – is to get me – the second category is because there was a – a sexual arousal with a – killing itself – that being an arousal also; and . . . thirdly, along with that . . . which came to me just a little while back, the third major reason is – is because – this is terrible – this is in no disrespect for the girls – dead people tell no tales. No witnesses.'

'But that was the very – it doesn't seem to me when I get that feeling – that's a very strong . . . reason for it. There was a more stronger, personal, emotional rage – arousal from that.'

The 'nice girl' victim surprised Bianchi. She harbored a sexual fantasy about police officers. As she had earlier confided to friends, she thought it would be fun to be so desired by a police officer that she would be arrested, handcuffed, and then, instead of taking her to jail, the man would be overwhelmed with desire. He would take her somewhere, the place was unimportant, and together they would have sex. Then he would return her home, the reason for the arrest long forgotten.

The victim genuinely believed that Bianchi and Buono were police officers, and she thought she was about to live out the fantasy she harbored. She was not a virgin, and apparently saw herself as a willing participant in the sex play, not a victim of rape. She was so enthusiastic that Bianchi (or 'Steve,' the alleged personality committing the violent crime) lost his erection. He wanted his victims not only helpless and about to die, but knowing that their lives would soon be ended. When the victim seemed to be enjoying herself, Bianchi panicked. When he and his cousin made clear what was happening, when the woman knew she was going to die, her terror restored his erection.

Bianchi was eventually arrested in Bellingham, Washington, where he had followed his girlfriend and their son. He had become a security guard and member of the sheriff's auxiliary, his checkable record indicating that he was honest, with a work history that would make him a good risk. The only aspect of his training that was troublesome was his enthusiasm. Law enforcement officers working for agencies with full police powers – city police, sheriff's department, highway patrol, and the like – are given more extensive training than security guards whose arrest powers are far more limited. Even as an auxiliary member, his training, and responsibilities, were quite limited.

Among the training programs for full time law enforcement is a course about abnormal sex acts, especially those that can lead to death. The heavily illustrated training includes photographs of what looks like crime scenes where the victim was tortured, often in elaborate leather clothing and various items attached to the genitals. Perhaps the most common is an autoerotic practice involving the temporary cutting off of oxygen in order to experience a 'rush' before or during masturbation. A noose is fashioned and placed around the neck of someone sitting on the ground or standing on a chair or other object. Then the person, sometimes naked, sometimes wearing special clothing, lowers his or her head enough to tighten the noose. The carotid arteries are compressed, blood and oxygen briefly cut off, and the lightheaded sensation is supposed to heighten the feelings of masturbation. What the person often does not realize is that this action is extraordinarily dangerous. There is a point prior to unconsciousness where the body does not respond to the mind. The person knows he or she only has seconds to loosen the noose but waits just too long, so that the hands no longer work. Unconsciousness comes and the person suffocates.

The death from autoerotic stimulation appears to be a suicide. More elaborate methods, which may include restraining devices, can appear to be torture/murder to the untrained eye.

The same course deals with other sexual practices the officers may encounter, including bestiality. The photographs are all evidence photographs, sometimes taken with surveillance cameras when a repeat offender is under observation. The lecture is a great curiosity among students in police academies, and it is also something most officers find unpleasant to witness. Thus they were surprised when Bianchi, in full uniform, attended one of the classes despite it not being a part of his primary or ongoing training. It was not the presenter's job to know who was and who was not appropriately at the training. But officers present were bothered by Bianchi's attitude enough to mention it prior to his crimes being discovered.

The final two murders were of two young women employed by a large discount department store. He convinced them that he needed them to house-sit a home where the security system was temporarily turned off during some repair work. There were expensive items in the empty home and someone needed to provide a physical presence for a few hours. The pay he offered them was high enough so that they never considered refusing.

Later questioning revealed that the story, though false, could have been true. The house selected, once known to be on a watch list of the security agency for which Bianchi worked, was of a value that such concerns were possible. The money offered the two women was also in line with what might be spent for such a service – if it was needed.

The differences between the Bellingham murders Bianchi planned and the ones in Los Angeles were two-fold. Los Angeles was a major city with extensive activity. Residents were less aware of their neighbors. People were unsure which sounds meant a problem and which were the normal noises of eccentrics drawn to a city with a reputation for an 'anything goes' lifestyle. In Los Angeles, it was possible to kidnap a victim on the street in a manner that would not arouse suspicion.

The second difference was that, in Bellingham, Bianchi decided to select his victims in advance. He not only targeted them, he talked with them, telling them not to alert anyone else concerning their short term job. He failed to understand that small town life was such that the women knew who they could trust. They did leave word with a friend because they were happy about the money they would be paid, and the friend would not tell anyone else. They also left notes that would ultimately connect them with Bianchi.

It was 8:30 a.m. on Friday, January 12, 1979, when Bellingham Police Chief Terry Mangan was alerted to the disappearance of Karen Mandic and Diane Wilder, both students at Western Washington University who were working their way through school. There was no reason to suspect a problem since many college students came down with skiing fever in January. Taking off for a long weekend without letting anyone know was common. The difference with Karen and Diane was that their work ethic would not have allowed them to leave their jobs without some notification. The chief decided to take the disappearance seriously, knowing that if the young women were skiing, the search would prove a good training exercise. He ordered a 'by the book' investigation, and because of that, all evidence was eventually gathered. This included a still wet footprint in the Bayside area home where Bianchi had taken the girls for their 'job.'

It was 4:30 in the afternoon that a woman listening to a local radio station heard the report of the missing girls. By then Chief Mangan felt certain that the girls were likely to be kidnap victims who were probably dead. He wanted as much coverage of their disappearance as possible, and the radio report paid off. The listener realized that when she had left for work that morning, a Mercury Bobcat automobile matching the description of one of the girls' cars had been parked in a cul-de-sac. The area was just off a main road, yet so densely wooded as to not be readily seen by passing motorists. The dead bodies of the missing young women were in the back of the car.

Bianchi, the last known person to be involved with the young women, was arrested soon after the discovery of the bodies. However, what he did not know was that Chief Mangan was friendly with Sister Carmel Marie, OP, a parochial school principal in Los Angeles. Mangan was a former priest and police chaplain who had left the clergy in order to pursue a career in law enforcement. Through Sister Marie he had met a man who maintained the books for the diocese. That man, he learned later, had a 14-year-old daughter named Sonja Johnson. The girl, along with her 12-year-old friend, Dolores Cepeda, had disappeared from the Eagle Rock shopping center near Los Angeles. They were eventually found murdered, two victims of the Hillside Strangler.

By the time of Bianchi's arrest and the gathering of information concerning his family, where he had lived, and other details quickly obtained, Chief Mangan was suspicious of a connection. His call to the Los Angeles authorities led to international headlines. It also created the first major serial killer media celebrity.

There would be many women excited by the prospect of meeting Ken Bianchi. He was eventually transported to the high security medical wing of the Los Angeles County Jail where he was allowed unlimited visitors during set hours. Anyone could come to see him, and soon there was a line of women waiting to visit. It was a phenomenon that shocked his defense attorney, a public defender who had not previously witnessed such adoration for a man who raped and murdered. It was as though the handsome Bianchi fulfilled a fantasy that belied the violence of his crimes.

Veronica Lyn Compton had never been a killer groupie. Bright, beautiful, she was an aspiring actress, writer, and producer who, in 1979, had spent four years trying to break into the film business in Hollywood. She had worked as a model for painters, sculptors, photographers, and advertising companies while paying for acting lessons with Lee Strasberg at the Hollywood Strasberg Institute. She worked as a film production assistant, performed in concerts and stage productions, and was a screen writer. She had an office in Beverly Hills, her own secretary, and was a guest at the 'in' clubs, ranging from Pips and Sergios, to the Hugh Hefner mansion in Holmby Hills.

There was another side to Veronica, a past filled with memories too painful to share with her friends, too frightening to revisit long enough to heal. Her first sexual assault was experienced at the age of five. Her first rape occurred when she was 12. There was never anyone to reach out to her, to help her heal. When she was forced into circumstances that should have ended the nightmares, she was too loaded with drugs to think. As she would later write:

'I had run away from home repeatedly. I had been committed to an insane asylum, lived on the streets, been raped countless times and beaten countless times for resisting and then raped anyway. I had been used by a child prostitution ring posing as a modeling agency, had been cured of gonorrhea, had surgery for breast and cervical tumors – the doctors discovered early cancer – and I had given birth to a child. I had become a narcotics addict and dealer, become a compulsive Baccarat player in Las Vegas where I supported my habit by being a madam. And later, a partner in an international marijuana smuggling operation.

'By the time I was nineteen and enrolled at the Strasberg Institute, I had made large amounts of money, done a lot, been to a lot of places. But at the bottom line, when I totaled up the pluses and minuses as every success-monger does, there was a sense of false gains and real losses. I was driven to be somebody, though, and to my way of thinking that could only come about by the acquisition of money and fame.'

Veronica was driven to achieve financial success in her chosen field, and to that end, she began studying the business of screen and stage writing. She came to understand that certain types of projects were cyclical, and if you wrote for the current popular category, you had a better chance of success. Horror was big in 1979, and so she decided to write a stage play entitled 'The Mutilated Cutter.' As she later related:

'I studied criminology and forensic investigation; I talked with Homicide detectives and doctors; I researched schizophrenia and serial killers.'

It was during this period when Compton saw a news show about Ken Bianchi. There was a film clip of his tearful leaving of the courtroom in Bellingham, Washington, following his confessing to the murders. She learned that Bianchi was probably a multiple personality, and she was fascinated to find that the various psychiatric interviews were conducted in front of a video camera. She immediately called Detective Ed Henderson, Chief of the Hillside Strangler Task Force that had been assembled to try and locate the tape. Instead, Henderson gave her Bianchi's booking number and address, suggesting she might try to interview him directly.

In order to convince Bianchi of her seriousness when writing about a serial killer, she let him read the finished draft of her play, 'The Mutilated Cutter.' She knew she might have to rewrite after talking with him because she was trying to capture what she defined as the 'pathos' of the serial killer. But to her bemusement, he made the mistake made by many non-writers. He assumed that writers only work from their own experience. He thought that the play reflected her past as a murderer. After meeting, he looked deep into her eyes and said, 'I think . . . I think you are no different than me.'

Veronica did not care what Ken believed. She wanted his help to make the play a financial success. Once it was in production, she would also write an interview article with him, using the money for what she considered more important work.

She did not know that each would begin using the other. Ken was a manipulator, seeking power over others the same way he had become aroused only when his victims knew that his power was absolute. He also wanted to leave jail, his mind filled with the fantasy of going through a few months of psychiatric work, then being released. At one point he sent a cassette tape to his former girlfriend and their son, talking about the book and movie deals he would make, the fact that they would be millionaires. He had no sense that between his confession to murders and the evidence against him, he would be behind bars for the rest of his life. Even if he could be cured of his compulsion to kill and rape, the horrors of what he had done so shocked Kelly that she wanted nothing further to do with him. She also had no intention of ever again letting their son visit him or, ideally, even know the story of his biological father.

Veronica also was a manipulator, though with a difference. She wanted to use the play to further her career and she was delighted to have a real serial killer act as unpaid technical adviser. However, her own background had been filled with pain. She had been an abuse victim, and a few weeks before the arrest of the Hillside Strangler had been attacked one night in her home. She felt that her professional success was proof of her coping, but in reality she was falling into a world where her vision was clouded by drugs and alcohol. As she later wrote:

'I went home that night [after seeing Bianchi], full on cocaine, and began drafting some notes; a loose structure for the article to come. Took some prescription pills and began to drift off to sleep. I was awakened by the phone early in the morning. It was Ken, quite upset. I poured a triple scotch [sic], tooted more cocaine and told him to tell me his troubles.' She did not realize that the request was the first test of how far she would go to get him out of jail.

Bianchi wanted Veronica to call his mother, a woman who refused to believe he had killed anyone. He said that she was quite ill from the stress of his arrest, and he wanted Veronica to tell the woman that she was helping Ken prove his innocence. He said that the words would give her a will to live, and if the worst occurred, she could die in peace.

'I quickly objected – Ken wisely suggested I calm down and reconsider – pour another drink, do a bit more cocaine and take a couple of pills.' Bianchi knew she was a chronic drug user, knew that her inhibitions would be lowered. What she did not realize was that not only was his mother in no danger of dying, she was willing to use the story Veronica gave her as a tool to influence the press.

Veronica, outraged, confronted Ken Bianchi in the visitors' area. This high security arrangement consisted of a large locked room overseen by Sheriff's Department deputies, and a series of cubicles with glass walls separating the visitors from the inmates. Each side of the glass had a telephone for two way communication. The nature of the glass was such that neither side could hear the other except by using the telephones. Bianchi, after hearing Veronica's tirade, got down on his hands and knees and, with tears in his eyes, pantomimed begging to be forgiven. Veronica later wrote:

'Over the next few months, ounces of cocaine, freebased, PCP, Quaaludes, gallons of Scotch, hundreds of Talwins and tranquilizers later, I was eaten alive and had become the extension of the Hillside Strangler. His "woman", his ace in the hole. Four months of near daily visits that extended into hours, daily phone calls, letters and a complete tearing away from all my family and associates. I lived and breathed the Hillside Strangler. In my ever diminishing rationale I accepted the role of creative playmate. It was a game, it was all a fantasy – it was just a man in jail, locked behind towers and steel, we exchanged only words, ideas, fantasy – no more. What a story. What a book. A story, not a real life. From one lie and a brilliant psychological play of manipulation, a mirror game, brainwashing, Ken had undone me. Held by part fear, fascination and lies I was consumed by his will. My growing hysteria I tamed by more and more intoxicants.

'I rationalized that I had worked with other writers in collaborations. Ken became just one more, all was capable with the drug cloud I lived in until he demanded I take the fiction into reality.'

Bianchi wanted to have a look-alike murder created in order to 'prove' that the Hillside Strangler had not been caught. As Veronica remembered the discussion, he said: 'When I was arrested I told them I had alibis for the times the women were killed. I told them I was with a woman, a woman in her 20's, with dark brown hair who met me in Universal City. You could be that woman, Veronica. You could be her.'

Veronica, in her drug induced stupor, began researching the murders in the manner she had once applied to play writing. She went to the libraries and looked up the newspapers for the days when Ken was killing young women throughout Los Angeles. She wanted to know the weather conditions, the daily events, and other information. If they decided to say they had been in a particular part of the city, how long would it have taken to get there given the conditions that existed? If they went to movies, what was playing and when would it have started? What clothing might they have worn? What food would they have eaten? She wanted to create the 'memory' of lovers who were sharing a new relationship.

Nothing was left to chance. Ken gave Veronica examples of his handwriting so she could arrange to fake receipts from the days in question. They plotted to bribe bartenders in order to get the types of receipts they would need, creating fake bar tabs signed with what would pass as Ken's handwriting. They would arrange to have copies of the receipts placed by bribed individuals in areas where they could be 'discovered' with other old receipts. If they got lucky, they might find people they could pay to act as witnesses to their presence together.

What mattered to the plotters was that the hard evidence against Bianchi was not that involved. There were a few eyewitnesses to a man who fit Ken's description but could not be positively identified as Bianchi. There were some footprints, hair samples, and semen information. But this was before DNA testing when truly conclusive results could be obtained. It was true that Bianchi had confessed, including giving information to this author prior to his meeting Veronica, but he could have been 'abused' by the authorities and he could have lied to me to impress me. What mattered to the two conspirators was that no matter what worked directly against him, some other piece of evidence more solidly contradicted it.

The plotting took the lines of a play rehearsal. Each discussed intimate details of their bodies so they could 'recall' identifying marks. They discussed the clothing they routinely wore, as well as clothing they might select when planning sex. They talked about how they had enjoyed sex, an issue that might arise if the police talked with others who had been intimate with them. Then they recreated their 'dates,' their love making, and the dialogue they 'remembered.' They wanted their created past to become so real, it could be spoken naturally – like the lines of a script brought to life by professional actors.

During this same period, Veronica was becoming extremely disturbed. The drugs prevented normal rest. She developed sleep psychosis compounded by panic attacks, hallucinations, and other problems. She entered Good Samaritan Hospital for tests, but she was not totally candid with them. None of the drugs she was taking were hallucinogens so she did not mention them. The week of testing was enough to rid her system of the short life prescription and recreational drugs she was abusing, and no one was able to learn the problem. When she left, not realizing the true cause, she decided she was 'mad, insane,' and 'demented,' all terms Ken had used to describe her. She came to feel that he was the only person who understood her, who could help her.

'Ken calmed me,' she wrote later. 'Promised me he'd keep me connected to reality and protect me from the monsters. The creeping terror that panicked me with a real fear that the "Boogie Man" was after me. I couldn't escape the delusion that I was being stalked. The Boogie Man was real, hiding under my car seat, in my closet, under my bed, outside the shower. He was out to kill me and no one could save me but Ken. Ken was strong. He had powers, I could let him control my life and then the Boogie Man couldn't touch me. Just do as Ken commanded. He told me I needed more cocaine, more pills, more scotch [sic]. Just do it he said. Just a little more and think of him, how he could protect me.'

Veronica undoubtedly gave the impression of insanity. She lost weight and stopped caring about her appearance. She became a recluse, using a Walkman cassette player and earphones to try and create enough sound in her ears so she would no longer hear voices.

The people with whom she worked did not want to see her.

'As the surrealistic world fused with the disorganized voices, their combined power found higher ground where energies were under their control. My own mind became more and more vacant as the thoughts of others were gathered. Life was purposeless; all was magic. There were no choices in life, only the passive sleep of an abducted consciousness. With weak eyes and a soul battered to complete helplessness, I was carried from one visual and audial [sic] horror to the next. I had no power whatsoever to halt the taking of the familiar world. It was being torn from my eyes, ears and body, and nobody had answers to what was wrong . . . no one but Ken. Pills, injections, more pills, cocaine and alcohol. Talk. The visits became confessionals. In the Name of the Father, the Son, and the Holy Ghost gave no consolation. In the name of the Hillside, the Strangler and Ken, there was at least a man, a voice, and given direction.'

July, 1980. Note made by Veronica as part of an ongoing series of notes that ultimately helped prove her guilt and her drug induced psychosis. 'Ken is everywhere; he knows my every move. He follows me. On the company yacht at sea, the radio transports his voice. At the Beverly Hills Hotel Polo Lounge, the phone is brought to my table. At the office up the road on Robertson Boulevard, the phone rings as I enter the reception room. At my father's home, he meets me, then later driving home in the limousine, he's on the car phone. Says he'll call me at home in half an hour. More booze, more cocaine, more pills. There is nowhere he can't find me. There is nowhere to get away to and to what end anyway. To meet my lunacy alone? More pills, more cocaine, more booze.

'My husband will do nothing; I must be all right. When I begged him to commit me before I start killing

73

people, he cried and said he couldn't. Maybe there is nothing so wrong that I should worry. What more can I do? The doctors know that I'm losing control but they haven't locked me up. What's happening? What is right; what is wrong? What is good or bad? I don't know. I don't know anything but Ken and Ken is God. Ken is my savior and salvation. He knows that nothing is so real that we can't overcome it. More pills, more cocaine, more booze.'

Eventually the sleep psychosis became so pronounced that she did not sleep for a week. A doctor gave her an injection that resulted in forced sleep, but when she awakened, she felt only strong enough to go back to the drugs.

Gradually, with memories of the attack she had endured before meeting Bianchi still on her mind, Veronica used the Boogie Man as the new reason to not sleep. Staying awake was no longer a problem. It became a matter of survival. No sleep meant she could be on guard against the Boogie Man. She no longer thought of herself as suffering from a psychosis. She decided that she was protecting herself from violence, not destroying herself.

Somewhere in the distant past Veronica had known that Ken Bianchi was a serial killer. That was why she had first approached him. And somewhere in the distant past Veronica had come to accept the idea of Ken's innocence, albeit an unprovable one without her supplying him with an alibi. But now, with Bianchi recognizing that all judgment had been shattered by her drug abuse, he could be honest with her. He began sneaking her notes and subtly teaching her what she would need to know in order to murder as he had. He even used a homemade belt of string to show how he had strangled his victims. He wanted her to be able to copy his method exactly.

Bianchi removed some of his hair and planted it

between drawings he made and sent to her. Then he used a kitchen worker's plastic glove for masturbation, sealing his semen in one of the fingers. It was ingeniously made a part of a string knotted rosary, then hidden in a book back binding.

Like all serial killers, Bianchi had retained souvenirs, only some of which had been found. He remembered what had been missing from his victims, then had Veronica obtain something that might pass. Among these was a woman's bra which Ken remembered, not only in size and style but also that it had been purchased at the Fred Meyers store. A combination of repeated washings and exposure to ultraviolet light would properly age and wear the item.

'Ken gave detailed sketches of Angelo Buono's house in Glendale. Why didn't I go there and break into this crime scene. Break in and obtain the rug fibers that matched the ones found in one of the victim's eyes. Perhaps take some wall paint chips as well. Yes, return to the scene of the crime, enter the rooms where torture and rapes and murders had occurred.' Bianchi even suggested that Veronica obtain dirt from the underside of the house to imply that an object had been buried, then removed.

Bianchi wanted to create the illusion of a killer still on the loose by having Veronica use the 'evidence' in an elaborate scheme. She was to find a willing actor, get him drunk, then have him read a script into a tape recorder. She would say that he was auditioning for a play, but the words would be ones which, when the tape was carefully edited and spliced, could be converted to several confession tapes. Each tape, along with one of the created souvenirs, would be sent to a different person involved with the case. The script, which Ken helped write, had details only the killer could know and which had not appeared in the newspapers. The police would have to believe that only Angelo Buono was guilty. That Ken Bianchi was not an accomplice. He was the wrong man to be in jail.

'My mind was a mishmash,' Veronica later recalled. 'I needed a drink, a pill, a drug to stop the nagging dread that loomed over my life. I needed rest but there was none, only voices that spoke gibberish, only visions of monsters and dark foreboding imagery that spun wildly out of control.'

Of all the murder groupies who would make so many other killers their friends, Veronica was perhaps unique. She was not insane in the normal sense. Her madness had come from the destructive lifestyle she had begun living rather than using therapy or some other constructive means to confront her past problems.

Veronica was also not trying to prove anything to her family. Many of the 'lovers' of convicted killers, such as Christine Lee, the 'fiancee' of the Night Stalker, exploited the murderer's notoriety. Filled with low self-esteem and great anger towards those who allegedly had abused them in their life, the closeness to such a criminal gave them celebrity status and strength. They were sought after by television talk shows, written about in the press, and flown to major cities for appearances. At the same time, they horrified, embarrassed, and/or terrified their families because of the implied danger from the killer.

Veronica was different. She was a victim of bad choices and bad timing. Yet the more self-destructive her actions, the less rational she became and the more she was willing to be manipulated by lies.

Veronica was convinced she could not commit a look-alike murder in order to create doubts about Bianchi. At the same time, she believed him when he said that he was scheduled to be moved to another jail facility where a contract on his life by Angelo Buono would result in his death. The fact that Buono, though guilty of working with his cousin during the Los Angeles murders, lacked the background, the friends, and the connections for such a 'hit,' if he wanted to commit one, was unknown to Veronica. In fact, some experts suspected that Angelo Buono fit the definition of a sociopath, a man who lacked a developed conscience. He would do whatever gave him pleasure, and he would not do what failed to provide that pleasure. By such a definition, Buono went along with his cousin because he had never killed, was curious, and apparently gained pleasure from the murder. Being caught and jailed was not fun, and so Buono quite probably would never kill again. Whatever the truth about his motives, there never was the possibility that he would seek revenge against his cousin for the testimony that helped put him behind bars for life.

Finally Bianchi convinced Veronica that she would not have to kill. She was to find the victim, subdue her, 'and at the crucial time repeat his name over and over and he would arrive and enter me and then do the deed. The voices in my head agreed it would work. The ugly pictures that danced about the shadows and flew through light before my eyes said yes. Ken was omnipotent. Ken could do magic. Ken was all powerful, I had to obey.

'I flew to Washington later that week in September of 1980. Twenty-three years old, nearly a year had passed since I had prepared to leave a family picnic. Nearly a year since I saw him on the television apologizing through his tears for his evil deeds. Nearly a year since I chose him as a subject to study.

'September [19] 1980, I had met a barmaid, given her drugs, Quaaludes, pot and lots of alcohol, then offered her cocaine in exchange for helping me play a joke. All she had to do was let me tie her up and take pretend bondage photos.

She agreed.

'I was so scattered I barely was able to tie her wrists

with a shoe lace type of bow knot. I didn't want to hurt her. I asked if the rope were too tight and she said no. I took a few photos with her lying on the bed [of Compton's room in the Shangri-La Downtown Motel, 611 E. Holly St] and then I slipped a pre-made noose about her neck. Whispered 'Ken, Ken' and pulled the rope as I straddled over her. She naturally panicked, got her hands free and struggled. I fell off of her onto the floor. She screamed at me, questioning me why I had done that. Why had I done that? 'He told me to.' I tried to explain.

'I saw the noose still about her neck. I rose to remove it. She drew away and I crumpled back to the floor crying, begging her to forgive me. I was sorry, so sorry. It was as if dawn had finally come into my dementia and I could see the previous telepathic thoughts I believed were coming from her earlier that evening were lies. She didn't know why I was there. The voices had lied to me. The voices I had heard prior to entering that room. Lies all lies she didn't want me to kill her and I didn't want to kill her anyway but Ken did and Ken never arrived. I said his name like he had said but it didn't work. He didn't come and now I was lost. What had happened here. What had I done?

'She tried to calm me and get the story out of me but I couldn't make sense of it myself. I kept saying he made me do it, he'd kill me if I didn't. But what did it mean? I couldn't put the pieces together. Veronica was in a strange room and had just tied to hurt, no, had tried to kill, an innocent woman. How did it all happen? I told her to just go – just go and call the police. I didn't care, just go. She hesitated, I was insistent. She was at the door confused and wanting an explanation, I nudged her out the door and locked it behind her, crying. I staggered across my motel room to the half gallon of wine and guzzled. I took some more pills, nosed more cocaine. I couldn't think. I laid on the bed sobbing.

'Gradually I recalled telling her to call the police. Had she? I couldn't stay. I had to go. I removed the disguise and gathered my things and left to walk through the night's heavy downpour of raid. I'd walk until it was morning and I'd fly back to California.

'I managed only a block or two until I collapsed by some bushes. A couple in a car saw me and came to help. They brought me to their car. I was incoherent but I did say my real name. They found the motel key and drove me there. They then directed me back to my room, watching me as I tried to unlock the door. The inside chain lock was in place, the room's interior was dark but I could see two naked bodies on my bed engaged in sex. A man jumped up and came to the door. I told him it was my room, he apologized and asked I give him a moment to dress. I staggered back to the car I had come from, two figures quickly left the room and vanished from the area. The driver told me I could go back in. I did and fell onto the bed passing away into a heavy drugged out sleep.

'When I awoke that morning I followed routine, I did more cocaine, drank more booze, took more pills and then I went to the airport. I then remembered I had still a tape to mail. What did it say? Who cared, just get rid of it. I paid some desk clerk at the airport to mail it for me and boarded my plane. I didn't learn till trial that the couple I found on my bed that night was my victim and a man we'd partied with earlier that evening. Evidently she had returned to see me and when I was no longer there she and the man used my motel room as their own. But why? Why have sex on the same bed I had hours before assaulted her on? Why didn't they stay when I did return to the room? Why didn't they call the police? Why was there an empty bottle of booze under that bed that I never brought into the room? So many whys and no answers, only speculations.'

The story of the assault was news only in Bellingham, Washington, so information about what occurred was provided by Veronica, who lied to him. She said that he had done exactly as he had instructed, tying the woman, strangling her, planting the sperm and hairs. It was the perfect look-alike crime and Bianchi was convinced that, because of his brilliance, it had occurred flawlessly. He said that he would obtain the Washington paper in order to read about it. Then he shared his plans, his hopes, and his dreams for the life that he and Veronica would lead after he was released from jail.

It only took a few days for Veronica Compton to be arrested. She had left too many clues behind. As a result, the arrest was made on October 2, 1980, by a combined force of Los Angeles Sheriff's deputies and two officers from the Bellingham Police Department. The only new twist was that the victim reported that Compton appeared pregnant.

By October 3, it was discovered that Veronica Compton had given an interview to Michael Housego, a Los Angeles based freelance British reporter. The interview, taped on September 23, had her explaining that she had been with Bianchi on every night of the Hillside Strangler murders in Los Angeles. She said that she had known Bianchi since 1977, before the murders, and that he was framed. 'Every night a woman was found dead (in Los Angeles), he was with me, and many more nights besides,' she told Housego. 'I've never been interviewed by the police because he never told.' She was adamant about the 'fact' that he had never murdered a woman.

Housego asked Compton about the Bellingham, Washington, murders for which Bianchi was arrested. Apparently that question caught her off guard and she refused to answer, saying only that 'I am saying the Washington police also made a mistake.'

Compton stressed that she knew the violent side of Bianchi, the 'personality' called 'Steve.' It was Steve that she first got involved with prior to the series of murders. 'It was like love at first sight . . .' She added that they got engaged around June or July of 1980, right after her divorce was finalized. She said that she was the one who proposed.

Since Compton's testimony could have cast doubt on the case against Bianchi, she provided an explanation for why she had never been mentioned. Hinting at the danger from the uncaught 'accomplice' she and Bianchi had created in their fantasies, she said:

'I suppose if you were going to be convicted of several murders, you would give an alibi. But some people are different, I guess. Especially when you know the person you love more than anyone else in the world is going to be killed if you talk. And that's what it came down to.'

During this same period, more information about Compton came forward. Her father, Armando Compero, was the political cartoonist for the Spanish-language daily newspaper *La Opinion*. He was also a friend of Mayor Tom Bradley who was approached by Veronica in August about helping free Ken Bianchi because he was 'innocent.' She also contacted Governor Edmund G. 'Jerry' Brown, Jr about a release. Yet the idea of a long term relationship was shattered by a search of her trailer home. The note, dated July 23, 1980, read:

'What an incredible journey my life has been at this time. And now I will be embarking a new course, a very new road of which I know not where it is to lead me. So many different roads are open to me. I must not fill with negations nor pessimistic ponderances.

'How can I marry a mass murderer?'

During this same period, Compton's Bellingham victim was identified, and the story she gave to reporter Teresa Allen of the *Bellingham Herald* was somewhat different. The woman, named Kim Breed, was the single parent of two children.

'I wasn't prepared for anything weird when I struck up a conversation with her,' Breed was reported as saying.

'I was just out on a Friday night, having a real good time, and I started talking to her about her pregnancy, because I'm a mother and I was interested.'

As reported by Allen, Breed, who still had faint marks on her neck from the strangulation attempt, was jumped when she arrived at the motel after having met Compton in the bar. She was a part time cocktail waitress at the Coconut Grove nightclub, but her primary work was with the maintenance crew of the Parks and Recreation Department, a fact that resulted in her having greater physical strength than her relatively small size would indicate. She was reported as saying that both her hands and feet were bound with rope before the strangulation attempt. She freed her hands, fighting off Compton and avoiding losing consciousness. She managed to get up from the bed and out of the room.

'All I remember is getting out the door and running,' Allen reported Breed as saying. 'It was bizarre. The whole experience was very bizarre.'

By October 9, 1980, Ken Bianchi was taking advantage of Compton by writing a 43-page 'letter to the world' proclaiming his innocence. No one involved with the investigation and prosecution believed him, especially since he had confessed. The only concern was with the trial of Angelo Buono, his alleged accomplice in the ten Los Angeles cases. Bianchi was a primary witness and the prosecution hoped he would be credible.

Compton, still under high stress though with somewhat less medication in her body, spoke of her joy with Ken. They would be married in March, and they hoped to have a daughter. She told how good he was with children [In truth, he adored his son and was viewed as an excellent father.]. 'He's generous and strong – he's the strongest man I've ever met,' she was quoted as saying. 'I'm saying that Kenneth Bianchi is stone cold innocent and he hasn't killed any of the girls he's accused of killing. I believe that fervently.' She also stressed that she was not guilty of the Bellingham assault. She had been set up, she claimed, by Angelo Buono's friends in the underworld.

In November, Compton gave an interview to Bill Johnson of the *Bellingham Herald*. Published on November 23, she was quoted as saying, 'Beyond the fact that I love Kenneth Bianchi, and that he is serving a sentence for something he did not do, I think that I owe it to so many people, and I owe it to America . . . to put the real murderers behind bars.

'If I had any doubt in my mind that Kenneth Bianchi was guilty – I don't care how much I love him, and I love him enormously – I would still pursue it to find the truth, because I also love other human beings and I love God and I couldn't live with myself if I didn't come forward.' She added that her arrest was the result of guilt by association, that she was innocent of the attack.

Very early in 1981 'Ken and I had given interviews to the *Herald Examiner* in Los Angeles. Having smuggled letters through legal staff, we had conspired to create a new twist in the plot. We would both say we were set up by Angelo Buono. I was indeed the missing brunette from Universal City of years past, the one that had Ken's alibi. I never came forward to help Ken at the time of his arrest because I was in fear of my life. Buono had a contract on my life and Ken out of his true love for me would not pull me into the picture. So now here we were ready to tell the whole truth. (After all we had created the fantasy life at the onset of our conspiracy.) Though I recalled very little in terms of actual dates and locations etcetera, I just went with the sham Ken spewed out. Yes, he told the paper. Yes, he wanted to marry me and have a family with me. Yes, he only wanted to keep me from harm's way. The bullshit was so pathetically thick only a moron would not question its stench. But it was all I had to cling to. Illusions and lies. Lies and illusions. Mind fucks and soul rapes. Life was like a Dali painting.'

By March of 1981, with the trial in progress, Kim Breed, the intended victim, was discussing the experience in the courtroom. She explained that from Veronica's appearance, she assumed she was pregnant. She said that she would have fought harder from the start if she hadn't been worried about hurting the baby she thought Veronica was carrying.

Breed's testimony differed from Veronica's in the details leading up to her fight for life, but the basic story was the same. According to Breed, the two went to Veronica's motel room after several hours of drinking in various bars around Bellingham. She was facing away from Veronica when she felt her hand being pulled behind her. 'Do you mind if I do this?' she remembered her assailant asking.

'I was under the assumption she was going to make me feel the baby. Then she grabbed my other hand and I didn't think that was peculiar. I mean it didn't arouse any suspicion in me at the time. I mean it wasn't something to be concerned about. 'I mean I trusted this person. I mean we had a rapport going. I thought we were friends.'

Kim Breed was confused when her wrists were bound, but whatever her fate was to be, she did not think she was going to be the victim of violence. She was convinced that Veronica Compton was pregnant, and she could not imagine a mother-to-be trying to kill her. Once she realized she was in danger, having been pushed onto the bed, her face on the covers, breathing becoming difficult, she was terrified. 'It felt like my eyes were going to pop out of my head. I knew I had to do something real fast. I knew I was going to die if I didn't do something real fast.'

Kim Breed did not say why she let herself be tied, even as loosely as Veronica claimed she secured the rope. There was a suspicion that she was drunk, though experts estimated that Breed's blood alcohol level was 0.01 in a city where legal intoxication starts at 0.10. Dr Robert Gibb, the Whatcom County Medical Examiner, said that the confusion Kim Breed showed after the assault was consistent with the emotional confusion of someone in a highly agitated mental state. Except for the blood alcohol level, which proved she was far from legally drunk, it would be easy to confuse the normal confusion of an assault victim with someone who had been drinking too heavily.

Breed said that she managed to push Veronica off her, get to her feet, and run for the door, her hands still bound. Veronica chased her, looping the rope around her neck, forcing her back on the bed. 'She was on top of me with the rope. It was a frenzy, it was all a frenzy. It happened real fast.'

Kim Breed was convinced that Veronica Compton was determined to kill her, yet in the midst of the struggle, suddenly Veronica fell to the floor, crying. Kim Breed, in great pain, sat on the bed looking down at her.

'I asked her, "Why, why did you want to kill me? I thought we were friends." '

Breed continued, 'She talked about "him" like he was the main element in the whole thing. She didn't say who he was. She just kept sobbing and crying about this person, this man.'

How serious was the assault? No matter what her intentions, the struggle between Kim and Veronica was such that the strangulation marks remained after the police arrived. Dr Gibb, who had performed the autopsies on Diane Wilder and Karen Mandic, the two Bellingham victims of Ken Bianchi, testified that the marks remaining on Breed's neck were similar to those on Bianchi's victims. The technique for strangling, including the location of the marks, was identical. He also said that he saw some hemorrhages in Kim Breed's eyes during his examination of her following her escape, and these were consistent with what he saw in the eyes of Karen Mandic. Such hemorrhages were not found in Diane Wilder's eyes, though, and they could have been caused by something other than the strangulation.

The similarity of strangulation was important. Coroners' investigators had been exploring the issue of multiple strangulations during this period. They had found that when they had a serial killer, mass murderer, or professional killer who strangled several people over a few days, weeks, or months, there seemed to be a pattern as unique as fingerprints. Studying the strangulation cases throughout the world, it was found that if you knew the order in which a killer strangled his victims, you could positively link the strangulation marks between the first and second, second and third, and so forth. What you could not tell was a link between the third and the tenth or some other combination out of sequence. The theory had been tested in cases where the same person was known to have strangled several victims, the victims had been found in the order of their death, and before the killer was caught, a seemingly unrelated strangulation occurred. If the marks matched the other murders, the presumption of guilt was made. In every case, when the killer was eventually caught, he confessed to the same strangulations the investigators had linked with the other victims.

Interviews with researchers indicated that they felt strangulation patterns were as unique as fingerprints. However, such pattern identification was not valid in a court of law if a killer, known for a series of strangulations, was denying his guilt in a case where the only evidence was a corpse whose strangulation marks fit the pattern. Had Kim Breed died, strangulation marks similar to those of the previous two Bellingham victims might have been enough to raise some doubts about whether the real killer had been caught. Of course, what Bianchi discounted or ignored was the fact that he had confessed, that there had been corroborating evidence, and that a look-alike murder would be seen as being just that.

Other evidence was released. The Reverend Richard Bergstrom of Samish Way Baptist Church in Bellingham had been sent one of Veronica's tapes. The male voice said: 'It started in California with Angelo.' He was speaking of Angelo Buono and the murders in Los Angeles. 'I'm asking for your forgiveness. I know I'll go to hell for it, and that's where I belong. I'm sorry, I'm really sorry, father. Please pray for me.'

Dr Ralph Allison of Davis, California, a man who had interviewed Bianchi after his arrest, was sent a tape that said, 'I can't take this goddamn pressure anymore – can you help me? I didn't know Bianchi had a wife and kid, but I did what I had to do.'

Again Bianchi forgot what had come previously when he schemed with Veronica Compton. He had been interviewed on both audio and video tape, during which time he had become angry, verbally violent, and confessed to the crimes for which he was sent to prison for life.

As the trial continued, the evidence mounted against Veronica Compton. On January 13, 1981, three months almost to the day before it was read in court, she had sent a letter to a Michael Lynch. Although not signed, police experts felt that it definitely was from her.

The letter was found after Lynch, a Bellingham resident, escaped from a minimum security prison where he was being held. The two had become friends, and she had written to him about her fears of going to prison. 'Will I ever be accepted as a normal human being and not a monster?' she wrote in the letter found in Lynch's cell after he fled. 'I do not anticipate I will do more than five years, and I still may be acquitted. I am not guilt ridden over [the accusation], so what the hell. We all do what we want to do in life right? I regret nothing I have done. Do you know the phrase "Can't do the time, don't commit the crime?" '

Veronica was remarkably candid in the letter, though warning Lynch to scratch out any statements that might be incriminating. He was more concerned with escaping than protecting her, so the letter also included the fact that she had strong expectations that short stories she was writing about 'gruesome murders' would sell well because of the notoriety.

The stories in and out of the courtroom kept changing. On March 18, 1981, Veronica Lyn Compton took the witness stand to try and explain what 'really' happened. The exchange among Prosecutor David McEachran, defense attorney Bill Johnston, and Veronica Compton was radically different from the statements she would make years later when dealing honestly with the events that led her to that courtroom.

Johnston: Veronica, did you attempt to murder Kim Breed?

Compton: No.

Johnston: Do you believe she is lying, testifying as she had?

Compton: I don't think she's lying in her mind. I think she's got things confused in her head to the point

88

where she's forgotten some things. And I think at other times the police have made her interpret it a certain way because her recollection isn't that good. That's what I think.

Johnston: Now I want to ask you some questions about the work that you do in California. Where do you work?

Compton: Well I worked at home, I was a writer. I had an office in Beverly Hills. With Intercontinental Films. I was under contract since 1979 to write eight screenplays. I wrote one of those screenplays over a period of about a year. So I worked in my office in Beverly Hills, which because I was teaching a lot in school, I [unintelligible] would write wherever I want to which was basically the teacher's lounge, because I didn't go in my office very often, and on the weekends I would go on the yacht – the company yacht with my producers in Marina del Rey . . . I would do camera shots and scene changes and that kind of thing.

Johnston: Could you tell us a little bit about your education?

Compton: Well for the past six years – it's been almost seven years now – I have been with Lee Strasberg's Theatrical Institute, and I was just accepted two years ago to study directly under Lee in his Master's Class. Dustin Hoffman was in it, Marlo Thomas, those kind of people were in the Master Class. With Lee Strasberg.

Johnston: And have you written plays and books?

Compton: Ah, yes I have. I have written plays and three screenplays. Some of those were musicals . . .

Johnston: What are some of the subjects that were covered in the books and plays.

Compton: Political, political issues, love, musical, comedy types of things, period prose, which takes place in the seventeenth century . . . murder, history, suspense type of things, psychological dramas – I am very much into psychology and psychological dramas . . . And as for the books I have written, I am completing an autobiographical work right now. And, ah, one on short story fiction. They are all murder stories.

Johnston: Can you tell us a little bit about your background until now?

Compton: Well, I grew up around television sound stages, art openings, nightclub performers, judges' chambers, because my family has been very interested in politics, those are my father's best friends – politicians and judges – and a lot of college campuses.

Johnston: Can you tell us about the writing business in Los Angeles and what a person must do to gain some notoriety there?

Compton: Well there's an axiom that is used among people in the business, and that is there is no such thing as bad publicity. All publicity is good publicity. There is no such thing as a bad review – as long as you get into those papers, then that's what gets you off. That's how you make the money, that's how you get the notoriety. That's how you get the acclaim. That's one of the ways that you are taught.

Johnston: Okay, thank you. I have no further questions.

McEachran: You met Kenneth Bianchi on a daily basis?

Compton: Yes sir.

McEachran: Also, you've indicated to numerous people, including a writer for the *Bellingham Herald*, that you love Kenneth Bianchi and that you would even go to jail for him. Did you mention that?

Compton: Ah, yes but there was a premise upon which it was made.

McEachran: You don't deny making the statement.

Compton: It was an exploitive [sic] statement.

McEachran: . . . Didn't you do this to show that Kenneth Bianchi was innocent of the Hillside Strangling murders here?

Compton: No sir.

McEachran: Didn't you feel that if a body was discovered here, strangled, same MO as the killings that have happened here for which Kenneth Bianchi was convicted, that would show that Kenneth Bianchi was not guilty of the crimes that were committed here?

Compton: Sir, I never anticipated a body being found here.

McEachran: Wasn't that the whole basis for your coming here?

Compton: No sir.

McEachran: As far as the situation that occurred, didn't you send tapes to a number of people?

Compton: Yes sir.

McEachran: One of those to Dr Allison?

Compton: Yes sir.

McEachran: Also to Rev. Bergstrom?

Compton: I believe so.

McEachran: Also, didn't you leave one at the Bellingham Airport?

Compton: Yes sir.

McEachran: Who is the voice?

Compton: I'm not sure. I'm positive his last name is Nesbitt, Rick Nesbitt.

McEachran: And where does he live?

Compton: Um, the last time I heard he lived at Rosemead, California.

McEachran: When you asked him to actually make these tapes, you gave him a transcript of what he was supposed to say, didn't you?

Compton: Of course I did. I coached him on it. He thought it was for a production.

McEachran: As far as the details on these tapes, there's a lot of details about the murders, aren't there?

Compton: Uh huh.

McEachran: The one to Dr Allison relates to the murders up here. Is that right?

Compton: Uh huh.

McEachran: Karen Mandic?

Compton: Um hum.

McEachran: And as far as where you got this information, you got it from Kenneth Bianchi, isn't that right?

Compton: Yes I did.

McEachran: As far as the specifics.

Compton: Yes.

McEachran: Wasn't this done in an effort to show Kenneth Bianchi wasn't the person who had done these crimes?

Compton: Well, my thought was that it would have implied there was another strangler on the loose. I mean it could easily, you could think it would prove Ken's innocence, or Angelo Buono's innocence, or it was some crazy person out trying to confess to something they didn't do, or I don't know I thought a lot of different things. Things just change.

McEachran: Angelo Buono wasn't the individual who was convicted up here of the killings up here of Karen Mandic and Diane Wilder, was it?

Compton: No.

McEachran: This was specifically Kenneth Bianchi's idea, not Angelo Buono's. Is that right?

[Johnson objects. Sweberg overrules.]

McEachran: You may answer that question.

Compton: That in a sense relates to Ken. Not that the tapes was professing other – it was professing that the person on the tape was the one involved in this. It hasn't proved anything.

McEachran: Wasn't this the first phase, first part of what you were doing that actually culminated in the strangling of Kim Breed?

Compton: No.

McEachran: Didn't you work this out with Kenneth Bianchi?

Compton: No

McEachran: As far as these details contained, you realize that these were not publicly known items.

Compton: I know. Well I had been doing research. I had been working with homicide investigators for a good four years. I know many of them on the Hollywood Task Force. I know Ed Henderson, I've talked to him in the Hillside case. I know many homicide detectives that I've talked to in research for numerous [years]. I'm saying I talked to many detectives about the Hillside case. I've gotten information from all over the place, confidential information that not everyone can get because they know me, they know who I am.

McEachran: Didn't you just say in your answer that you got the information from Kenneth Bianchi?

Compton: Some of the information, yes, but not all of it. Yes, some of it is not. But probably some of the most important things I got things that no one could get but I did get. And I did it with only one intent – as a writer. Not as someone who is trying to supply Mr Bianchi with an alibi.'

Ultimately the jury heard too many stories from Veronica Compton. Among her other statements was one that explained she was trying to function as a writer. 'Since I am an unknown writer, I embraced an idea for publicity. In that idea I grasped the most sensationalistic murder case I could because I had just completed a murder play, which I believe is very explosive, very dynamic. And I want it sold.

'I thought the best way to do it was to get the homicide people involved, make a big scandal and then have them say "Oh see, it's not really someone on the loose strangling people. It's just a writer out doing something dumb." '

At one point she said that the statements she had made about loving Bianchi were not real. They were just meant to gain publicity. She became outraged with the prosecutor, screaming at him, 'I tried to tell you guys I was innocent, but you didn't believe me. So my idea was to exploit the situation . . . I figured what the heck. Take the game all the way.'

There was also yet another story about Kim Breed's involvement. Compton said that after befriending the woman, she promised Breed two grams of cocaine as payment for telling the police that a man with the same description as Bianchi, along with a man who looked like Angelo Buono, attempted to strangle her outside the motel.

The problem came when Breed was so intoxicated that she became upset. She only intended to place the rope around her neck in the manner of a necktie, using the same type of knot, so that there would be some marks when the police arrived. But Breed forgot that this was all a ruse and thought Veronica was trying to kill her.

Veronica said that she wanted to have a look-alike attempt with Breed, and planned to do at least two more. One would be in Oregon and another in Texas. She would change her disguise when entering those areas, though, telling the courtroom that she planned to go as a nun, 'Sister Mary Carlton.'

The jury had mixed feelings about the case, though it did not take long for them to decide that Veronica was guilty as charged, the judge ultimately sentencing her to life in prison. There were many questions, including why Kim Breed returned to the motel with her boyfriend, spending the night, not reporting the assault immediately. However, as one unidentified juror was later quoted as saying, 'I believe she stayed at the motel that night because she had no place else to go. The victim, I think, didn't immediately report it to police because of a combination of the booze and the shock of what had just happened.'

What mattered most to everyone were the marks around Kim Breed's neck. No one took seriously the Medical Examiner's statement about Breed's level of possible intoxication, especially since no testing was done immediately after the assault. However, the fact that the rope had been pulled so tightly that marks lingered belied the idea that murder had not been on Veronica's mind. The neck abrasions were so severe, no one thought they could be connected with a publicity stunt with which Breed voluntarily cooperated.

Bill Johnson of the *Bellingham Herald* staff was the first reporter to interview Veronica in depth after the assault. She admitted she had hoped that she would be acquitted, that she would be in Los Angeles cashing in on her notoriety. 'Now I'm doubting whether I am a good actress,' she was quoted as saying. 'I guess I made a mistake by wanting the publicity, and I sincerely wish the consequences hadn't gone this way. But oh, it was exciting.'

Compton discussed the murder attempt that she was still trying to play down. 'I wasn't fooling around with Kim Breed's life any more than the people who put on *Candid Camera* fool with their subjects' lives. They are constantly blowing people's minds.

'When I set this thing up, all I wanted was the publicity. I was never trying to play myself off as a murderer. I didn't know I could be liable for obstruction of justice charges if Kim had filed the police report. Had I known what I know now, I wouldn't have done it.'

According to Johnson, Compton talked of wanting to be rich and famous. He said she claimed to have been studying ways to create publicity stunts for the previous four years. She alleged that had she pulled off the stunt, she would have gained notoriety much like Orson Welles had achieved when his *War of the Worlds* was broadcast on the radio, terrifying much of America. 'It was a terribly captivating story that, however, was full of holes – it was utterly ridiculous. And anyone with any common sense would have dismissed it as such.'

She also added: 'I am very good writer, I am very into myself, very much so. I love myself immensely – I am very narcissistic. Believe me, I had to have an enormous ego to do what I did.'

The judge and jury were more objective than Veronica, of course. And it would be after more than a decade in prison that Veronica would finally face the truth about herself, her relationship with the Hillside Strangler, and the fact that no matter what she intended, the depth of the strangulation marks indicated that Kim Breed truly was in danger of being killed.

In yet another twist to the life Veronica was leading, she had a 'pen pal' during her time fighting for the chance to stay out of jail. Shortly after her arrest and booking in Los Angeles, Veronica was sent to the Sibyl Brand Institute for Women. She went into maximum security, a section meant solely for women facing the death penalty. Because it was felt she was too dangerous to be close to other women, she was given a cell placed so that the cells on either side were empty. The length of the cell almost exactly matched the length of her body. The width was adequate for a toilet and sink. A dim light was always on so that the guards could always see whatever she was doing.

The cell had not been painted in more than ten years. One of the members of the Charles Manson 'family' – murderers of a half dozen people in Hollywood – had engraved Manson's name in the paint on the bars.

Nearby was a woman named Carol Bundy, awaiting trial for her participation in what the press called the

Sunset Slayer murders. In 1980, Hollywood's Sunset Strip was the scene of a series of sex killings. There were at least six victims, including some girls who were shot in the head while performing oral sex on Douglas Daniel Clark, Bundy's boyfriend. According to later testimony, after the murders some of the women were decapitated. Then Bundy made the heads more attractive with lipstick and eye liner so that Clark could continue to use them for masturbation until they putrefied. Carol Bundy had also had at least one murder solely to her credit. That was one where she had sex with a former boyfriend before shooting him, then using a boning knife to sever his head from his body.

Carol Bundy was convinced she had found a soul mate in the form of Veronica Compton. She was delighted to talk about her case and the killings that she knew about. She developed a code for talking so that she could be more open without the guards learning details they might otherwise not know.

'She was convinced I had been Keń's actual murder partner in the Hillside Case. That illusion gave her the freedom to speak through veiled code to me about the joys of her crimes, reliving their perversities and games,' Veronica later wrote. 'After five months of Carol's tales of beheading victims and sexual necrophilia coupled with the Hillside detectives' details of the murders done by Bianchi and questions of how I could protect such a monster, I felt my life utterly surreal.'

It was during this period that Veronica began receiving letters from a man named Daniel. Friendly, articulate, and caring, he was sensitive to her story. He said that her story reminded him of a modern day Romeo and Juliet. She began corresponding with him, and he wrote about his travels and insights into the cities he visited, the people he met. What she did not know was that Daniel was using a mail drop, not his real address, for he, too, was in prison. Daniel was actually

Douglas Daniel Clark, and when news of the relationship reached the press following her conviction for murder, Veronica was viewed as even more of an unhinged monster. After all, she was having affairs with two of the nation's most deranged killers, not just one.

'By the early 'eighties I was sent to California for the Sunset Slayer case. Again. My family had sent out an attorney. I took the 5th. Shortly thereafter I again flew to California for the Hillside case where I dismissed my family's private attorney and just admitted to my crime. I was too tired of covering the lies. Too tired to keep the truth at bay. My appellate attorneys were upset because the Supreme Court had agreed to hear my case and my confession meant that appeal was going to be abandoned. The D.A. threatened to charge me with multiple counts ranging from conspiracies to commit murder with Ken, to obstruction of justice and anything else applicable. Said he'd be sure I'd not see the light of day. My admission to Ken's conspiracy was a damaging point in Ken's credibility as star witness against Angelo Buono and it was Angelo now on trial. Still, how did I know if Buono was guilty or not? I didn't, but I did know first hand what was right – perhaps for the very first time in a few years. Just tell the blasted truth once and for all. That is what I did to the best of my ability. It was sheer agony to face the world again, but my life could make no progress until I began living in the real world of facts not fiction. Only by meeting the burden of punishment could I grow and mature, develop wisdom where wildness grew. I had reached the turning point in my young life and turned my back on one road I was never to travel upon again. The road that leads and dwells in the bowels of Hades. I had come through the hell fire a survivor.'

Veronica Compton was not the first woman to love Ken Bianchi, nor would she be the last. In addition to the numerous other female visitors were two other women who fell in love enough so he hoped he could manipulate them. Only Veronica Compton was disturbed enough from her drugs, alcohol, and emotional problems to be willing to possibly kill for him. However, even after she was jailed, even after the nationwide publicity about her case, women kept reaching out to Ken Bianchi, including Shirlee Joyce Book who eventually married him.

Shirlee had been touched by seeing pictures of Bianchi crying in a Los Angeles courtroom. She contacted him by mail when he was in Walla Walla Penitentiary in 1986. She gave him her address and telephone number so he could call her collect, the only way most prisons allow outgoing telephone calls for inmates. They also exchanged letters and tape recordings they made for each other. Finally he proposed marriage after approximately two years of communication. He arranged to send her an engagement ring and she accepted. She was 36 and had a teenage son. Bianchi was 38, and though he had fathered a son, his former girlfriend had left him.

The marriage occurred on September 21, 1989. He wore a rented tuxedo. She wore a traditional wedding gown and veil. They spent the first 30 minutes getting to know each other better since it was the first time they had met. Then they underwent a 15-minute ceremony in the presence of their parents, an attendant, and two convict friends of Bianchi.

Shirlee Bianchi moved to Washington state to be closer to her new husband. They also applied for a chance to 'honeymoon' in a trailer designed for conjugal visits of married inmates. However, publicity in the *National Enquirer*, the paper to which they gave exclusive interviews, and the *Los Angeles Herald Examiner* caused such a furore that the honeymoon was denied. The man primarily responsible for as many as 17 rape/

murders was denied the right to have intercourse one more time.

It took one full generation of Americans to go from looking at serial killers such as Harvey Glatman as reprehensible individuals who should be locked away or put to death, to seeing them as the new celebrities. And once the change occurred, it was as though a floodgate had been opened. Women made heroes, friends, and fantasy lovers of men who had raped, tortured, and murdered sisters, mothers, and daughters. They idolized men who, had they met them prior to their arrests, would have made them their victims. In the next chapter, some of those women explain the reasons why.

CHAPTER 3

TO LOVE A MURDERER

A serial killer is frequently the most concerned of friends after his jailing. He truly listens to the women reaching out to him. He tries to understand them, to learn what to say and how to say it in order to intensify their devotion to him. The fact that successful serial killers are generally master manipulators and con men when free – traits needed to gain the trust of their victims long enough to isolate them for murder – is seldom mentioned. In the fantasy of the women who contact them, serial killers are men who never ignore them, who elevate them to a level of importance they have not encountered with husbands and lovers.

Serial killers make no demands on them, other than perhaps an occasional request for money to spend within the confines of prison. They never criticize the women for being overweight, unkempt, sloppy house-keepers, bad mothers, or uncaring daughters. They never come home drunk, getting sick, passing out, or becoming enraged enough to beat the women over an imagined slight. They never make sexual demands. They always have time to talk, to listen, to make the woman's presence seem wanted. And when they listen, they are sympathetic, nurturing, and caring – or such are among both the fantasies and realities of the women who write to them. What is never considered is that most of the traits are forced upon the men. They are faithful because, unless they are gay or bisexual, there is no one with whom to cheat except by mail. They never see the violent side of the man because there never is the opportunity to see it. And though they may have read the trial transcripts or attended the trial, and though they certainly have read the newspaper accounts of the crimes the men commit, the women fail to put themselves in the place of the victim. Even those who have been raped and brutalized refused to recognize that given slightly different circumstances, the men who hurt them were no different from the men they now 'love.'

In talking with one woman who was aware that her serial killer lover had securely bound and gagged his female victims, raping them over a period of hours, beating them if they failed to cooperate ('The bitch thought she was too good for me and had to be taught a lesson.') and beating them if they tried to stay alive by cooperating, ('She was nothing more than a whore trying to come on like she was scared when she really wanted it. The cunt had no right to tell me she didn't want me when she couldn't get enough of me.') the denial was obvious. 'I wouldn't mind his tying me up and having his way with me,' she giggled.

'But several of the women were killed,' I reminded her. 'And others ended up in the hospital with broken bones.'

'That's what the police say,' she replied, angry with me for bringing up the truth of the matter. 'He told me the ones who died were accidents, and he's been honest with me about everything else so I don't see why I shouldn't believe him.'

'What about the ones in the hospital?'

'Rough sex,' she said. 'It's not my style, but I've had some friends who tried it. He wouldn't do that with me. He was just trying to please them. He's really a very gentle man. That's why things got out of hand. Men who always beat women know how far to go so they won't leave marks, won't get in trouble. The fact that those women went to the hospital proves how loving he is. He did what they asked for and didn't know how to do it right.'

For many women who get involved with serial killers, the murderers' notoriety adds a touch of fame to what may otherwise be perceived as dull lives devoid of glamor. A serial killer is the subject of newspaper articles, television programs, and, occasionally, books and movies. Having a connection with a serial killer can mean a chance for vicarious fame. At the least, your name may be mentioned in one of the annual follow-up articles most newspapers run on the anniversary of the arrest or conviction of their community's local historic murderer. At best, you become a guest on a segment of *Oprah*, *Donahue*, *Hard Copy*, or some similar program.

And in the most tragic of cases, a serial killer can become the only strong male figure in a little girl's life. He becomes father confessor, counselor, the all accepting 'Dad' or close uncle. The fact that the little girl is either too young to be allowed in a prison where the killer is not a relative, or so far away that she will never personally meet him, adds to the fantasy.

Perhaps the saddest correspondence was between a man who had been raping pre-teen and young teenaged girls from the time he was 20, and 13-year-old Nancy. His urges increased until he added ever more violent kidnappings, eventually murdering a girl who, despite his ski mask disguise, recognized his voice. She knew him from the neighborhood, said his name, and assured her death.

The girl's nightmare proved the killer's delight. He found himself experiencing ever more frequent urges to take a life. He became a serial killer, enjoying his victims' pain, their suffering, and their deaths. And none was any older than Nancy who looked to him for advice about her alcoholic mother, her erratic school attendance, her relationships with her friends, and the sex life that, at 13, had become so active, she rarely went a day without intercourse.

The child's story was chilling, for what she thought was normal could emotionally shatter any caring adult. Even more tragically, the girl was so well adjusted to the nightmare world in which she lived that she never came to the attention of social workers and school counselors. She fell between the cracks of the system, and the man who would have ravaged her body, then murdered her without hesitation were they ever to meet in the 'real' world, became her friend, her confessor, and her mentor.

'I was 9 and my best friend was Beth because we always went to school and did after stuff together. She got 2 brothers who was older then 9. George was my boyfriend and he was 17, but T.J. was like I don't remember. Not as old as George was because he can't drive us no where. Beth said if I can keep a secret she would tell me that George does sex to her sometimes and he wanted to do sex to me because he loved me alot. I liked him alot to because Beth said I would like it alot. But I didn't no what his peter would hurt to go in me down there because his finger was OK. Then his peter was in his hand going fast and he said to take my dress off and I did but I was scared when he was say for me to spread my legs and Beth was saying don't yell because she was watch for her Mom if she come up the steps. George's peter hurt me bad but I didn't cry to get him in trouble. He liked me alot the first time because when a girl let a boy be the first one to do sperm in there it means love all the way. So that how he was my first boyfriend and he was until we moved here when I was 11. George and me did sex so many times I don't no and I liked it. But I didn't no better then to say no to other boys because I wanted to be excepted, But George was my boyfriend and he said do it because they were our friends.'

The child's role model was her mother who had become promiscuous at 13, dropping out of school to marry her father, becoming a baby having a baby. The woman was a heavy drinker, perhaps an alcoholic, according to the letters, and her love life was more blatant than that which a healthy parent/child relationship would have tolerated. She explained that her mother:

' . . . got 3 boyfriends now and she does sex to all them. Andy is her best one and she stays all night with him sometimes. She goes to the bar with Brant and Norm and sometimes one stays here in her room all night. I can here her bed making them noises so I know she does sex to them. I think that is good for her to do sex, but she gets all pissed off at me for sex with a man.'

The child's relationship with her mother's friends was also sexual. One of the boyfriends agreed to stay in the house to take care of her for two days while her mother was in jail for drunk driving. The boyfriend had no interest in the child, but she was encouraged by her best friend, Janet, to have sex with him since they were alone together all night.

'I didn't know if he liked me like that, so we said I will just be sexy and hug him with a big kiss when I got home. When I did that he was all nervous and was shaking his hands, but he liked me right away because his peter was hard in his pants when I first rubbed it. So we do sex all the time now and I love him.'

The girl saw her 'pen pal' as a man to whom she could tell anything and from whom she could get information about life. She told him about her drinking, her sex life, her relationship with her mother and her mother's boyfriends. And her biggest goal, three years from when she began writing, was to get a driver's license and come to visit him. She said she could not wait to hug him. She had no sense that if she met him on the streets, he would rape and murder her without a second thought. He was her friend and she loved him.

As has been seen, the adults who write to serial killers have no illusions about what they did. These are women who have read the newspaper accounts of the murders, they have seen the television reports. In many instances, the women eventually read the trial transcripts or attend the trials, listening to the evidence. They learn the details about women who have been murdered at best, raped and/or mutilated before or after death at the worst. In many instances the sexual perversions to which the killers admit are so extreme, no rational person, no matter how 'kinky' in their sex life, could ever consider imitating them. Yet invariably the women are in denial about that aspect of their lives.

Sometimes the denial takes the form of religious beliefs. Letters from devout Christians stress the change that can come through Jesus. And the men, understanding how to manipulate the women who write to them, tell of their 'miraculous' conversions. These same men might be using drugs smuggled into prison. They might be violent enough to lose privileges and spend extensive time in solitary. In some instances, they teach other inmates with shorter sentences, and who will return to the streets, how to more effectively commit violent acts.

[It is not just men who fall into this category. Susan Atkins, a member of the Manson family who was believed by the prosecutor to have more influence than Charles Manson, was sent to Frontera Penitentiary in California. Women incarcerated in the same area were shocked to find that she was proclaiming herself a born again Christian by day and teaching other women how to kill with a knife in the evening. According to inmate witnesses, she said that she delighted in using a knife because stabbing someone was like cutting through butter. However, they were convinced that she was serious about her religious statements as well. She seemed to be a sociopath, someone without a conscience, yet because her discussions of violence were limited to other inmates, there was a period when Christian groups actively sought her parole because she had 'changed.']

At other times the woman writing the serial killer feels that he was pressured by others, that the victims 'asked for it,' that he made a mistake he would not repeat, or, as in the case of Alicia, they just don't want to think about it. 'I personally wouldn't want to dig up all the details from my past,' Alicia wrote her serial killer 'friend.'

'I feel better not thinking about things that upset me or make me feel insecure and out of control.'

Oddly, Alicia is someone whose background would normally not predict her response. She was a school teacher who said of herself, 'I live an average middle-class life – I'm in my 40's, married with kids.' She justified her writing with the fact that he 'actually confessed to what you did and expressed a little remorse about it.' She ignored the fact that, in more than 25 years, he was known to never to have been out of jail without kidnapping, raping, and ultimately murdering girls. He even made clear to anyone who asked that, if released, he would return to such violence.

Others felt as Alicia did, that hearing too much about what the killer did was not comfortable. 'It has a tendency to jolt me out of the warm & safe place that I have reserved for you & I, in my mind,' another woman wrote. 'There are things that I've done that I will never be able to be honest with you or anyone about. But who the hell cares anyway. I just feel so lucky that we are getting to know one another & are finding many similarities.'

Connie decided to blame 'her' serial killer friend's

problem on the victims. 'From what you have described of your girl friends, you have trouble making good choices in women because you're trying very hard to be accepted and loved.' She ignored the fact that the 'girlfriends' who lived were subjected to regular beatings and rapes.

Amy was involved with what might be called a dance of control with her serial killer, a man who regularly abducted women before his arrest. Like Ken Bianchi, the killer delighted in the reaction of his victims when they were helpless and knew they were in trouble. Some were left bound, partially naked, and terrified. Others were raped or mutilated enough to scar them for life, though they lived to identify him. Eventually there were no living witnesses, though souvenir photographs were a part of his crimes as well as evidence that helped result in his conviction. Yet Amy was convinced that she was in control of him, that he was in love with her, a man who was her emotional slave. She delighted in teasing him about the fact that he would do anything she asked, even though they had never met.

Ironically, Amy's attitude was not much different from that of Shirlee Book Bianchi. She was interviewed by reporter Diane Albright and discussed serial killer Ted Bundy, a man who was apparently her first 'love.' She told Albright, 'They killed him, an innocent man. They weren't Christians who done that to him.' Albright confirmed that Shirlee may have tried to correspond with Bundy but her efforts apparently led nowhere. Certainly she had no relationship with Bundy prior to his execution. Yet she told the reporter, 'I would still be with him if they hadn't fried him.'

Amy seemed to create a fantasy relationship, then project her beliefs on a man who did not share them. 'I can't picture you doing any of those things [rapes and murders],' she wrote, 'It's not a picture of a person that I've gotten to know.'

Trying to relate to the pain that drove her 'pen pal' to hurt women, she wrote, 'I wasn't a sexual abuse victim but I had an alcoholic father & I guess that's not the same thing. I was a victim of verbal abuse and that's bad too. A person never gets over those things but it does get buried deep within one's self and you block it out. At one time or another it re-surfaces.'

Amy was actually involved with two men, both violent, both in prison, but only one convicted of serial murders. The other had a chance for parole, and Amy repeatedly wrote to the serial killer about her plans to marry the other inmate when he was released. However, the closer to his parole hearing, the more she began to think she would not stay involved. She was a single parent, hard working, and looking to go into management after years on one or another forms of public assistance. She became increasingly fearful as she learned that the other man expected to have a physical relationship with her. She weighed, then rejected, the idea of his living with her. She considered his spending weekends, then confessed a fear of sex. She insisted she wanted to wait for marriage, then spoke of regretting writing the man who might be released. With reality about to strike, she declared herself wrong, that her heart truly belonged to the serial killer who would never leave prison (and who she had never physically met despite being on his list of approved visitors should she desire to go see him). She said that she did not need sex, had gotten along just fine without it, and would be faithful.

The lack of self-worth of many of the 'girlfriends' of the serial killers becomes evident in their histories and comments. 'My mind is so fucked up, I don't know if I am going or coming.'

'I felt anger & rage to the point of self abuse while stuck living with my mother, who sadistically & totally enjoyed raging & screaming at me – & at times enjoyed physically abusing me.'

One woman told her serial killer that her interest in him came from the compassion and sensitivity living a hard life had given him. Another, after seeing the man on the *Oprah Winfrey Show*, referred to the admitted murderer as 'very articulate, brave, sincere & very, very human.' She added, 'Something about you touched me & I am a woman.' Yet another commented that the man 'seemed genuinely to feel bad for the pain & anguish you had caused the families [of the victims].' She then went on to explain that while she knew that other people did not see his pain and the goodness within him, the reaching out to help others, she was more sensitive, both seeing and understanding it. (This was based on approximately two minutes of coverage during the evening news when he was shown in court.)

Another woman commented, 'I continue to think of you as a little boy (not that I'm speaking of immaturity) but a small, lonely & perhaps, lost, little child. I pray that you may connect the child within & find a very special man.' Yet another tried to relate to the man's violence towards women, agreeing that it was difficult to care for women. She expressed understanding that he was only treating them as he had been treated. Since he was alive and they were dead, it was yet another odd form of empathy.

Many penitentiaries are arranging for conjugal visits between inmates and their wives. There may be a mobile home for privacy, an out building, or some other arrangement. The sex is considered not only a reward for good behavior but a means of helping a man bond to his wife before returning to the free world. No matter what is said about prison being a place for rehabilitation, most lack the programs to assure that a man who has been locked away will become a productive member of society. Many lack basic literacy skills, crime being the only way they could ever earn much more than minimum wage. The fewer programs offered behind bars – literacy, GED courses, and specialized training in a job skill area that will be marketable on the outside – the more important it becomes to give a man the incentive to seek them upon his release. If he has a close relationship with his wife, he may do whatever is necessary to assure that he stays out. Halfway houses, the Salvation Army, and numerous other organizations will help men when they are released if they seek to use the services. But loving someone and being loved in return are important. The conjugal visit assists with all this.

The girlfriends, 'lovers,' and women who marry serial killers after they are caught are rarely permitted conjugal visits. The large number of victims, the often extreme brutality the victims endured, and the extensive publicity these cases receive usually result in prison officials denying the women the chance for sex with the men. It is an ideal situation for them because none seem to want intimacy. In many cases, the women were victims of rape, including incestuous rape. They have been battered by fathers, brothers, and/or lovers. The physical side of a relationship is unpleasant for them under the best of circumstances. They glorify the romance of love without sex, yet the truth is that often they have been victims of violence to such a degree that they fear intimacy. Having a 'lover' with whom they can speak on the telephone, write, and occasionally visit (though many do not) makes them feel 'normal.' They do not have to experience the counseling necessary to heal and lead a life where intimacy is possible.

Sometimes it is the fact that the woman knows the serial killer has been violent that is part of his appeal. Christine Lee is typical of such individuals. She is the fiancée of Richard Ramirez, the Night Stalker.

It was on March 17, 1985, when the Night Stalker first became known to the police. Not that Richard Ramirez, the man eventually found guilty of the series of violent robberies, rapes, and murders, was called that then. Nicknames require a series of crimes to take place before the police and/or press identify the unknown suspect by a special term. There have been the Boston Strangler and the Hillside Strangler. Both men strangled, but one terrorized the city of Boston while the other, though also killing by strangulation, dumped the corpses of his victims by hillsides and cul-de-sacs. There was the Sunset Slasher, and in the privacy of their offices, the Los Angeles Police Department's older Homicide Detectives will talk about the killer who murdered only homosexual men, leaving their remains in trash bags. Though the press used a term that was 'respectful of the gay community,' the police named the murderer the Fag In The Bag Killer.

There were only two crimes on March 17, 1985, the first being foreplay for the second. Daylè Okazaki lived with a young woman in a condominium in the community of Rosemead, California. It was typical of the bedroom communities ringing the city of Los Angeles at the time. The residents were urban people grown tired of the violence of the city. Their jobs generally forced them to commute which they typically did in upscale cars equipped with telephones, stereo systems, and tape players on which they are as likely to listen to language lessons and books as they are to music. Frequently they live together, splitting the high rent as a matter of convenience, or falling in love and being uncertain if they are ready for a commitment. Some are of Asian descent, others Hispanic. There are Blacks and Whites, and a sprinkling of wealthy immigrants from Europe. Most were born and raised in the United States, only their parents or grandparents sacrificing to assure they can live the American dream. Their wallets were filled with gold credit cards. 'Home cooking' meant eating in restaurants within walking distance of their condos, apartments, and houses. And their personal lives were usually more focused on sensual pleasures than community involvement.

So Dayle Okazaki's 'significant other' was shocked when she saw a man dressed all in black except for the dark blue of his baseball cap and the chrome of his gun. He was moving through the shadows when she used her remote control garage opener prior to parking her car. She left the car, confronted the stranger, and instinctively raised her hand as she begged him not to shoot. He ignored her, ignored the gesture, firing one shot. By chance, the bullet first struck the car keys, deflecting it just enough so she was able to live. Bleeding heavily, she fell to the floor, conscious both of the seriousness of her wound and the fact that he would undoubtedly fire again if he knew she was alive.

The woman waited until the gunman entered the building before getting up and forcing herself to run to the other side. As she moved, she heard a second round being fired somewhere within the home. She did not realize that the gunshot signaled Dayle's confrontation with the gunman, and that encounter resulted in instant death. Then, to her horror, the killer emerged, confronting her once more as she tried to hide behind a parked car. For whatever reason, the man placed the gun in his belt, turned, and fled.

By the time the sheriff's deputies arrived, Dayle was dead, his friend was hysterical, and the intruder's baseball cap was in their possession. It would be the first of many clues ultimately leading to the man's capture.

Serial killers, like most murderers, do not spend the evening going from stranger to stranger in order to commit their violence. Multiple murders in different locations are usually the handiwork of the grudge killer. Such killers are avenging a perceived wrong in their lives and frequently commit suicide after killing several of their enemies. Typical is the man who feels he unfairly lost his factory job and decides to kill selected management personnel and those co-workers he feels should have supported him. For serial killers, usually the single confrontation sates their appetite for murder, and it is a matter of days, weeks, or months before they strike again. Only the mass murderer will kill in more than one place on the same day. And the mass murderer, unlike the serial killer, has a finite list of intended victims, the only other people dying being those who accidentally get in his way.

The Night Stalker was a different type of serial killer. He did kill twice on the same night. After Dayle, he went to Monterey Park where the victim would be Tsai–Lian Yu. She was born in Taiwan, and was called Victoria by her American friends. At 34, she was one of the older students in her law school class where she was studying to become a criminal defense attorney.

This murder occurred not in her home but in her car, a yellow Chevrolet spotted parked on North Alhambra Avenue in Monterey Park. The car's lights and stereo were on, and Tsai was crumpled by the side of the car, her breathing increasingly shallow as the officer examined her. She died before the ambulance could arrive to take her to the hospital.

Once the homicide detectives came on the scene, they found that Tsai had been murdered by multiple gunshots. There was a bruise on her leg, her stockings were torn, and her shoes were off. But she had not been raped.

The Chamber of Commerce would never discuss the matter, but Los Angeles is a county that now has a fairly predictable killing season. The city was still small in 1958, the year both Harvey Glatman was executed for killing women and decisions concerning the building of a massive freeway system were made. Much of the territory was farm land. Many homes had oversized lots because land was so cheap, it was easy to buy a little privacy. And when the community became crowded, those lots sold for record prices. Homes began to be built close to one another, and commuting long distances became normal. The county itself had a mix of gambling casinos, mob dominated nightclubs, residential communities, retirement areas, and even large ranches used as adjunct film studios. Agricultural products, oil reserves, and motion pictures were the primary sources of income for the residents, and the county was a peaceful place in which to live.

After 1958, the population density increased. The city of Los Angeles began annexing areas such as the Sunset Strip. Both the city and the county saw construction rise. A highway system was built, and mass transit quickly was allowed to decline. A variety of businesses were opened, the entrepreneurs delighted with the warm weather, the closeness to the ocean, and the glamor of living near movie stars.

Progress brought what came to be known as smog. This was a combination of pollution (smoke, industrial waste, car exhaust, and the like) and the fog from the ocean. People with asthma, emphysema, and other lung conditions learned to keep oxygen for emergencies and to stay indoors when there was a smog alert. Otherwise healthy people found that the physical stress of smog days caused them to be short tempered. Alcohol and drug use regularly led to an increase in domestic violence, bar fights, and gang 'rumbles' at such times.

Eventually the police and hospital emergency room workers learned that there were certain seasons of the year when weather conditions caused people to kill each other with greater frequency. Eventually even drive-by shootings and violence between strangers jockeying for rush hour position on the freeways would be a part of the legend and stress of living in Los Angeles. Tsai's murder seemed to signal just another time when residents of the area would be more inclined to kill each other, stopping only for rain and the cooling breezes that signaled an end to the explosive tempers.

The horror of the serial killer became evident on March 27, 1985, with the deaths of Vincent and Maxine Zazzara. He was 64, 20 years older than his wife. She was a successful lawyer. He had undergone a midlife career change, switching from his investment counseling business to owning a restaurant that featured pizza. Unlike many would-be entrepreneurs who enter businesses they know little or nothing about, he thoroughly studied the industry and had a thriving location. Together they were very successful, living the good life in Whittier, another community where terror is supposed to be a stranger.

It was Peter Zazzara, the couple's son, who discovered the murder. He routinely stopped by his parents' home in the morning, and though he had his own key, he respected their privacy and normally rang the doorbell. He let himself inside only when he saw that their car was still in the garage and they failed to respond to persistent ringing.

The couple had been killed instantly. Each had been shot, and neither had been able to cling to life for more than a few seconds. She was naked on her bed. He was fully clothed on the sofa.

The deaths themselves did not cause the homicide investigators to recoil in horror. Instead, it was what happened afterwards. Although Vincent Zazzara's body was untouched, his wife's corpse had been carefully mutilated. Some of the wounds came from stabbing, especially a large gash in her left breast. More horrible were the ripping wounds, as if a deranged surgeon had had substituted brute force for a knowledge of anatomy when trying to enter the chest. The woman's eyes had been gouged out, and a series of small cuts were evident in the sockets.

Serial killers generally lack the rage evident in the murder of the Zazzaras. Some are rapists who kill following the pain and humiliation of forced sex. Others are killers who rape – men such as Ken Bianchi whose arousal comes only when the woman is helpless and about to die. If there is a ritual prior to the death, it usually involves some form of bondage, sex play, or humiliation. Cutting and slashing are rare. Gouging out the eyes following the death was almost unheard of. Certainly the investigators were troubled, and they were used to seeing the horrors of the damned inflicted by one human upon another.

The next attack which could be *linked* to the same killer happened on May 14. This time it was an Asian couple in Monterey Park. He was 66 and his wife was three years younger. Their home was one story, and their attacker gained entry by forcing open a window, then sneaking into the bedroom as they slept.

The attack brought new information about the serial killer. His targets were obviously women, the men in their lives being unavoidable nuisances who had to be killed quickly. In this case, the killer placed his hand over the mouth of the sleeping woman, and as his actions brought her to consciousness, she realized a gun was being placed to the head of her husband. Before she could try to scream, the gun was fired.

The man was not dead. A bullet fired at the head does not mean certain death. Usually it strikes an area that kills instantly. But the brain does not fit fully into the skull. There is enough space that there have been cases of a bullet entering the skull, bouncing around the perimeter, and no more than grazing the brain. The person may even be unhurt, though he or she will lose consciousness from the trauma. In this instance, the husband was gravely hurt, though he did not die right away.

The attacker grabbed the wife and began beating her. He tossed her around the room, striking her repeatedly, and finally demanding to know where the couple kept their money and jewelry. When she managed to speak, he forced her arms behind her back and immobilized them with thumb cuffs. Less common than handcuffs, though available in stores that sell such items, they painfully lock the thumbs close together, preventing movement.

The husband managed to regain consciousness enough to drag himself to the den where he managed to telephone the emergency number 9–1–1. Then he drifted in and out of consciousness, nearly bleeding to death before help arrived. He would die a few hours later in the hospital. His wife, her face and body battered, was found standing in shock, unable to speak coherently.

As the initial trauma diminished, the wife was able to give the first description of the man. He was a Caucasian, approximately 5 feet, 10 inches tall and perhaps 160 pounds in weight. He had dark brown hair and was probably somewhere in his thirties.

There was a problem linking all the crimes together, though. Los Angeles County is a massive territory of 4,083 square miles, easily dwarfing some of the New England states. Although it contains several cities, the largest being Los Angeles which has 464 square miles, the residents treat the entire county as their home. The city of Los Angeles never had a center in the manner of Eastern communities that were created in a downtown location, then expanded outward in logical ways. In fact, one writer visiting the city of Los Angeles in the 1940s called it seven villages in search of a city. This lack of a center, and the way all activities are wide spread, has made for odd police problems. The various cities that, with Los Angeles, comprise the county are all interlinked. Everyone commutes what are often long distances, and there is little awareness of suburban government by the residents. Someone in Whittier or Burbank is likely to tell a stranger that they live in Los Angeles, even though they technically do not. Yet the government workers themselves, and this includes the police department leadership, are often insular, refusing to share information with the big city of Los Angeles unless absolutely necessary. Thus key clues in investigations involving related crimes in different cities may not be shared, at least in the early stages of investigations.

Los Angeles County is also the first area in the United States not to be dominated by the descendants of White European immigrants in the manner of the East Coast. In 1985, for example, the Mexican and Mexican/American residents of Los Angeles County totaled 2,100,000, approximately the entire population of the state of Arizona just a few years earlier. There were enough Iranians and Salvadorans – approximately 200,000 men, women, and children for each group – to comprise major cities on their own. There were Filipinos, and Armenians, Israelis, Vietnamese, Samoans, Koreans, Chinese, and numerous others. Many of the first generation citizens lived together in their own communities where they shared a common language, common newspapers, and could express common concerns. This was no different than the experiences of immigrants coming to Boston, New York, Cleveland, Chicago, and similar cities a century earlier. What made Los Angeles County unique were the numbers of first generation individuals, the unusual number of languages, and the fact that the police had to learn to deal with many cultures.

Each ethnic group had its own history with government and the police. Sometimes they came from areas where there was a mutual respect. Other times they had fled oppression, the police being the criminals, doing whatever was necessary to keep private citizens supporting the current person in power.

The result of all this was that there was a reluctance on the part of many residents to call police even when they were suspicious of a stranger. The areas in which they lived were considered safe, the newspapers filled with stories of violence in Los Angeles proper, several miles away. Strangers were not necessarily embraced and made welcome, but if they seemed to be minding their own business, they were rarely feared. 'Real' crime was a problem of Los Angeles, not the other cities in the county.

Even worse was the fact that one of the links among the victims was evidence left at the scenes indicating the killer was involved with the occult. Pentagrams and other symbols seeming to relate to Satanism were found at the crime scenes. Since some of the cultures had a history of occult religions being practiced, news of what was being found could generate needless panic.

Law enforcement officers finally released a statement concerning a serial killer. They omitted most of the details of the murders that indicated one man was linked to all of them in order to ensure a conviction. If they said too little about what they knew, possible witnesses might not realize they had information of value to offer. If they said too much, they would be bothered by 'confessors.' These emotionally disturbed individuals have a desire to be punished, and they may also want public attention in whatever way they can get it. They regularly confess to crimes of which they are completely innocent. The more details they can obtain from the news media, the more accurate their confession. This means that someone who would otherwise be dismissed as a crackpot might have to be investigated – a waste of time and money.

Gradually, the investigators were able to determine

what they felt were provable connections among 15 murders beginning earlier than they thought. The first murder had been in Glassell Park, another suburb, and involved Jennie Vincow, a 79-year-old woman who had her throat slashed during a burglary. That one occurred on June 28, 1984, yet until previous unsolved crimes could be matched to later ones, it was listed as an independent case.

The other cases involved fairly consistent violence – beatings, forced sex, and several murders – in the course of burglaries. They were in a variety of communities, such as Monrovia, Burbank, Arcadia, Glendale, Sun Valley, Northridge and Diamond Bar. Always the husband or boyfriend was murdered or left for dead. Always the woman was brutalized, often left bound or in handcuffs. Money and jewelry were taken, but the burglary aspect of the crimes seemed less important than the violence. The man who came to be known as the Night Stalker deliberately entered homes when he knew he would encounter occupants, a situation very different from the average criminal who wants to sneak in and out undetected.

Adding to the violence was the occult aspect of the cases. In a number of instances following rapes or other violence, the women were made to swear they loved Satan. With the exception of the first murder, all the violence known to be connected with the same man occurred in a relatively short period of time – March through August of 1985.

The newspapers were filled with speculations about the identity of the killer. Several of the victims were Asians, leading some experts to conclude that the man was a Vietnam veteran, perhaps living flashbacks where he was still killing the enemy. The trouble with such a theory is that none of the victims seemed to have been chosen in advance. Instead they all lived near freeway entrances. He seemed to be traveling county roads, hitting wherever there was a conveniently located home providing a quick escape route after the murders. This was no different than what police had long found happened with gas stations and convenience food stores. The closer they are to freeways, the more likely they are to be targeted for robbery. The criminals want to be able to flee quickly, the reason similar businesses in congested areas are rarely robbed.

The stories of the Night Stalker created fear in Los Angeles that was far more valid than had gripped the city when killers roamed the streets in the past. The Hillside Strangler focused all his crimes within a 15-mile radius of the community of Glendale. People throughout the county lived in terror, and many people felt they could not sleep safely in their beds. But the Hillside Strangler never stealthily entered a home, never traveled very far, and was feared more for the myth than the reality.

By contrast, the Night Stalker was a roamer. While he never killed in the city of Los Angeles, he did travel the county. He liked to enter occupied homes. He liked to confront the home owner. And he liked to kill any man he encountered.

Sometimes he sexually assaulted children in the home. Usually he left them alone. But he was no respecter of age, gender, or living arrangements.

The purchases of hand guns increased during this time, though most people understood they might not have a chance to use their new weapons. Lock companies and alarm installers prospered. The sale of larger dogs increased. And many people added locks to bedroom doors as well as specially constructed security areas where they could flee and lock themselves inside.

Neighborhood Watch groups were established. People began looking out for their neighbors, confronting strangers, and recognizing that the police could only react. It was their job to protect themselves and those around them. And it was just this attitude that led to the capture of Richard Ramirez, the dreaded Night Stalker.

The beginning of the end for Richard Ramirez was the result of new technology. One of the surviving victims of the Stalker attack, a woman who had been repeatedly raped and brutalized after her boyfriend was murdered, managed to see him escape in a battered orange Toyota station wagon. Earlier that evening, a man who lived in the same neighborhood spotted the station wagon cruising slowly through the streets. Nervous about the Night Stalker and knowing that the car seemed out of place, he noted the number, then called the Sheriff's Department where a deputy wrote down the information. Nothing further was done because no crime had been committed. However, after the surviving victim's report, the deputy checked the license through the state's computer system. The car matched one that had been stolen in the Los Angeles Chinatown district while its owner was eating. Since the Night Stalker was believed to steal cars for his exploits, law enforcement officers began searching for this one.

It took two days for police to locate the abandoned station wagon. They put stakeout teams nearby, watching the car for 24 hours in case the thief decided to use it again. Once they convinced themselves that it was abandoned, they searched for fingerprints.

Among the most important tests for evidence are those involving fingerprints and blood. The fingerprints are unique to the person leaving them. The blood can contain information that narrows the search for the person who spilled it. DNA matches are especially helpful for convictions.

In the past, powder was dusted on areas that might have fingerprints, gently blown, and the residue left outlined where someone touched the surface. However, it was possible to remove them or to have them so faint that the powder method did not work.

By 1985, a new technique was in use for some investigations. Superglue, an unusually strong adhesive, was made from chemicals that had special properties when heated by the air. These reacted to even the slightest moisture left by fingerprints, turning them white. The Toyota was carefully sealed, then a quantity of the glue was placed on a saucer inside the closed car. The heat coming through the glass caused evaporation, and the chemical interaction was meant to reveal any previously invisible prints.

In addition, the Orange County Sheriff's Department utilized a laser beam device that could reveal even the faintest traces of prints someone tried to remove through careful wiping. Then the prints were checked in the state's computer system which held prints of men and women born after January 1, 1960. If he was older, the FBI lab in Washington would have to be used, and that could be time consuming.

The combination of techniques resulted in enough information so that within hours, Ricardo Levya Ramirez was identified as the primary suspect. His name had been Americanized to Richard Ramirez, and most of his friends called him Ricky. He was born around Valentine's Day in February 1960, a fact that would lead to his downfall.

Richard Ramirez had a police record as a petty thief. He also had a good photograph on file from past arrests. Copies of the picture were quickly made and circulated to all newspapers and television news departments in the county and throughout most of California. No location was overlooked, including the foreign language papers that abounded in the various ethnic communities.

Prints left at the scenes of unsolved crimes of violence were cross-checked against Ramirez's print using newly developed computer technology. The print itself could be cross-matched where, in the past, a suspect's name was needed for each case. Special searches could be made based on prints alone, and the result proved that Ramirez had been present at a number of the crime scenes. There was no question in the minds of law enforcement officers of his probable guilt. They would need more evidence to gain convictions, but they had enough to make an arrest.

Ramirez was not in California at the time his identity was discovered. But friends and former neighbors abounded, and they were soon being interviewed by both police and reporters. It was learned that he was 6 feet, 1 inch tall, weighed 155 pounds and was missing several teeth. The remaining teeth were stained and often rotten, a fact that would given him the foul breath many of his surviving victims described. He obsessively listened to heavy-metal rock music, was fascinated with Satanism, and he always liked to dress in dark clothes.

The foul breath had been so frequently reported that it was the subject of some of the questioning. Those who truly knew him explained that, when healthy, he liked to eat sweets and drink cola. The closest he came to healthy food was a love for yogurt. But everyone agreed that he never brushed his teeth. They also talked about his weight loss following his using cocaine during the previous year. He had started by snorting it, then began the higher risk activity of injecting it in his arm. He also drew what was described as a 'Satanic star' on his upper arm, and a 'witch's star' on his stomach.

Ramirez was known as a car thief, specializing in Datsuns and Toyotas. He allegedly had obtained a master key enabling him to open any lock on either vehicle.

The more Ramirez used drugs, the more he craved sugar. Friends who had seen him change in recent months talked of his increasing his consumption of candy cola drinks. He had little interest in anything other than drugs and sweets, and when a friend, worried about his diet, took him to a restaurant for a more balanced meal, Ramirez refused to eat.

Investigators learned that Ramirez had been raised in El Paso, Texas. He lived in a poor section of the community known as the Ledo barrio, having few friends. It was an active gang area, but Ramirez had no interest in such groups. He enjoyed the video arcades, and when he was a teenager, he liked to drive to wealthier communities surrounding El Paso, silently enter the homes, and steal everything he could. He avoided the owners, was never violent, but fortified himself with marijuana to get the courage. He was not always successful, and he ultimately spent time in reform school.

While everyone who knew Ramirez could picture him as a professional thief, no one thought of him as violent. He was remembered for being interested in martial arts when he was in junior high school, but he practiced in his backyard, usually while listening to rock music. He loved to read horror stories, and devoured articles about rock musicians, all solitary activities. Some saw him as cowardly. Others felt that if he was guilty of the rapes and murders, it was because he had been brain damaged by a bad diet and heavy drug use.

None of this information mattered when Ramirez arrived back in Los Angeles on August 31, 1985. He had been traveling in Phoenix, Arizona, trying to relax. He either had a supplier of cocaine in that city, or made contact with one. Whatever the case, he not only stayed stoned while in Phoenix, he bought a large quantity of the drug for use when he returned home.

Ramirez did not realize that the same day he returned to Los Angeles, every newspaper and television station was carrying his photograph, and every radio broadcast his name and description. When he stopped to buy a soft drink and some donuts from Tito's Liquor State about 8:30 a.m., other customers instantly recognized him from the front page photo on *La Opinion*.

The customers became vocal, Ramirez uncertain what was happening until he checked the other papers in the store. His photograph was on all of them – *Orange County Register*, *Los Angeles Daily News*, *San Francisco Examiner*, *Los Angeles Times*, *Sacramento Bee*, and *Los Angeles Herald Examiner*. The picture was his old mug shot and he knew he was in trouble. He fled the store while the cashier called the police.

Ramirez ran down the street, racing two miles in the next 12 minutes. When he stopped to catch his breath, yet another passer-by recognized him from the publicity. By 8:57 a.m., with sighting reports flooding the police department, the area where Ramirez had run was being cordoned off. Police helicopters were in the air. Police cruisers were trying to set up road blocks to keep him from escaping.

On Percy Street, just off Mott Street, Ramirez raced to the home of Bonnie Navarro. He begged her for help, speaking in Spanish. He was so winded and sweat covered that she thought he was a mugging victim. As she started to open her screen door, she looked more closely at him, realizing who he was. She screamed, slammed the door, and her 20-year-old son came rushing out. He tried to pursue Ramirez for a moment, then came back inside to call the police and comfort his mother.

Ramirez now turned to cars. He reached the 800 block of Indiana Avenue where he found a woman sitting in a car in a supermarket parking lot. He tried to pull her from the vehicle in order to steal it, but his desperate actions and the woman's screams caught the attention of people in the area. Arturo Benevidez was in his barber shop next to the supermarket, talking to a friend when he heard the screams. Arturo Perez was drinking coffee in a nearby donut shop. They left what they were doing in order to pursue the man at the same time that other passers-by, drawn by the commotion, also recognized him.

Ramirez began running, instinctively racing towards the low income Hispanic area of Hubbard Street. Why he chose this district is uncertain. Some think it reminded him of the El Paso neighborhood where he was raised. Others felt that his Hispanic features would help him blend in. Still others think he ran blindly. Whatever the case, it was the wrong way to go.

Hubbard Street residents are typical of Hispanic communities in the Southwest. The people are artistic, religious, and filled with pride. The young men often turn their cars into 'low riders' which can be driven with the chassis riding only an inch or two off the ground. They alter the mechanics, add special hydraulics which are sometimes rigged to operate independently, allowing the car to be bounced or dipped from side to side. They also paint them, the most elaborate having the artistic beauty of holy icons and, occasionally, having religious themes. Church is important in the community, and while gang members are there, family is more important. The people are hostile to outsiders who own businesses of one type or another, feeling that if they really cared about the community, they would make their homes there as well. They work hard and try to give a better life to their children as well as, in many instances, sending a portion of their income to family members still living in Mexico.

Richard Ramirez's second mistake was jumping the fence that separated the street from Luis Muñoz's backyard where Muñoz was cooking ribs and hamburgers on an outdoor grill. Outraged by the intrusion, he struck Ramirez with his barbecue tongs when the Night Stalker refused to explain himself.

Ramirez raced for the fence, leaping into the backyard of Faustino Pinon who was working on the transmission of his car. Before he landed, Muñoz struck his wrist, causing him great pain.

This time Ramirez shouted he had a gun, thinking he could scare the man and perhaps steal the car. Ramirez managed to climb inside, but the owner caught the wheel and sent the car smashing into the fence. Ramirez threw the car into reverse, but instead of escaping, he hit the garage, the car stalling. Piñon grabbed him, but Ramirez managed to escape.

Suddenly the chase was on. He tried to steal a Ford Granada from Angelina de la Torres who recognized him from his picture. As she screamed, her husband, Manuel, came out and took up the chase. Then came Jose Burgoin, along with his sons Jaime and Julio.

Ramirez was caught briefly, punched, then sped ahead of his pursuers, stopping briefly to turn and stick his tongue out at them. He quickly resumed running, but by then Manuel de la Torres, armed with a metal bar, managed to reach Ramirez and smack him on the head. Ramirez was not seriously injured, but he dropped, unable to continue running. Jaime and Julio held him down, and within moments Sheriff's Deputy Andres Ramirez arrived. Richard Ramirez, the Night Stalker, had been captured.

The evidence against Ramirez was overwhelming in the 15 cases for which convictions were gained. The trial was disgusting, a litany of rape, mutilation, terror, and death experienced by innocent men and women in what should have been the safety of their own homes. Yet not everyone was horrified. A number of teenaged girls and young women attended regularly. Among them was Bernadette Brazal, perhaps the most ardent of admirers. She was young, attractive, and like so many other 'lovers' of serial killers, she chose to ignore the facts in favor of fantasy. During an interview with an Associated Press reporter, she was quoted as saying, 'I feel such compassion for him. When I look at him, I see a real handsome guy who just messed up his life because he never had anyone to guide him.'

The young woman gave her age as 23 and said she was a student at California State University in Los Angeles. She had never met the 'attractive' Ramirez, a man she thought reminded her of a movie star. However, she had been writing daily love letters and sending photographs – 50 in all according to her statements. She thought that now that he was caught, he could learn to be good and to stop listening to bad rock music. However, he refused to answer her letters and she became upset with him.

Most of the other trial groupies claimed to be college journalism students. Others were trying to save his soul or share his interest in the occult. The oddest was Cindy Haden, a woman who would later relocate near his prison and visit him twice a week when possible after he was sentenced to death for his crimes. Haden went so far as to appear on the Phil Donahue show to declare her love, a fact made all the more unusual because she was a member of the jury that voted unanimously to convict him. During a later interview, Haden would allude to improper evidence used against him and the possibility that he was innocent of at least some of the charges.

Christine Lee was different from the other Ramirez fans. During interviews concerning her relationship with the serial killer, a relationship that includes her alleged engagement to be married to him, she revealed a past that indicated reasons for being with the killer. Those reasons had nothing to do with love. She commented:

'My parents have a lot of money, right? He [father] gave me black eyes a lot, and I'd go to school . . . like then . . . then it wasn't reported, you know what I mean? My aunt has home videos of when I was six and I had two black eyes, and I told her, and she just goes 'oh, shut up, liar.' You know what I mean? I don't even talk to them anymore. I just stopped a few months ago.'

Christine felt that her father's violence towards her was abnormal, not because she believed that parents failed to strike their children. Instead, she was convinced that most men hit their sons but think twice before battering their daughters. The idea that a father might love his children, nurturing them without violence, was almost beyond her comprehension. 'Family' meant pain, and fathers were the primary perpetrators of the violence that filled the nightmare most people call childhood.

'I felt like something was wrong [when her father abused her]. Like when I was 13 and I told my aunt, and she just like . . . "Yeah, yeah, yeah. You're a liar." And she told my father. And then I got in trouble for telling her. He punched me in the face.

'And then right after that I dropped out of high school, and had a baby, and I was like, I've got to get away from these people. I was like an "A" student.

'And now by being near Richard [Ramirez] it's like, *I feel like I'm embarrassing them, and I love it* [emphasis added]. You know what I mean?'

'And I love embarrassing them [her parents]. Like they've got really good jobs and they've got a lot of money, so this is like embarrassing them to death, and I love it.

'Like I've been on every talk show except *Oprah*, and some I've been on three times, like two or three times. *A Current Affair* like three times. *Inside Edition* . . .'

Christine has no illusion about the violent potential of her 'fiance.' As she explained about her visits with Richard, 'If he were to reach over and punch me, the guards would kill him.'

Despite this awareness of his potential for violence,

Christine refuses to dwell on his past. 'Another thing. I think serial killers are disgusting and I never think of him as one. At the same time I think of him like as a weapon, and I stick him in my parents' face and laugh. So, you know what I mean?

'I don't believe this is happening to me, though.

'The first time I saw him was four years ago [1989]. My husband was . . . like . . . he was an animal. And I left him and I moved out to California with my cousins.' She had been married a year, having just had a baby when she left her husband.

'The day after we got married, he totally changed. Right before, he was all nice, this and that . . . As soon as we got married, the next day he changed into a different person. Just an animal. He hit me a lot, like he threw an ash tray at me and it hit me right in the face and it split open my head, and I couldn't believe it. I was like a month pregnant then, but the whole time I was pregnant, he hit me. The whole time. [Christine was not pregnant when she got married. She got pregnant approximately a month into the marriage.]

'He was just an animal. We got married in November. I got pregnant in December. And I had the baby in August. And then from September through . . . what was it . . . December or November . . . the next three months I had to save up the money to move back out to California and get away from him. And then I went right near Richard, and for four years I've stayed with Richard. And that's what everyone's telling me now – "oh, you're just looking for safety."

'He [Ramirez] was really nice, like when I first met him, like the first year. When I first seen him on TV, I just felt he looked . . . I don't know . . . He looked familiar to me for some reason. I don't know why.'

'Like you know when you meet someone and you feel you've known them a long time even though you haven't. That's what I felt like with him. I don't know why.

'I saw on the news he was in San Quentin, and that was like an hour from where me and my cousin lived. And then I met my friend, my friend from New Jersey. She came up, too. And then one day we just went up there. But I thought it would be like a one time thing, and I just been going up for four years.

'He was just really nice, and then I felt sorry for him. Then I met his attorney, and his attorney told me, "He's innocent. He didn't do anything. I want you to keep visiting him." '

Neither Christine nor the attorneys believed in Richard Ramirez's innocence in the Night Stalker cases. Although there might have been some concern that the police would try to blame him for more crimes than he committed as a way of clearing older cases, no one doubted that he was a serial murderer. He left too many living witnesses, retained too many souvenirs.

'Everybody's telling me that it looks good for him in court, like I have two kids, and if he has a wife and two little kids, then he looks good. So that's what his attorneys want.

'One day a newspaper's up there and they took pictures of me, and *USA Today*, and they put it on Page 2. And this was only like a year after I met him. The day the newspaper article came out, my phone was ringing off the hook from every TV show. TV shows, magazines, everything, and since then, I've just been doing like all these TV shows. They wanted me to come on it and talk about my relationship with him.

'They all told me that because of my looks, it helps keep the interest.' She is a physically beautiful woman who looks like an actress who was appearing on the cover of *Playboy* magazine at the time. She is also not naive enough to believe in a future with her serial killer.

She told of dating others, including a law enforcement officer.

But as Christine admits, the main appeal of Richard Ramirez is much like the appeal of a large, vicious dog kept for protection, yet feared because he is unpredictable and could turn against the owner. As nervous as you might be having him close, there is also the comfort that comes from knowing that the potential for violence terrifies your enemies. '*I feel like I'm embarrassing them [her parents] and I love it.*'

The Girls are Not Alone

The women who love the men who kill can often be understood because of their past experiences with males. Certainly that is true with a woman such as Christine Lee. More important, the vast majority, though proclaiming their beloveds to be misunderstood, innocent, or changed, have no impact on parole boards and the public at large. They are seen as eccentric, misguided, or 'crazy.'

Sometimes they get a commercial voice. Sondra London became friend and lover (on paper) of Danny Rolling, then sold their writings to *The National Examiner*, a supermarket tabloid. Rolling committed five murders in Gainesville, Florida, in August, 1990, and confessed to them in court on February 15, 1994.

The brutality of the deaths was horrible. Christa Hoyt's head was found on a bookcase shelf. She had been raped, stabbed, and gashed from her neck to her stomach. Manny Taboada and Tracey Paules, both 23, were violently stabbed to death, Tracey also being raped. And the other two victims, Sonja Larson, 18, and 17-year-old Christi Powell, were hacked to death. Christi was also sexually mutilated after being raped. Yet despite this, Rollings had the fantasy that led him to write, 'Darling, don't ever harbor a thought that we shall never embrace. I still hold fast to the hope that we will be married one day soon.' And Sondra said, 'I knew Danny's fate was sealed when the jury recommended the death penalty. But I prayed that somehow there might still be room for a small glimmer of hope.'

Rolling's story was made more fascinating because he claimed that he believed he was possessed by a demon named 'Gemini . . . the Spirit from Hell that possess and corrupts the innocent soul unawares.'

The story was front page for the May 10, 1994 *National Examiner* which featured the headlines: 'EXCLUSIVE: INSIDE THE TORTURED MIND OF DANNY ROLLING', 'GAINESVILLE KILLER'S OWN STORY,' 'Chilling diaries', 'Eerie sketches', 'Kinky passions', 'Chat with Devil.' When the two-part series was over, Rolling remained infamous. His fiancee, Sondra London, gained more attention than her past writing and two failed marriages had ever brought her.

What is far more troubling is the growing series of commercial enterprises surrounding the murderers. Some of the enterprises are apparently attempted with tongue firmly planted in cheek, the entrepreneurs guilty of little more than bad taste. For example, in 1992, a California company introduced serial killer trading cards along the line of baseball trading cards. Each card had a photograph of the killer on one side, and brief 'statistics' concerning his victims on the other.

Charles Manson is perhaps the most widely merchandised of all the men involved with mass murder and serial killing. His past is well known, culminating on the night in August, 1969, where his followers forced their way into two homes and killed seven people. Among these was the pregnant actress Sharon Tate whose womb was slashed by her assailants. As was made clear in a best selling book on the murders and their subsequent capture and conviction, the Manson

Family cult was extremely violent, without remorse or regard for human life. At least two of the Family members claim to have 'found God.' Yet at the same time that one of them, Susan Atkins, was proclaiming herself 'born again' by day, reports from other inmates revealed that many an evening she was teaching women how to kill with a knife!

Zooport Riot Gear in Newport Beach, California, was among the first of the businesses to produce a Manson T-shirt. Sensitive to aspects of Manson's crimes, and not wanting to alienate their market, the swastika Manson carved into his forehead was retouched from his photograph before the transfer to the $17 shirt. The shirts have the slogans 'Team Charlie,' 'Charlie Don't Surf,' 'Charles In Charge,' [A play on the title of a popular television situation comedy] and 'Support Family Values.' Ten cents of each sale was set aside for Manson as a royalty.

Among the wearers of such a shirt has been Axl Rose, leader of the extremely popular rock group 'Guns N' Roses.' He has worn the Manson likeness during several concerts, fascinating his fans. Not only has this boosted sales of such items, including at the San Francisco store Ameba where Manson dresses, shirts, children's wear, jackets, headbands, and pants are offered, it also resulted in correspondence between Manson and Rose. The latter ultimately led to the use of a Manson song entitled 'Look at Your Game, Girl' on their album 'The Spaghetti Incident?'

Other prison inmates have developed side businesses. Numerous prisoners have become interested in particular aspects of the arts. The late John Wayne Gacy, for example, a serial killer of men and teenaged boys, was famous for his clown paintings. Ken Bianchi became interested in art, though he did not make it a cottage industry. One of his lawyers received some of the art work, but it was not so widely distributed as original

Gacy paintings. Charles Gervais, a multiple murderer in Louisiana, has used his art to express his feelings about himself and society. And numerous others have also tried to express themselves through art, sculpture, and writing.

In principle, there is nothing wrong with someone using a song by Manson. But this was not a song written in the penitentiary. Instead, it was a love ballad he wrote in order to help him lure young women into his Manson Family of cult killers. He would sing the love ballad to new recruits, and the inclusion of such a song was a direct slap in the face of every survivor and surviving family member of his victims.

Everyone involved with the Guns N' Roses album seemed to be aware of the potential for backlash, a fact which has made those hostile to the inclusion all the angrier. It was an uncredited cut on the Geffen Records label. Instead of noting the songwriter's name, the only connection is heard when Axl Rose ends the song with the spoken words, 'Thanks, Chas.'

The performers were also of a mixed mind about the song. After its release, lead guitarist Slash realized it was not a good idea. Axl Rose was defending the inclusion while Slash commented, 'We naively thought there was a certain dark humor in Manson singing those love songs.' He added, ' . . . Even though I was only 4 in 1969, I remember what a shock it was to my hippie parents that there would be someone like Manson out there.'

Manson might be the source of dark humor, yet the song's original purpose is constantly seen as a vicious swipe at the victims. More importantly, Manson's share of money from the sales of the album is quite large. For every $1 million in record sales, a very realistic number for the popular group, Manson was to earn $62,000. This was neither charity nor a way for Manson to help the survivors of his victims. It was a commercial venture for all concerned, and all that will keep Manson from collecting is a 1971 lawsuit by Bartek Frykowski, the son of one of the victims.

There is also a full album of Charles Manson songs. Performance Records of New Brunswick, New Jersey, became the distributor. The record, called 'Love and Terror,' has 12 songs and was originally recorded weeks before the Manson family murder spree. The marketing of the album has been for its historic value and the sales have been relatively limited. None of the money goes to Manson or anyone connected with him. Only charities are supported by what would have been the composer's royalties, and no effort is made to hide the identity of the person performing.

Television journalists have also supplied Manson with money for interviews, determined to help boost the ratings of their shows. More than $10,000 has been paid to him, and fans frequently send him money. These contributions have made him wealthy by prison standards, enabling him to enjoy commissary privileges in the maximum security Corcoran State Prison near Fresno.

There is a sick humor to all of this for some of the people involved in the creation of hats, beanies, stickers, and the like featuring Charles Manson's likeness. In fact, one of the Huntington Beach, California, stores selling this type of paraphernalia is named the Electric Chair. But there are also people who fail to understand the depths of humanity. Many serial killers are apparently affable, polite, often highly intelligent individuals. They may be drifters and they may be very well educated. Many have been loving husbands, sons, and/or fathers. They can be extremely articulate and sensitive in the vast majority of the hours of their lives. Yet they have already murdered, and if released into society, they will kill again.

The classic misunderstanding was that of author

Norman Mailer who, though posturing as a street-wise tough guy who has seen it all, seems actually quite naive when it comes to the reality of men of extreme violence. He befriended imprisoned writer Jack Henry Abbott, a brilliant, articulate writer whose book, *In The Belly Of The Beast*, was a best selling look at life behind bars. In that book Abbott told of his life in prison where, at 37, he had lived for more than 20 years, 14 of them in solitary confinement. He was a bank robber and murderer on the outside, and had stabbed a fellow inmate in 1966, adding 14 years to his sentence.

Abbott was a very clever man who was self-educated in the field of literature. He studied the scholars of history, and was apparently so cultured that Mailer became convinced he should be released. He seemed to feel that, though Abbott said in his book that he would kill again, a man of such brilliance could not be a danger to society. He worked for his release on parole – and succeeded.

Abbott was true to his word, though. He liked to carry a knife because knives used on human flesh resulted in no resistance. Cutting a man was the same as 'cutting into hot butter, no resistance at all,' he wrote, and he proved that on July 18, 1981. It was a that day that he stabbed to death a New York City waiter with whom he had an argument in the restaurant where the waiter worked. The disagreement was over the use of the rest room, and Abbott immediately fled the state. He was captured in Louisiana and, in 1982, sentenced to 15 years in prison.

Was the death predictable? Almost certainly. Would it have happened had he served his full sentence and then been released? No one knows. What mattered was that Abbott had no illusions about himself, no illusions about his being a man who would kill again. But Norman Mailer seemed to overlook everything except

Abbott's intellectual attainments, and the result was the death of the waiter.

Perhaps society is always at risk from such men. Many serve their sentences and are released. But the foolishness of the deification of the violent becomes obvious when a Jack Henry Abbott takes a life for nothing more than the issue of where he could urinate. It was compounded because Mailer seemed to look at the writing and not the man, a situation perhaps not dissimilar to the Axl Rose use of Charles Manson's love song for new recruits.

CHAPTER 4

WHERE DOES IT ALL BEGIN?

Jeffrey Dahmer did not want to live alone. He was 18 when his parents divorced, his mother moving out of state with his brother, a boy six years his junior. His father was working long hours as a scientist, and since Jeff was legally an adult male, no one thought about his feelings, about his loneliness. Yet there seemed no one willing to listen to his troubles, no one to help ease him through nights he frequently spent hating to go to bed. It was when darkness fell that the loneliness was most intense. And so, in the twilight hours of each passing day, he began to consume ever larger quantities of alcohol, trying to render himself unconscious until morning.

Dahmer could have gone on dates. He could have joined clubs or actively sought new friends after graduation from high school. But such actions, though obviously productive, would have exposed him to the risk of rejection. He had little interest in women, yet he had not fully accepted his homosexuality and did not know which men would agree to sex and which would refuse.

The loss of his mother was rejection enough in his life. And since he craved the physical presence of another person, not an interactive friendship, his thoughts turned to an alternative. He began to think about killing someone. As Detective Patrick Kennedy of the Milwaukee Police Department's Homicide unit noted in his report:

Jeff Dahmer 'states that he received physical pleasure from being with the victims when they were alive and he would have preferred that the victims remained alive; however, he states that it was better to have them with him dead than to have them leave. He states that when he felt when they were to leave, that is when he would decide to kill them.

'Regarding the fact that he stated that he had infact (sic) eaten the parts of one of his victims, he states that he feels that by eating parts of the victim, this was his way of keeping them with him even longer and making his victims part of himself.'

'It's hard for me to believe that a human being could of done what I done, but I know that I did it. I want you to understand that my questions regarding satan and the devil were not to defuse guilt from me and blame the devil for what I've done, because I realized what I've done is my guilt, but I have to question whether or not there is an evil force in the world and whether or not I have been influenced by it. Although I am not sure if there is a GOD [emphasis in original report], or if there is a devil, I know that as of lately I've been doing a lot of thinking about both and I have to wonder what has influenced me in my life.' (Confession of Jeffrey Dahmer to Milwaukee Police Homicide Detective Patrick Kennedy; 08–08–91.)

Jeffrey Dahmer possibly fits American's perceptions of a serial killer. He was a loner. He was a homosexual. His victims were mostly dark skinned, not from prominent families, and frequently sharing Jeff's sexual orientation. In addition, his biological mother was alleged to be emotionally disturbed according to many reports, adding to the image of a one-off, a 'bad seed'. And Jeff not only killed his victims, he kept some body parts as souvenirs, consuming others. For example, he was excited by the biceps of one of his victims. After murdering the man, he saved one bicep for a souvenir, then took the other, coated it with Crisco, added meat tenderizer, and fried it for a snack. As he confessed his actions, each victim brought another recipe from hell, a fact so horrible that it quickly became material for late night comedians. There were sick gags about a Jeffrey Dahmer cookbook with titles such as 'To Serve Mankind.'

'He [Dahmer] related that there were other times in which he had eaten part of the victim. The first time was the person he identified as *CASH D (Raymond SMITH* – Victim # 5). He related that he eat [sic] this victim's heart. He related that it tasted kind of spongy. He indicated that the next victim was the person he met by the bookstore, (Victim #7 – *Ernest MILLER*). He related that this was a person he really liked. He indicated that he had fileted his heart and thigh muscle of this subject, but it was so tough he could hardly chew it. He then purchased a meat tenderizer and used it on the bicep. He stated that it tasted like beef or a filet mignon. The next person who he was going to eat, and in fact tried, was victim #15 – *Oliver LACY*. He stated that on this victim he ate his bicep. This also tasted like Filet mignon. He stated that he would tenderize it first. He stated that he did keep this individual's heart and bicep. We asked him if he had eaten the body parts, just plain. He stated that he would use salt, pepper and A-1 Steak sauce on them. He stated that the reason he ate these parts was because he was curious but then it was because he wanted to make them a part of him. He stated that this way he could keep these people with him. He stated that he ate only the people that he really liked and wanted them to be a part of him or with him all the time.'

There was another side to Jeffrey Dahmer, though, a side most people were reluctant to discuss. His father was a scientist with a Ph.D. His biological parents were estranged, though not until he was in his late teens. If his mother had been as terrible as the press seemed to indicate, then that implied that Dr Lionel Dahmer either distanced himself from his son or refused to protect his son. Either way, an issue of neglect has to be raised.

There is also the question of whether or not the father was physically or emotionally abusive, a question no one is comfortable asking because he is well educated, respected on the job, and maintained a 'nice' home for his family.

Then there are those around Jeff growing up. He was known to hang out in school with other boys whose primary interest was smoking marijuana. In his early teens he became fascinated with animals killed on the road. He would take dead dogs and disembowel them, sometimes hanging parts of their bodies on trees. One dead dog was left impaled on a stick near the Dahmer home in Bath, Ohio, when he was around 14 or 15 years old. Later, when he was of legal age to drive, he would deliberately run down animals with his car, then 'experiment' with them. His talk in school was about using taxidermy skills on a human.

Jeffrey also began practicing dismemberment. He had no training, could find no literature on the subject. Instead, he started his studies with dogs, and when he felt a degree of competence, switched to humans.

Jeffrey first experimented with homosexuality when he was 14. He began drinking heavily when he was 17, a year younger than the legal age. Teachers, other parents, and various adults in the community were aware that Jeff was a troubled youth, yet none reached out to him. No one tried to see what was causing him to engage in self-destructive, anti-social, and illegal behavior.

Ultimately there is the question of personal responsibility. This is the one issue that is rarely raised by police, prosecution, or defense when a serial killer is caught and goes on trial. Did the man have a choice? Was he insane? Was he compelled by inner demons? Was he, in fact, possessed by the forces of evil?

Most serial killers have experienced one or another forms of child abuse growing up. Some have been the victims of neglect or unusually brutal punishment when they have gone against their parents' wishes. Others have been victimized by abnormal punishment, the same infraction of a family rule sometimes resulting in a savage beating and other times resulting in their being smothered with love.

The most blatant example of what can happen is the case of Leslie Williams and his sister, Dorothy. Both were raised in extreme brutality. Their mother was a prostitute. They were both beaten, raped, and endured horrors at the hands of family members. Both were highly intelligent. Both suffered from low self-esteem.

Dorothy fled home and became a promiscuous alcoholic in her youth. Gradually she gained an education, recognized that she did not have to destroy her future because of her past, joined Alcoholics Anonymous, and became a successful mother and career woman. Leslie Williams chose to take out his anger against his mother – whom he now claims was the perfect parent – by attacking girls. He went from being a serial rapist to being a serial rapist/murderer before he was caught and sentenced to life in prison.

Both Leslie and his sister remain highly articulate. Leslie spends much of his time answering fan mail from women and an occasional gay male seeking a lover who will abuse him. He has given a mother sex advice for her teenaged daughter at the parent's request. And he has agreed to television appearances on Oprah Winfrey's television show. He has also written extensively about his crimes to his sister who, to her horror, has come to see his actions as a deliberate choice.

Jeff Dahmer also made choices. Like many other serial killers, he placed himself in positions where help was available, then rejected it. For example, Ken Bianchi sought psychiatric help when he was 18, then did not like what he was learning about himself. After he quit going to the sessions, three little girls were murdered.

Another serial killer, Edmund Kemper, of Santa Cruz, California, had a superior intelligence along with a history of violence. On August 27, 1964, when Kemper was 15 and living with his grandparents, he picked up a .22 rifle and shot his grandmother just to see how it would feel. Then he shot his grandfather and called his mother to tell her his grandparents were dead.

Kemper was sent to Atascadero State Hospital for the criminally insane that December. Five years later, despite the advice of the hospital staff, he was turned over to the California Youth Authority which allowed him to live with his mother.

Kemper began a spree that led to a series of rapes and murders. He also found that having sex with dead bodies, especially if he decapitated them first, was exciting for him. Eventually he murdered his mother, left Santa Cruz, and called the police to arrest him.

Kemper, like Bianchi, knew he was disturbed. He began seeing a psychiatrist and came to understand that there was strong hatred for his mother. Rather than seeking help to get on with his life in a productive way, Kemper murdered his mother, placed her body in the trunk, paid one last visit to the therapist, and left the area. When he turned himself in, he explained that he had understood his choices but felt that murder was a faster way to handle his problems than going through therapy.

The police report on Jeff Dahmer also reflects the issue of choice. The first murder he committed could only have been avoided if school authorities, family members, or others in a position to help him had intervened. That killing occurred in June, 1978, almost a decade before he killed again. The victim, Steve Hicks, was hitchhiking on Cleveland–Massilon Road when Dahmer picked him up and took him to his home to drink beer. They drank in Dahmer's bedroom, but when Hicks wanted to leave, Jeff struck him on the head with a barbell. This was followed by strangulation.

There was no sex, then. It was just Dahmer's determination not to let Hicks leave. He put the body under the crawl space of the house, later dismembering him and putting the parts into three garbage bags. Two weeks later the bones were broken up and dumped in the woods. The knife used for dismemberment was tossed in the river. The killing had been an act of passion, not something carefully planned in advance. Dahmer also was filled with remorse, though he chose to avoid getting help. The report of the Homicide detective interrogating him about the time states:

'... when he [Dahmer] first moved to West Allis with his grandmother, it was at this time that he decided to try to put behind him the nightmare he had constantly re-lived regarding his first homicide. He stated his grandmother was a religious woman and at this time he began attending church with her and apparently was looking into religious ideals in an attempt to change his life. He stated he recalls reading the Bible and attempting to look for a job and to live the so called "straight and narrow life." He stated that although he constantly tried to delve into the religious aspects of life, he constantly had fantasies of homosexual activity and mutilation of human beings. He stated that eventually during this period of time the fantasies and the urges for, as he called them, "the darker side," bothered him and that he decided to quit attending church and looking into religion, and for a while he delved in the occult. He stated he felt he did this because he felt that since religion wasn't working, maybe he should just delve into the occult and to satanism. However, after reading several books and dabbling in it, he realized this was not for him and then he again gave in to his homosexual tendencies. He stated he began by going to the bookstores where he obtained information regarding gay areas in Milwaukee. He stated he also started reading gay and homosexual pornography and eventually became acquainted with the bars in the homosexual areas of town. From there he began to frequent the gay baths and was a regular member of the gay baths and spent the night several times. He in fact stated that several times he used a liqueur [sic] which had been tampered with by his sleeping pills in the gay baths, however he did not commit any violent acts while there. He only druged [sic] some of his gay friends who he had met and spent the night with in the gay baths. He stated he believes this is the reason why there was such long span between homicides, as he was going through all of these mental changes, trying to leave the old life behind and that once he finally again gave in to his homosexual desires, that it slowly began to escalate over years until he finally gave in to his fantasies of killing and dismembering men after homosexual acts and culminated in his first homicide here in Milwaukee at the Ambassador Hotel.' (From report by Milwaukee Homicide Detective Patrick Kennedy dated 7-30-91.)

Jeff Dahmer was contradicting himself when describing his motivations. Finally he admitted to police 'that during the time that he was cutting up his victims and attempting to dispose of the bones that he was feeling several different emotions. He indicated that the emotions were a combination of fright, for fear of being caught, and excitement knowing that he had done what he had done. He stated that he also had the feeling that the victims could not leave him anymore because he had complete control over them.'

The basics of Jeff Dahmer's life seemed both ordinary and showed a young man with a good work ethic. He was born on May 21, 1960, in Milwaukee, Wisconsin's Deaconess Hospital. He moved to the Akron, Ohio, area and went to Revere High School from 1975 until graduating in June, 1978. He worked part time at the Holiday Inn and attended Ohio State University for one semester. On December 29, 1978, he joined the army as a Private E1, being sent to Military Police School in Fort McClellan, Alabama. However, he did not complete the eight week course. Instead, on May 11, 1979, he took the full six week course needed to become a Medical Specialist at the Army Hospital School at Fort Sam Houston, Texas. From there he was stationed in Baumholder, Germany, from June 1979 though March 24, 1981. Two days later he was discharged at Fort Jackson, South Carolina and flew to Miami Beach, Florida. He only stayed until September of that year, but during that time he had his only heterosexual relationship.

Dahmer went to work at a sandwich shop called Sunshine Submarines. There he met a young British woman named Julie. They became friends, taking walks on the beach and going out to dinner, though never having any sexual attraction. He was only interested in men, and she seemed to be attracted to the manager of the sandwich shop.

The problem was that Julie was illegally in the United States. She would be deported if discovered unless she married an American citizen. She suggested that she and Jeff marry, divorcing as soon as she had full citizenship. However, he felt as though even such an arrangement would imply a commitment to a relationship he was not ready to make. He never considered her a girlfriend.

Dahmer moved back to Ohio, living in Bath, a suburb of Akron, until moving to Milwaukee. There he stayed with his grandmother in the suburb of West Allis, Wisconsin, for the next several years. He did not leave her home until May of 1988, shortly afterwards being arrested for Second Degree Sexual Assault. He was taking sexual pictures of a minor, was caught, and sentenced to five years' probation and a year in a work release program. His term began in June of 1989, and he was freed in March, 1990, living with his grandmother for the next two months. Then he obtained his own apartment at 924 North Street where he eventually would be arrested for murder. He also obtained a job at a candy factory.

During this period, 17 people would die. All were males. All allegedly were either involved with homosexuality, a counter-culture lifestyle, or willing to pose for pictures for a price. Two were white. The rest were dark skinned Hispanic, Asian, and Black. Jeff claimed that the victims were choices of convenience. However, other aspects of his life make this statement questionable. They also blatantly reveal the problems law enforcement officers, sociologists, and psychologists have when dealing with serial killers. Once they catch the guilty parties, there is little interest in truly trying to understand what happened. While each killer is unique, there are also some consistencies which are often overlooked.

The Devil made me do it

Interview by Milwaukee, Wisconsin, Police Homicide Detective Patrick Kennedy, 8-8-91:

'At this time DAHMER started to talk about the movie which we found in his apartment, that being the *Exorcist II*. I asked him at this time why he in fact purchased the *Exorcist II*, and he stated that he had seen the movie when it was first released and that he was fascinated by it. He stated that he enjoyed the movie so much, that when it was first released on video cassette he spent approximately $100.00 in order to purchase a copy of it. I asked him what his fascination was with the movie, to which he stated he was unsure, but he knows that he felt a tremendous amount of guilt, because of his actions. He stated he felt evil and throughly [sic] corrupted, body & soul, because of the horrible crimes he had committed against people. He stated that everytime he would try to overcome his feelings of wanting to kill and dismember people, they would haunt him and overcome him, almost like an addiction. He states that he felt that he could not fight that feeling and wondered if in fact the devil had anything to do with his evil thoughts. He states because of this he watched the movie *Exorcist II* on almost a weekly basis, for approximately 6 mos., and sometimes 2 and 3 times a week. He states that in the movie he could tell that the devil was angry for being condemned and that he could relate with the devil, because he felt that his life on earth was condemned. He went onto [sic] state that the main character in the movie appeared to be driven by evil and that he could relate to this character as he felt that his life was driven by evil.'

Jeff Dahmer admitted to law enforcement officers that he was involved with Satanism. His story of how deeply he was involved changed a little from interview to interview, though he was not a Satan worshiper, nor did he belong to a cult. His most important reference was to 'The Nine Satanic Statements' in Anton LaVey's *The Satanic Bible*.

The Satanic Bible was written by LaVey, a brilliant man, self-taught musician whose work was usually for such counterculture activities as the circus and, at least for a brief time, a striptease show. He was also a photographer for the San Francisco Police Department and the leader of a study group on Satanism. When he formed the Church of Satan, he became the focus for serious scholars, dabblers in Satan worship, the lunatic fringe, and others. When he wrote his book, it became extremely popular throughout the United States, especially among teenagers who were fascinated by messages quite different from the ones provided by their parents, teachers, and religious schools.

The statements probably did not mean much to Dahmer despite his comments. They are found at the front of the book and read:

'1. Satan represents indulgence, instead of abstinence!

'2. Satan represents vital existence, instead of spiritual pipe dreams!

'3. Satan represents undefiled wisdom, instead of hypocritical self-deceit!

'4. Satan represents kindness to those who deserve it, instead of love wasted on ingrates!

'5. Satan represents vengeance, instead of turning the other cheek!

'6. Satan represents responsibility to the responsible, instead of concern for psychic vampires!

'7. Satan represents man as just another animal, sometimes better, more often worse than those that walk on all-fours, who, because of his "divine spiritual and intellectual development," has become the most vicious animal of all!

'8. Satan represents all of the so-called sins, as they all lead to physical, mental, or emotional gratification!

'9. Satan has been the best friend the church has ever had, as he has kept it in business all these years!'

The points are relatively innocuous. Some people find them thought provoking; others find them a little humorous or the comments of a cynic. A few find them mildly blasphemous. The serial killers who have studied

The Satanic Bible or indulged in creating their own occult groups based on it, are highly selective.

This is not to say that *The Satanic Bible* is an 'innocent' book. The real danger of serious Satan worship, beyond the moral issues involved, is that it is a totally self-centered religion. It justifies any personal pleasure, no matter how perverted or painful to others. And though LaVey's writings have never encouraged violence, they create a psychological environment in which a deviant, psychopath, or other disturbed individual can feel justified for inflicting what may be the horrors of the damned on another person.

There is also a mixed message in some of LaVey's writing. He will talk about symbolic sacrifice, and he will talk about genuine sacrifice. Just as you think he is stressing the former to the exclusion of the latter, he will discuss when murdering is appropriate. (He does *not* use the term murder, though that is an accurate term for causing the untimely death of another person.) For example, on page 88 of the Avon Books edition of *The Satanic Bible* (copyright 1969) he writes:

'The use of a human sacrifice in a Satanic ritual does not imply that the sacrifice is slaughtered "to appease the gods." *Symbolically,* [emphasis in original] the victim is destroyed through the working of a hex or curse, which in turn leads to the physical, mental or emotional destruction of the "sacrifice" in ways and means not attributable to the magician.

'The only time a Satanist would perform a human sacrifice would be if it were to serve a two-fold purpose; that being to release the magician's wrath in the throwing of a curse, and more important, to dispose of a totally obnoxious and deserving individual.'

The problem with the second paragraph of the quote from the chapter entitled 'On the choice of a human Sacrifice' is that it gives the disturbed individual justification for his behavior. The reader who is filled with anger can take the text as a message to kill instead of exploring alternative ways of healing.

This is not to say that the censorship of such books is critical for safety. That would be denying the free will of the killer, the choice that he has made, and the fact that hundreds of thousands of others have read the same material without feeling compelled to kill.

Retired police captain Dale Griffis, Ph.D., is an expert on cult and occult related crime. He is a consultant for law enforcement agencies throughout the United States. He has found that there are several types of Satanists, beginning with the Traditional. The Traditional is also the least likely to be found among serial killers or violent individuals of any type.

There have been many stories about the origin of Satanism, and many periods in history when a new leader or approach to worship arose. The Knights Templar were accused of creating a Satanic cult instead of staying loyal to the Pope. Aleister Crowley defined Satanism in the first couple of decades of the twentieth century. And Anton LaVey, the founder of the Church of Satan, created his own twist in the 1960s. But the formalization of the religion dates back to the third century AD as specifically opposed to the practice of Christianity. It was a counter religion, the worship of the dark side, the bad that was necessary in order to also have good.

Satanism has always been a self-centered religion, one that allows for self-gratification. There is Satan worship, of course, but the self is as important as the Devil. Law enforcement officers who have studied the Traditional worshipers have found truth in Detective Sandi Gallant's (San Francisco Police Department's Intelligence Unit) belief statement:

'Satan's goal is to defeat God's plan of grace, to establish a kingdom of evil to ruin man. Satan needs men alive to do his work for him, that is to destroy the good in and good spirit of mankind. Men must be predisposed to doing evil; Satan cannot absolutely overwhelm a good person to do evil.'

The Traditional Satanist is no more likely to kill anyone in the name of Satan than the traditional Christian is likely to murder in the name of God. The groups organize themselves in a manner not unlike that of churches. Participation is a family affair, and membership often extends over several generations.

Traditional Satanist groups have various degrees that can be earned, with definite time limits. There are ritual practices, individual leaders, and the members may be prominent in the community. The groups are no more linked than many Christian groups, and there are serious congregations of Satanists who either lack affiliation with other groups or the affiliation is so loose as to be meaningless. Such groups do not have a central leadership, nor is there the equivalent of the Black Pope which Anton LaVey has occasionally been accused of being.

The important Satanists are those who are sometimes called Dabblers. It is among these individuals that the serial killers are most likely to be found.

The Dabblers are self-styled Satanists. They may develop their own following, bringing two or three friends to rituals of their own creation. Or they may do what Richard Ramirez did, utilizing Satanism as a way of avoiding a sense of responsibility for his own actions. Blaming Satan means that you don't have to face your potential for change, for making choices that are not self-destructive.

Sandi Gallant handled a case in San Francisco that, on the surface, seemed to be connected with Satan worship. The corpse, found with his throat slashed, had been sexually mutilated and murdered on June 21, the Summer Solstice. Traditional Satanists seldom consider the holiday one of great importance. It is also not a holiday where extremist groups dabbling in their own version of Satan worship are known to murder.

Had the murder occurred on Easter Sunday, the law enforcement might have initially considered other possibilities. Since Satanism runs counter to Christianity, the most solemn day of the year for Christians – Good Friday, the day Jesus was put to death on the cross – is a joyous celebration of new life for many Satanists. Those who involve themselves in an animal or human sacrifice, and their numbers are limited, will likely murder on Easter Sunday to make a mockery of the Resurrection. Thus the death, with its ritual trappings including a pentagram carved on the body, seemed more likely to be the work of murderous Dabblers.

A week later another man was murdered in the same way. He was a derelict, and this time, though the ritual concept was present, it was obvious these were not Traditional Satanists.

Eventually the murderers were caught. There were several, the leader being a violent sado-masochistic homosexual who thought it would be fun to experiment with human sacrifice. He formed his own group, and together they kidnapped a transient man who was placed in a cage. He was used for sex acts, then forced back in the cage so he would remain readily available to them. When the leader decided to kill the man, he used his own created ritual.

It was the thrill of the murder that led to the second killing. And that proved so exciting for the leader, he decided to have others join him. He contacted gay men who he knew enjoyed sado-masochism. However, this time he went too far. Very few gay men take pleasure in such activities, and none that he encountered wanted to cause real pain. Upon realizing that the leader was talking violence and murder, the police were alerted.

Neither the Satanism nor the fact that the leader and his first followers were homosexual had anything to do with the crimes. The leader had the desire to kill and he committed the murders in a manner that enabled him to claim to himself that he had no personal responsibility. Yet he would have killed regardless of his sexual orientation, the presence of the others, and the ritual trappings.

Traditional Satanists may have children with psychological problems, but they do not grow up to commit murders any more than the children from extremist Christian groups. The difficulties for law enforcement officers comes from understanding what they are seeing in its context.

For example, many serious Satanists believe that life is found in blood, and that when a child drinks blood, he or she is stronger. Thus there may be the use of animal blood or even human blood when possible (though not from murder), and it may be consumed as is or mixed with more palatable liquids. Yet this is seen as being no odder by the followers than the idea that the drinking of the wine and the eating of the wafer of bread in a Catholic Mass is the ingestion of the body and blood of Jesus. Rituals where children drink blood during what are often regular Friday night services may eventually cause emotional turmoil for the adult coming from such a background, but the actions, in the minds of the true believers, are as loving as a Mass. Likewise, there are other rituals that require genital cleansing which, to an outsider, are obvious sexual molestation. Yet these are cleansing rituals and the adult involved does not think of them in a sexual manner. Again, the problem is that the child comes to maturity accepting as 'normal' what the greater society rejects.

It is the extremely disturbed individual who becomes involved with blood sacrifices, the ritual killing and mutilation of animals, and in some cases, the murder of humans. The rituals created are personal ones that

157

reinforce as 'positive' the violence the leader would commit regardless of ritual.

Unfortunately, when a suspect is located, a search warrant is difficult to obtain at times. The warrant requires that the investigating officers specify what they are seeking relative to the alleged crimes, and that they remove from the home or office nothing more than is stated in the warrant. The Dabbler serial killer may have any number of books, ritual objects, restraints, and the like used for the murders. But they will be based on his fantasies, not something that might be consistent with serious study groups and Traditional practitioners.

Dr Griffis notes that the rituals of the serial killer are quite different from those of a 'self-respecting occultist.' There is rarely a Book of Shadows which will be kept by serious occult practitioners. This is a personal book of spells and incantations along the lines of a prayer book as used by several Christian religious groups. Just as The Book of Common Prayer is an integral part of the Episcopal Church, for example, so the Book of Shadows is an integral part of the Satanist's regular worship. The difference is that the Book of Shadows is sold with blank pages on which the occult practitioner writes personal rituals. Christian prayer books come printed with those prayers and rites understood and followed by all like minded believers.

The type of symbols left at the scene of a serial killer's murder will often be different from those used by a Traditionalist. Often they are symbols that most people connect with the occult, yet they come from unrelated traditions: Satan Worship, Wicca, and various pagan religions, none of which are connected.

Los Angeles County Sheriff's Department Deputies Gerald Biehn and Thomas Kerfoot prepared a reference manual for investigators looking into possible occult related crime including homicide and serial murder. Their experience has revealed consistency in the types of objects and circumstances that will be found when there is a true relationship, not just a Dabbler's involvement. According to their findings, officers approaching a crime scene investigation should look at the following:

'Clues Unique to the Black Occults in General:

1) Mockery of Christian symbols.
   (inverted cross, vandalized Christian artifacts)
2) Use of stolen or vandalized Christian artifacts.
3) Discovery of candles or candle drippings.
4) Unusual drawings, symbols on walls/floors.
   (pentagram, etc.)
5) Non-discernible alphabet.
6) Animal mutilations including removal of specific body parts. (anus, heart, tongue, ears, etc.)
7) Use of animal parts (feathers, hair, bones) to form signs and symbols on ground.
8) Absence of blood on ground or in animal.
9) Altar containing artifacts.
   (candles, chalice, knife, etc.)
10) Effigies like voodoo dolls stuck with pins or otherwise mutilated.
11) Bowls of powder or colored salt.
12) Skulls with or without candles.
13) Robes, especially black, white, or scarlet.
14) Rooms draped in black or red.
15) Books on Satanism, "Magick" Rituals, etc.

Homicide Investigations:

1) Location and position of the body.
2) Missing body parts.
3) Location of stab wounds/cuts.
4) Branding iron or burn marks.

5) Wax drippings on victim or ground.

6) Oils or incense found on body.

7) Human or animal feces consumed or found on victim.

8) Blood letting.

9) Stomach contents analyzed for – urine, drugs, wine, potions, etc.'

Teens and young adults who kill are looking for power. They have been desensitized to life by a variety of factors including distant parents who fail to supply strict moral values. A charismatic killer who creates the trappings of a cult can give other teens an artificial family. They will experience discipline and emotional support lacking in their homes. They can easily be drawn into helping a charismatic serial killer who wants to use the trappings of the occult to commit his crimes.

In talks with some Dabblers who have involved others in their crimes, they have stressed that they chose their followers based on their willingness to debase themselves. If they could get interested teens, often partially desensitized by drugs, to be the recipient of oral or anal sex with the leader, to drink from a chalice containing urine, and/or to sacrifice an animal, usually either drinking the blood or sharing in the eating of the heart or other body part, then they could rely upon them for murder. It was also felt that the murder helped unify the group.

Charles Gervais of Louisiana explained that the victim of a ritual-style murder had to be a stranger in order to fully unite the members of the group. It was hardest to kill someone you know nothing about and about whom you have no strong feelings. It was easiest to kill someone you know and dislike. Once the first life was taken, and it was often done in such a manner that each member of the group contributed directly to the death (e.g. multiple stab wounds, each of which missed a vital area but together caused irreversible trauma), then the members were quite willing to kill as often as the leader desired.

Griffis has felt that the potentially violent teens who may get caught up in ritual murder often send cries for help. He noted that the various privacy acts often intimidate adults who should get involved. He notes that judges frequently allow battered children to return to an abusive home life because they feel that the natural environment is best. He mentioned one teenaged girl who could tolerate her abusive home life no longer and sent her teacher a cry for help. The girl wrote a note saying she was going to kill herself. The teacher went to the principal with the note only to be told that it was best to not get too involved. There were privacy issues and other factors that could result in an embarrassing situation. Two days later the teenager was dead by her own hand, and at the funeral home, the principal said to the superintendent of schools, 'I guess we should have told you.' Yet tragically it is also possible that no one would have gotten involved.

Privacy issues are also raised when a troubled teen becomes familiar to more than one agency. Since they are not allowed to share information, often what seems to be an isolated incident is a pattern of serious, over-looked abuse.

Does Satan worship lead to murder? There is no evidence that it does. However, just as there are those who may kill because they hear the voice of God urging them to do so, there are also those who dabble in the occult to make themselves feel that the murders they commit are somehow blessed. Richard Ramirez, the Night Stalker, followed this pattern. And books such as *The Satanic Bible* are occasionally found in the possessions of men arrested for serial killings. But it is important to note that the serial killer would be murdering regardless. Instead of the one influencing the other, the one simply justifies the other in the mind of the murderer.

During the research for this book, the issue of pornography and its impact on serial killers was raised. Just as many serial killers have been found to have *The Satanic Bible* and other works related to the occult in their homes, so many have pornography in their possession.

Sometimes the pornography is of the simplest, most common type available in all adult bookstores or 'adults only' sections of regular bookstores. These are what one police chief called 'fuck books.' The pictures range from full frontal nudity, sometimes with the woman shown playing with her nipple and stroking her vagina, to pictures and stories of sexual intercourse involving two or three consenting adults. Magazines devoted to the extreme acting out of sexual variations often combine articles or stories with photographs that support what may be deviant behavior. This ranges from bestiality to acts of sexual violence supposedly leading to sexual pleasure.

Reading the text gives a false impression of male/female relationships. There are a number of variations, but the general idea is that the woman wants a man to dominate her. How he does this will vary with the story. Sometimes he forces her arms above her head as they lean against a wall or stretch out on the bed. Sometimes he will punish her with a spanking that may be gentle or rough enough to redden her bottom. Sometimes he will handcuff her, chain her to the ceiling, spread-eagle her on the bed with rope or leather straps, or elaborately tie her hands and feet. The latter can range from images that look like the 'damsel in distress' pictures in true detective magazines to elaborate bondage rituals with ropes encircling the breasts and wound around the vaginal area.

In the stories or captions, the woman may be presented as a scold, a shrew, a bitch. She may be condescending to males in general and the protagonist in particular. She may even openly ridicule the man when they are at work together or out on a date. However, when the man either has had enough and explodes with violence, or when he decides to 'teach her a lesson,' she is shocked by his manliness. She secretly wants him to take charge, to overpower her, and when he does, she is overwhelmed with lust.

One problem with all this is that the stories usually involve sexual games that are considered normal variations of a healthy, consenting sex life between long-time lovers. However, they are taken to an extreme that, if duplicated in real life, would be criminal assault, rape, and battery.

For example, books on sexual fantasies and variations, from Nancy Friday's *My Secret Garden* and *Women on Top* to Gael Greene's *Delicious Sex* to Alex Comfort, MD's classic *The Joy of Sex*, all discuss bondage games. These range from the man or woman pretending to be tied to the bed to more elaborate games where one partner restrains the other loosely enough so that there is no pain, yet securely enough so that resistance is difficult. A gag may also be used, ranging from a scarf tied lightly over the mouth to muffle sound to something placed between the teeth to effectively stop speech.

The books describing the sex games variations of normal, consenting adults, usually have a set of rules accompanying them. The couple is invariably warned to be careful, and to have a signal that the bound partner can use to indicate she or he should be freed. There are other rules, including never leaving the restrained partner alone, and never going to sleep while one person is tied and/or gagged.

The violent pornographic versions of such sex games

give quite different messages. Instead of being a willing partner experimenting after mutual trust has been well established, the aggressor may be on a first date, an office co-worker, a neighbor, or someone else who has not established more than a nodding or business relationship. The bondage does not result from long term intimacy and a mutual decision to experiment. Instead, it comes because the woman 'wants' the man to take her despite the fact that she is always saying 'no' in the story.

The scenarios vary with the imaginations of the writer and photographer (older publications of this type relied upon an illustrator using pen and ink). The woman belittles the man, telling him that she would never go out with him because he is not assertive enough. Or the man lusts from afar, sees her making a fool of herself with the wrong man, and determines to save her against her will. Or some other scenario is used, though always starting with the clear understanding that the woman has said 'no' to the man.

The kidnapping again is whatever the writer decides. Some publications go into elaborate details about the tying up process. Some show that the woman's foolish resistance 'forces' the man to be so firm, the ropes causing pain she will later ignore when overwhelmed with passion. Still others have the woman resisting in a manner that requires excessive force – slapping, spanking, or even a brief but violent beating to render her silent. The woman never gets a black eye, broken jaw, broken ribs, and/or intensely painful bruising as would happen in real life. Instead, the violence brings her up short, making her scared yet impressed with this previously unknown, deeply 'macho' side to the man. The trembling with fear, the whimpering, or whatever else she does also has a hint of sexual arousal both the woman and her aggressor recognize. Once helpless, of course, the sexual arousal dominates and she fights her restraints only because she desperately wants him, his teasing (slapping, spanking, tickling, etc.) only making her hunger for his body.

The items used to silence the victim are also elaborate. The face may be covered in a leather mask with only openings for the eyes and nostrils. A ball gag may be used, a commercial device sold in some sex shops, which has a leather strap, cloth, or some other material with a rubber ball like object in the center. The ball is placed between the teeth in the woman's mouth, and the ends of the gag are tied securely behind her head. A variation has a penis shaped object, much like a dildo, which the woman holds in her mouth. Some advertisements call this a 'training gag,' the idea being that ultimately the woman will be bound while the man's penis is placed in her mouth for forced oral sex.

Whatever the circumstances, the women in the photographs may seem battered and in painful restraints, but their faces do not reveal this. Some seem to be happy with their predicament since they will soon have sex with the man. Others have blank faces, revealing neither pleasure nor pain despite the fact that the average person, restrained in the same manner, would experience great discomfort. Often the passivity or tolerance to the pain is caused by drugs given to the models. In fact, some are what are known as 'coke whores' (or heroin whores, etc.) and will let themselves be photographed in exchange for the drugs they receive before, during, and/or after the photography session.

Other models for the photographs are prostitutes, lovers of the photographers, or victims of white slavery – women forced into prostitution and other sexual activities against their will. But who poses is not of a concern except for law enforcement officers and social workers. What matters is the impact of seeing violence as a natural part of an interpersonal relationship.

There are three types of men who routinely buy hard

165

core pornography. [X-rated videos sold in chain video stores fall into a different category. Many such X-rated videos that do not include violence are rented by married couples, sometimes actively involved in the community. They use them as foreplay, to build fantasy, and to get ideas for varying their own activities in bed.] The first individual is the man who is curious. The magazines are expensive, often selling for from $10 to $25 or more, depending upon what is depicted. They are too costly to want to own more than one or two. And the ones selected are usually carefully selected to either match the buyer's fantasy or to enable the buyer to see a fantasy acted out about which he is curious. If there is any harm from such use, it is not evident.

The second buyer uses the 'fuck books' to masturbate. Some men are married or in a long term sexual relationship. Others are single. Either way, they lack the courage to ask their sex partner to try the variation or they have been told that the partner will not do it. Rather than hire a prostitute, they masturbate while looking at the images.

And the third buyer is the one who is most likely to be involved in some form of sexual assault. This is the man who has no socialization skills. Often a loner at a time when others his age were dating, he is both lonely and has no idea how to act towards a woman. He believes the stories he reads, the 'proof' of the words being the photographs of the willing, often happy women. He knows that if he refuses to take no for an answer, if he physically asserts himself, the woman will become intensely passionate.

All of this seems nonsense to a person with normal socialization experience. But there have been several instances in recent years where men have been arrested for either rape or, more commonly, attempted rape as they try to treat a date in the manner learned from such material. Because they are not truly criminals, nor are they insane, there usually is a point short of forced intercourse where reality overcomes the pornography fueled fantasy they are trying to act out. By then the woman has been terrified, perhaps struck, handcuffed, or otherwise restrained. When she rightfully cries rape, shock sets in for the perpetrator.

Serial killers frequently have some form of pornography as a part of their lifestyles. Ken Bianchi had a 'fuck book' in his truck when arrested in Bellingham, Washington, while working as a security guard. He also had a semen stained towel he was using for masturbation. However, Bianchi also had an active, normal sex life with his wife. And rape was never a part of his murder plans, though his murder kit contained condoms because he came to realize that he had an overwhelming sexual arousal once the victim was helpless and knew she would be killed. Leslie Williams, the Michigan serial rapist/murderer, also liked pornography. Hard core magazines of one type or another have been found in the possessions of others too.

Interviews with the serial killers do not link the pornography with their drive to do harm. Serial killer Ted Bundy, just prior to his execution in Florida after killing and mutilating numerous women throughout the United States, tried to blame pornography for his crimes. It was his version of 'The Devil Made Me Do It,' but it did not have the sound of authenticity. His violence and the fantasies he acted out predated his interest in pornography. And the crimes he committed, which included using his teeth to rip and tear the breasts of his victims, had no relationship to the pornography he enjoyed.

Some serial killers look upon pornography as a way of easing sexual tension. They have said that if they can masturbate while looking at photographs of women in apparently painful bondage, they sometimes delay going out in search of a victim. This is quite different from those 'experts' who feel that pornography is used like foreplay, turning a meek individual into an unstoppable, sexually driven animal.

Pornography may not be a healthy form of recreation and relaxation, especially in the hard core form. And there are serious concerns about the physical and emotional well-being of the women and men depicted as victims or 'willing' participants. But that is a separate issue from the relationship between pornography and serial killings.

The one area of growing concern that is just beginning to be studied is that of the relationship between serial killers (and other violent offenders) and electronic communication systems. Internet, CompuServe, and other forms of computer Wide Area Networks linking computer users who are often thousands of miles apart have been found to be a possible support system for violent individuals.

Few members of law enforcement have been willing to go public with their concerns because the situation is too new and they do not want to appear overly alarmist. Some, such as Dr Griffis, and Steve Gilbert, Director of Computer Security And Electronic Intelligence for Sigma Group, Inc., have been more forthcoming. Their feeling is that having advance knowledge of what is taking place may allow law enforcement to more quickly stop a problem when it arises. No matter who is right about discussing the problem in depth, the fact is that some violent loners have been able to use computers to create a support group for their perversions.

Death on Line

Wide area networks available through the use of computers and telephone connectors (modems) are best understood as serving two familiar functions. The first is as a giant library of information. Instead of going to a local library with its finite offering of books, periodicals, and other documents, the computer user connected with Internet or other systems has access to seemingly unlimited resources. You can browse in numerous libraries of the world. You can gain access to the latest research papers in colleges and universities thousands of miles from where you live.

The second function is as a social club, convention center, meeting place, and the like. Through the use of what are known as bulletin boards, like minded individuals can talk about topics of special interest. Sometimes research scientists and business executives share ideas and learn from each other. Sometimes there are special programs where an expert fields questions from 'callers' sitting at their computers and typing in what they want to know.

The one concern almost everyone actively using these systems has is that there is no censorship. It is the ultimate exercise of first amendment rights under the US Constitution, and because of that fact, there are some rather unusual bulletin boards. Various groups of Satan worshipers and followers of the occult (or people who claim such things – one aspect of the bulletin boards that is never clear is who is serious and who is playing a fantasy game) are on some of the boards. Collectors of toy cars might be on another. Yet another will discuss a variety of sexual perversions. Another will discuss recreation areas for nudists, including people to be contacted and places to stay during a visit. And still others have photographs scanned into the system, pictures which can be obtained by other computer users. The latter include images of bondage, sado-masochism, kiddie porn, and the like.

There are also files detailing how to make incendiary devices and bombs from commonly available items. A sample of available material includes such items as a military explosive similar to nitroglycerine, explosives such as Composition B which is similar to TNT (the explosive ingredient of dynamite), Composition C-4, and Fire Fudge which is an incendiary for igniting hay, paper, rags, and other combustibles. The ingredients are harmless enough that they can be obtained anywhere, yet in combination are deadly, often over a large area.

The areas of greatest concern fall into three categories. The first is the writing about sexual perversions that is readily available to teenagers and anyone else who can use a computer and modem. For example, a group calling itself the 'Cult of the Dead Cow' placed a readily available story on line that discussed two young men having anal sex with a rabbit. The sex act involved torture and sexual arousal increasing as the rabbit screamed in pain before dying. Among the least disgusting statements made in this tale of perversion was: 'David's manhood tingled with every slight movement of the now half alive rabbit. He began rhythmically sliding in and out, moaning with pleasure on every thrust.' It went on to discuss the sex act in graphic terms, as well as the way in which the rabbit was being battered. Ultimately, again in graphic detail, the rabbit is tortured to death.

Another story was entitled 'Toxic Shock presents the Fetus by Bloody Afterbirth.' It is the story of the creator, the coathanger, the fetus, and Adam and Eve's first sexual experience.

The same 'Toxic Shock' had yet another story, this one being a personal story of a teenager and his two girlfriends. It details seven months in their relationship, starting with the boy having sex with his girlfriend's best friend when his girlfriend is present, to his having sex with his girlfriend, to all three enjoying each other. Again the sex is graphic, a combination of oral sex and various forms of intercourse.

The story continues with the trio deciding to break

into homes after the residents are asleep, tying and gagging them, then raping them. As is typical of such pornography, no matter what occurs, all parties react somewhat favorably, despite the obvious horror of the situation if it really were to occur. For example, 'We found the first bedroom of the house, a nine-year-old child slept soundly. We left her alone. We came to the parents' bedroom. As the couple slept (we had no idea who the fuck they were) we bound their hands and feet to the bedposts. We gagged them and then shut and locked the door. As Tracy and I yanked on the bonds to tighten them fully, Suzanne pounced on the man and ripped his clothes off savagely . . .

'I watched for a moment, and then the wife turned to me. She tried her damnedest to scream but the gag prevented her . . .'

The story continued with explicit descriptions of sexual violence, as well as telling of a second break-in where teenagers were the victims. It also detailed the precautions taken to prevent discovery.

The identity of the writer was not given, and though a telephone number was provided for access to the information, the nature of computer sources is that the telephone number was not necessarily that of the writer. The number was for an electronic bulletin board, the computer equivalent of a small town bulletin board or posting area where anyone, from elected officials to private citizens, can leave messages for others to read.

If no similar crimes occurred in recent months in the community where the bulletin board was accessed, they could have occurred thousands of miles away. The rapist could then have sent the story to the bulletin board in a manner that is currently untraceable. Then anyone calling the number would be able to read it.

Or the story could be false, the violent sexual fantasies of someone who might still be a virgin. Individuals using the Internet and other, smaller services such as CompuServe, range from doctors, lawyers, business people, and students to men and women completely lacking social skills. Their work often involves computer use to the exclusion of others. They do not date. They have few, if any, close friends. If they take their meals in restaurants, they rarely talk with anyone, including the serving staff. It is only with the anonymity of the computer screen that they lead lives of excitement, adventure, and even romance. Since there is no chance of accidentally meeting the people with whom they are communicating, they can pretend to be anyone they wish.

Steve Gilbert, a computer expert whose work has frequently been used to successfully fight computer based crime, managed to trace some of the more perverted writings. He wanted to know who was involved and what was happening.

As disgusting as the pornography might be, the type of writing was not Gilbert's concern. A large enough number of people take pleasure in writing perversion filled fiction so that variations of what appeared on the bulletin boards could be found in various magazines. The mildest forms are in magazines that feature sex oriented 'letters' supposedly written by readers or in sexual lifestyle magazines such as *Hustler*, *Chic*, and *Climax*, the latter billing itself 'America's No. 1 Couples Sex Magazine.' Sometimes the letters are true. Usually they are not, the writing being the result of reader fantasies acted out on paper.

The biggest difference between bulletin board sex and magazine sex is that the most disgusting perversions will be edited from the text before the material is printed in magazines. Computer users do not have editors.

The concern Gilbert has raised is more serious. He

has found that some of the writers of sexual violence material are also involved with the bulletin boards offering information on explosives manufacture. In addition, they are connected with some of the available photographs of sexual violence.

It is extremely rare to find someone who is fascinated by the combination of talking and/or writing about sexual perversion, taking and obtaining pictures of sado-masochistic acts, and the making of explosives who is not acting violently in his daily life. One interest or another is not unusual. The combination of all three is troubling. It almost always reflects someone who is violently acting out his fantasies.

In the past, it was not uncommon for a man to be obsessed by an idea that ran contrary to the moral code with which he was raised and the society in which he was living. He might collect pornographic publications, especially of women in what appear to be painful bondage. Or he might collect books that describe various sexual acts with children and/or adults. So long as the books only contained written stories, not illustrations, they were legal. Supreme Court Justice Potter Stewart, during the time between his retirement and his death, frequently lectured reporters and others in the media concerning first amendment freedoms. Anything can be published, though some things may violate state or federal law, resulting in prosecution of the publisher, photographer, etc. after the fact.

The problem that is created by bulletin boards is that in addition to obtaining materials that may be dangerous, obscene, illegal there are also other people to reinforce that pleasure. (It is against the law to photograph children in sexually explicit ways. Yet the nature of bulletin boards is such that it is rare for investigators to be able to locate the people offering them over the computer. Publishers need a distribution network. Advertising such images, offering them through stores,

173

and other non-electronic means of placing them before the public all leave a traceable trail. But presenting them through systems such as Internet protects the manufacturer and seller.) A man may write about his fantasy with a group of like minded individuals who encourage him to act it out. Someone who is on the edge of doing violence may be pushed over the line through the encouragement of others hundreds or thousands of miles away.

For example, there have been conversations on bulletin boards concerning bondage and sexual violence. An encounter is described, and a Polaroid photograph of a woman tied, gagged, and being whipped, spanked, or otherwise abused is scanned into the system. Then one of the men participating in the conversation, after downloading the picture for his own collection, is encouraged to both act out his own fantasy and to place a photograph in the system for sharing.

What happens next is unknown. The picture appears, the woman being treated in the manner described prior to the acting out of the fantasy. But is the woman a consenting individual, whether wife, lover, or paid prostitute? Or is the woman drugged? Has she been kidnapped? Is she dead? This is the deadly unknown with computer network users.

The most horrifying example of what can happen is the case of Charles Ng, Leonard Lake, and Lake's ex-wife, Cricket. Lake and Ng were San Francisco area serial killers who liked to kidnap, torture, and murder women, all the while recording their actions. They obtained a rural cabin specifically for the purpose of acting out and photographing their violent fantasies. Women were kidnapped, kept in handcuffs and chains, raped, and otherwise used for their violence until they were murdered days or weeks after being kidnapped. They were also videotaped.

The private recording sessions evolved from more

public activity. Recognizing that many men and women had sado-masochistic fantasies that they wanted to experience vicariously, Lake and his wife, Cricket, set up a business of violent pornography made to order. The customer would supply his name and desired fantasy. Cricket would act it out with the help of whatever man or men were needed, and as she performed as desired, she would say the man's first name. He could fantasize that she was his, that she was delighting in playing with him as he had always desired. It was the type of business that reinforced the idea that violence could be exciting to women, and because they supplied this service in the early 1980s, they were ahead of the computer offerings of the time.

Although Lake committed suicide before it could be proved, it is believed that he had a business separate from the violent sex to order, using his wife as actress. What is known is that he kidnapped men and women, then raped, tortured, and killed them, all while they were being videotaped. Then the tapes were either copied or edited and copied for general sale. Because the victims were killed anyway, there were no limits to what could be done to them. Cricket had to be kept alive and unhurt for the business they ran together. Kidnap victims could be subjected to any perversion, any pain, 'enhancing' the excitement for the buyer.

Leonard Lake was probably the first person to offer such a service, although still photography to order has been a staple of many harder core men's magazines for many years. The advertisements, usually shown in a photo classified section, often establish the parameters of what is available. Some show a woman with very big breasts photographed from a low angle to exaggerate them. Others may show women comfortably bound and gagged on a chair, a bed, or the floor. Or they may show someone restrained in a painful way. Or someone having intercourse. Or the picture may focus on the genitals of a woman as she masturbates with dildo or vibrator. Post office boxes were used for contacts, personal letters requested, and clients were frequently warned that only contacts from men and women using home addresses would receive responses. The idea was to protect the sellers from a possible law enforcement undercover 'sting' operation.

Leonard Lake, and contemporary computer bulletin boards such as 'The Farmer's Daughter,' often got more violent. Lake's work always showed the woman as willing or unwilling victim. Bulletin board photos such as 'The Farmer's Daughter,' are unclear as to the willingness of the woman. One image shows a semi-naked woman elaborately tied, her arms behind her back, her wrists presumably tied, and the cord passed around her body so that it encircles her breasts and goes between her legs, pressing into her vagina. The fear among law enforcement professionals is that some of what appears on the bulletin boards is more like the deadly images of Lake and Ng than the 'helpless-to-order' images for which Cricket posed.

Kathy Allen was one of the Lake and Ng victims. She was kidnapped because her boyfriend, identified as Mike Carroll in the murder videotape that was a part of Lake and Ng's ritual, could not pay them money owed, apparently for a drug deal. They took her to their cabin in Wisleyville, California, one of the wilderness areas of northern California favored by nature lovers and survivalists. The first images were apparently taken after she arrived at the cabin. They were her instructions for behavior, and they were given to her as she sat on a chair, her wrists handcuffed behind her back. The voice that was heard was that of a man who is not seen. The focus is strictly on the victim.

The voice on the tape stated: 'Mike owes us and unfortunately he can't pay. We're going to give you a choice, Kathy. It's probably the last choice we're going to give you. You can go along with us. You're going to cooperate and in approximately thirty days – if you want a date, you can write in your calendar the fifteenth of May – we will either drug you, blindfold you, or in some way or other make sure you don't know where you are and where you're going, and take you back to the city and let you go. And what you say at that time, I don't care. My name you don't know. His name is Charlie [Ng], but screw it. By then, hopefully, Mike will have disappeared gracefully. If you don't cooperate with us, we'll probably put a round through your head and take you out and bury you someplace. No witnesses. You will give us information on Mike. Basically Mike will move off in the horizon.

'While you're here you'll wash for us, you'll clean for us, you'll fuck for us. That's your choice in a nutshell. It's not much of a choice unless you have a death wish. You'll probably think worse things in the next few weeks.'

After the instructions, the rituals begin. These were repeated in one form or another with several other women. In this case, Leonard Lake is seen attaching leg irons to Kathy Allen so she can not run. Then he removes the handcuffs, has her undress, and Charlie Ng comes to take her to the shower so he can use her sexually there. The tape is turned on and off at different times, including four days after she was first taken to the cabin. At that point her fate is obviously sealed for she is strapped to the bed and Lake is berating her for trying to escape the cell they created in the cabin. She had apparently found an object she managed to use to bend the lock hasps, though not enough to escape. Naked, the tape has Lake taking still pictures of her before killing her. Mike, according to what is said, has already been murdered.

While women were the primary victims, one of the corpses found was two-year-old Lonnie Bond, Jr, the son of victim Brenda O'Connor. They killed the child when they kidnapped the mother, taking him out of the mother's sight and hearing so they could claim the baby was safe with a family in another city. They did not want the women to be so upset that they would put up a fight. They liked them to be submissive, sex slaves with just enough hope that they would one day be freed that they did not try to resist what they were ordered to do.

The men allegedly planned to build a series of bunkers in the hills of the community of Miranda, located in Humboldt County, California. The bunkers were to be used for protection against radiation and any enemy soldiers (or unprepared Americans fleeing the cities) during the holocaust the men felt was coming to America. They were going to settle the bunkers with like minded individuals, stockpile food and weapons, then have a section containing sex slaves. These would be carefully chosen, kidnapped women who would entertain the survivalists by performing any sexual act requested of them. The trouble was that Lake and Ng were serial killers, probably unable to end their sex slave training sessions in any manner other than the deaths of the women they captured.

Not all the victims were women. Lake liked to lure victims in a variety of ways. He placed classified advertisements offering to sell video equipment, torturing and murdering those who came to the cabin in response. Likewise, he agreed to purchase used cars that were for sale, then murdered the person who delivered one for possible purchase.

Lake kept a cyanide suicide capsule hidden on his body so he could swallow it if captured. The police learned about the capsule too late to prevent its use, though some of his background was learned following his arrest for shoplifting in June, 1985.

Lake was both physically and psychologically a victim

in his early childhood. He was raised primarily by his grandmother, a strict disciplinarian, both his parents coming from alcoholic family backgrounds. This became a serious problem when, at the age of six, he was sent to live with his grandparents. His parents lacked the money for all their children, keeping one son and their daughters at home. This meant that Leonard had to win the approval of a man who wanted him to fear punishment to the point where he would obey any command instantly. Since the grandfather was frequently drunk and abusive, Leonard's childhood was extremely troubled.

Donald Lake, who was raised at home, was a viciously cruel teenager. He physically assaulted both his sisters, tortured animals, and committed arson. He showed all the tendencies that would be expected in a serial killer, though he was murdered by his older brother before he could violently attack anyone else.

Leonard Lake was compulsively clean, taking several showers a day and making certain his sex and torture victims showered before he hurt them. He also kept extensive notes and a diary in addition to the pictures.

Even the photography seems to go back to his childhood. He was raised to enjoy nude bodies, was given a camera, and frequently photographed girls, including his sisters and other relatives, in naked and near naked poses. All the still photos of young women were kept in a series of albums.

As an adult, after serving in the Marines (he was discharged because of emotional problems), Lake was somewhat of a drifter. He is believed to have committed two series of killings, the ones done with Ng and an earlier series in Humboldt County. He earned a living from thefts, his ex-wife occasionally selling the goods and using or selling the credit cards. Because she was needed to act as a witness against Ng and to fill in the holes in the case against her late husband, law enforcement officers were careful to not try to learn too much of what she might have known about Lake's activities when she was his fence.

The question that has since arisen is whether or not men like Leonard Lake have taken their high tech fantasies to the world of the Internet and other computer systems. Lake was arrested by chance while shoplifting, the discovery of weapons eventually leading to the truth about his crimes. Evidence was found in and around his home, including bags of bones from his victims kept in a trough near the cabin. Someone using computer bulletin boards can find support from others for their violence, sell their pictures, and run even less risk of detection. This is one of the great concerns of police as they view the photographs available to anyone through such bulletin boards.

The primary issue with Leonard Lake, aside from the reinforcement he received from his customers, was whether or not the childhood created the monster. His brother was equally disturbed, raising the question of genetics since they were raised apart. Yet because most parents raise their children as they themselves were raised, it could readily be said that the home environments of both Leonard and Donald were similar.

Leonard had survivalist fantasies and a desire to control women. But he also was healthy enough to enter the Marines and to serve without serious problems for several years. His murders seem to have started following his discharge, which lends support to the idea that help had been available but was not provided. Certainly the Marine doctors knew something was quite wrong, yet they felt that it was best to be rid of him.

Daddy dearest

'I have started this letter so many times trying to save my son but also my husband, but no matter how I try, it comes out the same: Danny was an abused child. From the day he was born, my husband was jealous of him. He never wanted me to hold him or show him love in his presence. Danny was told from the time he could understand that he would be dead or in jail before he reached 15 years of age. His self-esteem was destroyed by his dad's constant belittling.' (Part of a letter from Claudia Rolling written to the Florida court where her son, Danny, was being charged with the serial killings of five people.)

Danny Rolling was always violent. He was an armed robber who had served time in Georgia and Mississippi. He spent time in an Alabama mental hospital. And he tried to murder his father. No one ever disputed those facts. The only question was why.

Retired Shreveport Police Lieutenant James Rolling was known as a strict disciplinarian, but not a violent man. He was short for a police officer, just 5 feet 8 inches tall, six inches shorter than his oldest son, Danny. Why there was hostility between the two (Kevin, the second oldest son, a year younger than Danny, reportedly had few problems with his father) is unknown. Fellow police officers claim to have seen nothing. At the same time, neighbors reportedly claimed that James Rolling hated his son. Another neighbor was quoted as saying that she witnessed Danny, as an adult, 'get on his knees like a little child,' crying because he could not win his father's approval. The same neighbor, a woman named Lillian 'Bunnie' Mills, told of Danny having to remove his shoes any time he wanted to walk through the family home. She said that one day he had to lace and unlace his shoes seven times because of frequent trips he was making to the kitchen. And one relative of the family claimed that Claudia Rolling was not allowed to cook meals for her oldest son, nor was she allowed to wash his clothes.

The domination of the father was the important factor in all plea arrangements. Rolling married young, fathered a child, then had the marriage fall apart as he began committing robberies. Eventually he returned to live with his parents in July, 1988. Why he returned to such an environment is not known. He was in his early thirties, seemingly capable of finding his own home if the living arrangement became intolerable.

Whatever went on within the family came to a head on May 17, 1990, two days after Danny was arrested for possession of marijuana, then released pending trial. He and his father were in the family car when a seemingly minor incident led to violence. First James asked Danny to roll up the window of the car. Danny refused, the argument leading to screaming. Finally James Rolling, who was carrying his service revolver, fired a round into the air and went inside. It was assumed he planned to call the police to have his son arrested, though for what was never clear. Before the call could be made, Danny kicked in the front door, grabbed his father's revolver, and shot him between the eyes. The elder Rolling did not die, though he would be partially blind and deaf in one ear from the bullet.

Rolling 'stomped' his father, according to a police spokesman, and shot him in the abdomen, missing vital areas. While James Rolling was being rushed to the hospital, Danny went to the home of Steve Clausen and Louisa Biedenharn, a Shreveport couple Rolling knew fairly well. Although not friends, Rolling had worked as a handyman around the couple's home. However, instead of ringing the doorbell, seeking help, he broke into the home through a set of French doors. Then he sneaked upstairs to the bedroom where the couple was watching television.

The sight of Danny Rolling was terrifying. He wore camouflage fatigues and combat boots. He had a gun in his hand, a second gun hidden in his clothing, and a four-inch hunting knife in one of his boots. A bandanna was tied around his head, and he announced that he was in 'big trouble' for having killed his father.

Steve and Louisa convinced Danny that they should go downstairs to the kitchen, where they talked for two hours. Rolling began in a somewhat maudlin mood, declaring his love for the couple, and then became verbally abusive. Steve convinced him to hand over the gun, and just as the couple relaxed, Rolling became agitated, drew his previously hidden second gun, and took back the one he had given up. 'He would turn sweet and put the gun down, then he would get mad over something and pick it up,' Biedenharn told a reporter for *People* magazine (February 11, 1991). Eventually he left, taking an old jacket, some cookies, and an apple. He might have been a kid taking a snack and warm extra coat before going off to sleep away at camp.

Rolling headed for Florida where he began committing crimes of which the police were first aware in September of 1990. In Tampa, Rolling found a sliding glass door he could open, entering what proved to be an apartment occupied by Ray and Patricia Rio. They were sleeping at the time, and Rolling did not try to awaken them. Instead, he ate a banana, leaving the peel displayed on the chair as proof he had been inside. Then he stole two watches and the keys to their 1983 Ford Mustang.

From Tampa, Rolling made his way to Ocala, Florida, 30 miles south. He entered a Winn–Dixie supermarket where he stole $2,000. He used a blue-steel Colt revolver loaded with four bullets, but was spotted by police after returning to his car. He then fled, traveling at speeds of up to 80 miles per hour, before losing control and smashing into a parked car. He was arrested immediately.

Rolling went to Marion County Jail because of the

armed robberies and past violence. There he became enraged, taking a toilet bolted into his prison cell, ripping it from the door, and heaving it against a window in the day room.

The violence led to a demand for psychological testing. It was also found that clothing, hair samples, and personal items had been located in a campsite near the University of Florida, Gainesville, campus. The campsite was such that it seemed to place Rolling near the school ten days earlier.

The date of the Gainesville location – late August, 1990 – was significant because five students had been murdered at that time. Three, all female, attended the University of Florida. The other two, a male and female, attended the Gainesville Santa Fe Community College. The murders were so shocking that the community became hysterical. Many students fled the city, returning home to their parents. Others talked with worried parents so often that the telephone lines periodically could handle no more calls. Weapons, especially Chemical Mace and handguns, were sold in large quantities. And hardware stores had a run on locks and various devices that could be used to better secure doors and windows. The fact that the murders included mutilation, rape, and, in one instance, decapitation, added to the fears. Since 34,000 students attended the University of Florida alone, and since three-fourths were in off-campus housing of the type where the victims were found, there was cause to panic.

There was no way to ease the fears that gripped the area. Even the University president, John Lombardi, saw no reason to lie about what was taking place in the name of public relations for the school. He gave a statement to Ron Word of the Associated Press, saying, 'It's clear this part of the country has some maniac on the loose. It reminds us of a natural catastrophe. The killer is selecting victims by criteria that are not clear to us.'

Over time, more information came out, including that the victims had been bound with duct tape. More important, though, was the fact that the tape was removed after the murders. In addition, bleach was poured onto the genitals of the four female victims to eliminate semen traces left from the sexual acts, as well as other biological evidence. 'I've never been associated with a crime scene that has so many violent attacks and so little evidence left behind,' said Dr Michael West, a deputy medical examiner. 'This individual that perpetrated these crimes is not your average criminal. He's very methodical, and very neat. He doesn't leave any traces of his presence in the crime scenes.'

Rolling had listened to his father and his father's friends enough to know what aspects of his actions could leave evidence that would lead to his arrest. He also left enough clues so that the police would know the cases were linked, though not enough to identify the killer. It was an action that made no sense until investigators learned that Rolling was the son of a police officer.

Other information came out over time, once again raising questions about shared responsibilities in cases of highly disturbed career criminals. Rolling would have spent the rest of his life in jail even if he had not murdered the five students. He was a habitual offender under Florida laws, a determination that means he had to be sentenced to life in prison with no chance for parole because of his robberies. However, as his background was explored further, it was found that he had long been a heavy drinker and drug user. He was haunted by visions of the devil, and had been known to scratch himself until he bled. Although the issue of Rolling's belief in the devil would come out in his trial, as was shown in Chapter 3, the fact was that it was not a ploy. Evidence of severe disturbance was found repeatedly in his past, and certainly would not have been overlooked by his parents during the time he lived with them prior to shooting his father.

The full story ultimately came from a former death row inmate named Robert Lewis who had been involved with writer Sondra London. Lewis gained infamy in Florida because he once escaped death row, not being captured for 11 days. Ultimately his sentence was commuted to life in prison.

Lewis's story was told in a autobiography *The Life and Crimes of Beautiful Bobby* which London was said to have published. In describing himself, he said: 'I've been in every kind of crime all my life. There is no crime I can think of that I have not done at least once . . . And I was damn good at what I did! I've always lived by my own rules. I never wanted to be a doctor or a lawyer or a preacher. I wanted to be an outlaw from the start and I worked hard for it.'

The death sentence, later commuted to life, was the result of the January 27, 1976, murder of a Jacksonville, Florida, drug dealer. However, it followed five previous felony convictions and 14 arrests for Lewis over the years, his crimes dating back to the age of 16 when he quit school for the financially more lucrative businesses of pimping prostitutes and dealing drugs.

Rolling confessed to Lewis before anyone else, including his attorney. Ultimately investigators went to the jail where they would ask questions, and Lewis would answer on behalf of Rolling. Whenever a question could not be answered because Rolling hadn't given the information to his friend, Rolling would whisper the answer to Lewis. Then Lewis would repeat it.

Why Rolling made his confession in that manner is not known. Later he talked freely in the courtroom, Sondra London by then representing exclusive publishing and movie rights to Rolling's story.

And in the end, as with most serial murderers, there were questions of who should have intervened. Neighbors told reporters for various publications about the years of emotional abuse endured by Danny Rolling. Claudia Rolling told of her son's problems. James Rolling was aware of his son's criminal activities and drug abuse. Yet no one wanted to get involved. Instead, everyone seemed to sadly shake their heads, then be shocked by the terrible tragedy that might have been prevented had anyone bothered to get involved.

If the killer disturbs you . . .

The idea that many organizations which should be involved with helping the potentially violent may abdicate that responsibility is not new. That portion of the homeless who are severely mentally ill, sometimes violent towards themselves or others, are on the streets because of 'enlightened' laws. In the 1960s, it was felt that the severely mentally ill should not be housed in hospitals where their care was usually paid for by tax money. They were released in the name of giving them complete freedom, as well as freeing the taxpayers. Aggressive acts, suicides, and homicides often resulted from the wholesale releases that began in the 1960s.

Likewise, many treatment facilities do not want to work with individuals who disgust them. Richard Chase of Sacramento believed that his mother had fed him laundry detergent, causing his heart to reverse itself and be turned to stone. He regularly went to hospital emergency rooms to get help for what he thought his mother had done to him. He was outraged when they sent him to a psychiatric facility instead.

Richard decided that he needed to find alternatives to medicine for curing his health each time he was released from treatment. At first he thought that nutrition would save him, especially vitamin C. However, rather than eating the appropriate foods or taking vitamin supplements, Chase bought several fresh oranges each morning. Then he would wrap them in a scarf and place them on his head in order to directly gain their benefits.

Later he decided that he needed fresh blood in order to recover from what his mother had done to him. While walking on the grounds of a mental hospital, he began capturing live birds, biting off their heads, and drinking the blood. This so sickened the psychiatric staff who witnessed what he did, the hospital released him well before he could be effectively treated. It was then that he switched from birds to humans, quickly killing six people including an infant, in order to gain their blood.

Once the 'Vampire of Sacramento,' as he came to be known, was finally locked away for the murders, he was still convinced he needed to cure himself of the damage done by his mother. He decided that the anti-psychotic medicine he was being given in jail was actually the cure for his heart. He saved the medicine for several days, then swallowed it all at once. The overdose was fatal, yet Chase would never have been in a position to murder had the staff of the psychiatric hospital not released him after being disgusted by his actions.

The other difficulty occurs with prisons. The idea behind the penitentiary in America came from that least violent of all religious groups, the Quakers. Given the nature of their society, it was reasonable to assume that a man who had done wrong within the community would change – become penitent – if forced to be locked apart from others and given time to reflect on his actions. The men they jailed were rarely involved with extremely violent crimes. They were also the known deviants in the community, and so even after their release, everyone knew to watch them. Those who were open to help were aided in returning to a productive life in the Quaker community. And those who were still a potential danger were avoided by everyone since all the residents knew who they were.

Today, with prisons costing more to house an offender each year than the cost of room, board, and tuition at only the most expensive colleges and universities, many people resent tax money being spent for more than isolation. They resent prison rehabilitation and education programs. The younger a man is when released, the more likely he is to have less than a high school education, no work skills, a history of child abuse, and unfocused anger. He is also likely to be extremely immature relative to his peers who continued through school, yet streetwise in the world of violence. When he makes the choice to act out violently rather than seek help, society is endangered.

However, most experts interviewed for this book repeatedly stress that there is almost always an element of choice in the action of the serial killer. They feel that the person who is so obsessively driven to kill that he can not control himself regardless of how he tries or what he does is the very rare exception. The obsession to kill is outside the control of the average serial killer. The violent background that usually precedes the acting out of crimes cannot be changed. But there is still a choice as to whether to seek help or begin taking lives. Whether or not the person can stop after the first murder is committed does not change the fact that there is almost always a moment of choice. Perhaps almost as great a crime is the failure of therapists, hospitals, and the like to fully treat all the people who come to them for help prior to making the choice to murder if the emotional disturbance is upsetting, as was the case with Richard Chase.

Serial Killers and the News

The idea that the news media creates serial killers has been growing in the United States ever since men like Charles Manson, Ken Bianchi, and others developed cult followings. Their pictures have appeared on tabloid publications, their family members, friends, and lovers offered large sums of money to tell their stories on one or other talk shows. When David Berkowitz began shooting people with a .44 magnum, then claimed to be the Son of Sam, a man who received orders from a dog to kill, the state legislators finally reacted. So-called 'Son of Sam' laws were enacted in a number of states around the country to assure that killers could not profit from their crimes. Even law enforcement officers began questioning whether the press was responsible for the seeming rise in the number of serial killers.

The truth is that the American press has never been as idealistic as journalists like to pretend. Until the end of the nineteenth century, printers were also the reporters and writers of news. They were well educated, highly respected professionals. And while there were exceptions in publishing, such as William Randolph Hearst, most of his excesses came after the turn of the century. (It was Hearst, for example, who sent illustrator Frederic Remington to Cuba to document the violence that preceded what came to be known as the Spanish–American War. However, none of the kidnappings, rapes, torture, or other violence Hearst hoped to have illustrated had taken place. Remington wired Hearst, asking for instructions. Hearst allegedly sent the artist a telegram reading, 'You send the pictures. I'll create the war.')

At the start of the twentieth century reporting became a job in itself. The reporters were not well educated. They were aggressive, and they would do anything to get a scoop on the opposition. They wanted a story they could tell dramatically, even if they had to lie, cheat, and steal to get one. Even the photographers liked to create the news, whether by shifting the victims, weapons, etc. in a scene or by creating a 'composograph' in the darkroom, combining several different pictures to make one that never existed. It was common for a press photographer to move a corpse, a weapon, a car, a sign, or something else to make a more interesting picture. In some instances the police were bribed to move a victim to a different street so the first photographer on the scene could have an exclusive. The fact that such movement ultimately could hinder the finding of the killer was not a concern. Likewise, the composographs – retouched photos – were never successfully challenged in court.

In 1928, Ben Hecht and Charles MacArthur brought Broadway a true-to-life comedy of reporters in search of the 'big story.' Although they based their play, *The Front Page*, on a Chicago newsman whose name was changed to 'Hildy Johnson' in the script, the New York press delighted in the story because they felt it was just like their own. Among other activities, the real life reporter/character model with whom Charles MacArthur had worked in Chicago, broke into an empty jury room, checked the ballots to see the outcome of a trial, then called the paper to scoop the other reporters. However, because he knew they would likely do as he did, he then took fresh ballots, changed them from the originals, and replaced the genuine with ballots that would show a different verdict!

In an even more outrageous situation, the reporter on whom the play was based paid a death row inmate $200 for exclusive rights to his story. As soon as he had it all, he challenged the man to a game of Gin Rummy, during which he won back everything he had paid. The $200 was legitimately from the Chicago *Herald & Examiner* for which the reporter worked, but when he won it back, he pocketed it as a bonus. The story did not come out until the inmate met with a Catholic priest and warned the priest to never play rummy with the reporter because the man cheated.

Reporters seldom bothered with facts if they needed fancy to make a more interesting story. For example, when the *New York Daily News* sent Arthur Pegler to a rooming house to learn about a man's death, Pegler discovered that there was no story. The man had died of natural causes. Rather than disappoint his editor, though, Pegler created the fiction that the dead man was Nicola Coviello, an Italian opera composer who was traveling to Saskatchewan, Canada, for the performance of some of his work. He was in New York only long enough to see a few sights, but made the mistake of traveling to Coney Island. There he heard the new form of American music becoming so popular with youth – jazz. The sound was so horrible, Coviello died instantly.

Serial killing was little in the news prior to the Harvey Glatman case because the focus was usually on single murders. The press liked to feature high profile stories, such as a murder of someone famous in Hollywood, or a bizarre crime scene. Publications such as *The Police Gazette* covered police stories among the unknown as well as the famous, but most others liked to have a touch of gossip. Low income families understood domestic violence from the stress of living in overcrowded tenements. They witnessed neighborhood fights ending in one or both participants dying from knife wounds or other injuries. And they were familiar with the extortion murders increasingly common in first generation ethnic neighborhoods. When they bought a newspaper, they wanted to know that those who had money, power, and prestige could suffer as well.

During the same period, the movie industry was male dominated. As motion pictures became an eagerly sought after form of entertainment, the action/adventure movie rarely showed women as anything other than victims. Even the strongest of the female characters, such as Pearl White who starred in *The Perils Of Pauline*, would frequently be left dangling from a cliff, falling from an airplane, or bound and gagged near a bomb whose fuse was rapidly burning to the end. The damsel in distress was by far the most popular approach to suspense, and that situation has changed little in modern times. Women in jeopardy stories sell far better in Hollywood than any other form of entertainment. Even talk show subjects frequently revolve around women being battered by their spouses, women who were kidnapped, women who were victimized by their children, women who had to fight Satan worshipers threatening their loved ones.

Despite all this, there were some constraints on the presentation of news reports prior to the early 1970s. Certain subjects were considered taboo by the reporters.

For example, most American Presidents had scandals in their lives, frequently involving women. These were well known to the reporters who wrote about them, yet there was an unspoken agreement that they would not be printed. All the Washington press corps knew that Franklin Roosevelt was having a long term love affair with Missy Lehand. However, out of respect for both Roosevelt and his wife, no one would say anything.

Dwight Eisenhower was severely criticized by President Truman for his affair during World War II. Many of the White House correspondents learned of the prolonged incident that almost led to a divorce from Mamie, yet it was not made public knowledge until well after his death.

When Jack Kennedy was a Senator attending the Democratic National Convention in Los Angeles, columnist Walter Winchell was among the reporters who witnessed one of his sexual liaisons. Winchell filed the story with his New York paper, but the editor refused to run it. The editor did not doubt that the man who was being touted as the next Presidential candidate was having an affair. However, he said that the item could not run because Kennedy was a married man and the paper's policy precluded writing scandals that would hurt such an individual.

Associated Press correspondent Jim Bacon was among those who knew many of the scandals. He was assigned to Los Angeles, covering both the movie industry and the politicians who came out there. He was well aware of the John Kennedy/Marilyn Monroe relationship, for example. But he wrote nothing about it, explaining later that 'it wasn't until Richard Nixon was doing to the country what Jack Kennedy was doing to women that we [the press] felt the need to write about it.'

It was in the 1970s that American publishing began to radically change. A nation shattered by dissension concerning the Vietnam War and the subsequent retreat which left former allies at the mercy of their enemies, made the public become insular. Demand for international news seemed to reach the lowest point since the Depression years prior to the start of Hitler's attempted conquest of Europe. Instead the American public wanted their heroes to be created by the media. When there were horrors taking place, they wanted the coverage to be such that the experience was more like watching a movie of the week. And in response came tabloid news such as *People*, *US*, *The Star*, *National Enquirer*, and numerous others. Over time, tabloid television became a hybrid of news and entertainment with shows such as *Entertainment Tonight*, *Hard Copy*, *Inside Edition*, *America's Most Wanted*, and similar ones. There were dramatic recreations of stories using professional actors as well as some of the participants involved. Editing techniques matched those that might be used when producing an action/adventure movie. A nation that prides itself on a history of never paying for stories suddenly found that the tabloid press and the tabloid television shows would pay big money for information. Serial killers were courted like sports stars (One California company even produced serial killer trading cards identical in concept to baseball cards, football cards, and other sports collectibles. Anyone who knew a serial killer, whether as a friend, co-worker, or family member could obtain a fee for going on camera.

A desensitization towards men obsessed with killing gradually affected the American public. It was as though the victims were nothing more than plot devices, carefully created clues to be studied while the reader/listener/viewer was apparently playing a game. Details about knife wounds, rope burns, bruises, and bullet placement were used to deduce who might have done the deed, how, and why it was done. No effort was made to show compassion for the victims. No effort was made to help the victims come alive so that the person hearing about the killer would show sympathy or mourn the loss.

The media does not make the serial killers. Men and women driven to kill again and again are thinking about nothing other than the violence. They are not driven by pornography, Satan worship, an obsession with violent rock music lyrics, or anything else, though they may use such things to reinforce what they would do regardless. They also do not think about making money from their stories because they do not expect to be caught.

However, in the frenzy to tell a dramatic story, reporters and their speculative musings often get in the way of the police effectively investigating a case. In addition, as they buy information from any source possible, there is a risk that a fair trial cannot be had with certainty. A jury may believe that a witness telling the truth about a case is actually lying because he or she has received several thousand dollars for appearing on television or selling a story to the tabloid press.

In some instances, panic is created in a community because the press exaggerates the problem, as happened with Ken Bianchi, Angelo Buono, and their Hillside Strangler murders in Los Angeles. At other times, the press tells of fears that are non-existent, such as was the case with the Donald Chapman story, told in full in Chapter 6. Chapman, a serial rapist who served his full sentence, then was released talking of returning to violence, wanted to return home to live with his parents. Interviewers for national news media throughout the country carried the story, implying panic in his New Jersey community. And while the police were rightfully concerned, especially since the therapists at the hospital where he had been locked away agreed that he was still dangerous, the neighbors were not. It was as though they had less reason to fear him than others who might be violent because they knew the young man. They had lived with Chapman over the years, would recognize him from a distance, and could simply avoid an encounter. They had no illusions about the danger he posed. They just felt greater fear from some violent stranger who had yet to be discovered.

This was especially blatant in the Hillside Strangler murders. Among the news reporters in Los Angeles was Jim Mitchell who went from being a general assignment and investigative reporter for KFWB Radio to working for CBS Television. Aggressive, intense, his nervous energy obvious in fingernails that appeared to be bitten to the quick and in the cigarettes he smoked almost one after another. His off air speech was rapid, and his dogged intensity resulted in many awards. However, when the sight of the corpses and the nature of the Hillside killings affected his emotions, his personal

beliefs and presentations on camera added sensational-
ism rather than reason.

One victim, a teenager named Judith Ann Miller,
particularly affected Mitchell. Miller was a runaway, a
girl who was bored with school, frustrated at home,
enjoying the street life which, for her, was like something out of the 1960s hippie existence. She used pot
or pills occasionally in order to 'mellow out.' She hung
out in the Hollywood area because that was where she
thought the action was. She expected to be discovered
by a producer or director, or at least picked up by a
movie star. Friends said that sex was a natural part
of her lifestyle, sometimes charging, sometimes giving
herself free.

Judy's death occurred on Monday, October 31, 1977,
when she was either hanging out or engaging in prostitution, no one is certain which, the corpse dumped in
the area of Terrace and La Crescenta. It was a location
just outside the city, and that meant that it was a Los
Angeles Sheriff's Office homicide unit case. As one
Sheriff's homicide detective explained about how they
found the body,

'We knew immediately that two people were probably
involved. The position of the body was one we often
see when two people carry a dead victim. There is a
natural way to carry someone under these circumstances, one person taking the arms and the other the
legs, using the knees like handles. If one person carried
the body, that person would have to carefully arrange
it, and that almost never happens. Besides, there was
evidence on the ground that two people had been there.
Somebody might have gone later and found the body
without reporting it, but that doesn't make much sense.
We assumed we had two killers from the start or at least
a killer and somebody who helped. We also assumed
that one killer was a man because we suspected she had

been raped. We just didn't know if it was two men or a man and a woman.'

The Sheriff's department was anxious to release specific information only. They wanted the public to know that two people were almost certainly involved with the murder. That knowledge might bring forth witnesses who would not come forward if they thought only a single killer was involved. They might assume that what had aroused their suspicions the night of the murder was inconsequential or related to some other, less serious crime.

The one place where the detectives tried to hold back was on the issue of subtle marks on the body. In Judy's case, for example, the autopsy revealed bits of adhesive on her face. This was not immediately obvious at the crime scene, and the press was not told. All it meant was that she was gagged with adhesive tape, but such a detail would only be known to the killer who obviously freed her mouth before dumping her.

There were marks on her wrists and ankles indicating she had been bound. There was no way of telling if any of this was voluntary, perhaps part of a bondage game she was paid to play as a prostitute. But it was again something the killer might know. And in some instances there were different marks indicating two or more types of restraints – handcuffs, wire, rope, cloth, etc. A killer who would discuss using different restraints, identifying them accurately according to what investigators found on the body, would also ensure that the investigators had the right person.

But Judy Miller's case was one where investigators wanted the public to know that two people were probably involved. However, Jim Mitchell was one of the most often watched television reporters whose personal beliefs overcame law enforcement efforts. As Mitchell explained,

'I had never, in all my experience, found a rape and

murder victim like that. I had never heard of such a thing. That is, simply, she was lying in this little parkway between the curb and sidewalk.

'She was completely nude and she was sprawled out on the grass almost as if she were about to engage in an act of sex with a man. The knees were up in the air, her legs were spread apart, the hands were at about a forty-five-degree angle from her sides, almost in a position of supplication. They weren't out straight in crucifix fashion, palms up, and my first reaction when I saw her was it was probably an OD, because when I drove up there I didn't know what had happened . . . Then when I realized that she had been strangled, I said, now wait a minute, something has gone wrong here. And I had a conversation a short time later with one of the police detectives and I asked him.

'I said, "I have never seen anything like this before in my life." He said that he had never heard of it either and I said, "Do you think it could be some psycho?" And he said it could be. So at that point I did the story but I made no reference to the possibility of a psycho.'

Mitchell also did not mention that two people were probably responsible. He was not aware of that fact. Yet just as reporters such as Mitchell inadvertently spread misinformation that created concerns where none needed to exist, so there were people who deliberately misled the press. As the late Supreme Court Justice Potter Stewart lectured to reporters after his retirement, there is no public right to know in the United States. There is only a right to publish anything. Misleading the press during the course of a murder investigation in order to prevent the public from knowing so much that it is difficult to gain a conviction, is a valid action by law enforcement.

As one investigator explained about Mitchell and the others, 'We tried to help the press as little as possible. Our first responsibility is to build a case and get the killer off the street so the public is protected. An erroneous conclusion on a reporter's part was encouraged. It meant that if the real killer ever confessed, he or she would mention details that had not been read.

'The reporters who saw deep significance in body placement simply weren't as experienced or well trained as we were. We knew immediately that the body position meant two people even though it looked grotesque with her nude and all. It's like, the coroner found two different marks on her wrists. We knew she had probably been both handcuffed and tied, but we weren't going to give that detail out. Most people would use one method of restraint or the other; the double use was an extra clue.

'The almost microscopic particles of adhesive on her face helped, too. It was logical to assume both that she had been gagged and that the gag involved tape. We saw most of these things right at the crime scene and learned the rest through autopsy. But kill an erroneous conclusion by a reporter? Never!'

Publicity following the arrest and before the trial is also a problem. The information in the press can create risks the prosecutors fear, as well as opportunities the same prosecutors like to exploit. The more information the public has about crimes, the more the public is prejudiced when a jury has to be selected. Even a change of venue – moving where a trial is held from the location where the crime occurred to another city – does not guarantee impartiality. Sometimes the story has been a national one. At other times the case is little known outside where it occurs. But the moment a new community is chosen, the local press likes to explain why the trial is being held there. The murder cases will be rehashed, and any available photographs will be shown in newspapers and on television. There will also be an explanation of how the accused became a suspect, why and how the arrest was made, and other facts.

Once the jury has to be selected, knowledge about the case may be fresher in the minds of the residents of the new community than it was in the minds of the residents of the city where the murders occurred.

Prosecutors like to show some of their evidence to brag about their efficiency, especially since many of them are political. They need to justify their successes, and they know that the act of making an arrest implies the guilt of the accused to many people.

Defense lawyers want to suppress evidence that works against their client. They also want to stress that which might be in their client's favor. Both defense and prosecution thus have a stake in cultivating the media.

At the same time, the popularity of news/entertainment hybrids on television is caused in part by their cost. A successful half hour comedy or drama becomes increasingly expensive with each season. The stars demand higher and higher pay for their work, and so long as the ratings are strong, the money must be provided. Otherwise either the stars will quit or, depending upon the ownership of the show, it may be taken to a rival network.

The news/entertainment hybrid has one or two hosts or anchors who are the highest paid people involved. Reporters, producers, videographers, researchers, and related personnel are all largely invisible. They can be replaced without the public being concerned. In addition, by going on location instead of needing to have large sets constructed and lighted, overall costs are drastically reduced. One episode of a successful situation comedy can cost more than a full season of the news/entertainment hybrid.

Serial killers attract viewers because hearing about them is much like reading a horror novel. The details are terrifying yet there is a psychological distance that convinces the viewer that he or she will not encounter such people.

This is also why serial killers and people connected with them are popular guests on television talk shows. The killers are recorded in prison or interviewed via satellite. Everyone else is in the studio. And the topic is always titillating – 'Women who love serial killers.' 'My daughter (mother/sister/father/brother/son) was a victim of a serial killer.' 'The growing menace of serial killers.' 'What motivates a serial killer?' etc.

The material is always dramatic. More important, while the subject matter is sometimes considered inappropriate for prime time viewing, it can be presented earlier in the day in the guise of news or public service programming. Thus the content of the shows can be more graphic than is considered proper for many families – especially with children – yet the news aspect allows it to be shown where a less explicit made for TV movie might be rejected by the networks. At worst, the afternoon talk show host might have to offer a statement saying that the information to be discussed might be too intense for some younger viewers. Parental discretion is advised. And with such precautionary statements, the audience is certain to be increased.

The tabloid and television fascination with serial murder does not lead to further serial murders any more than pornography or other sources. It is not a reason for the seeming rise in serial killers. This is the result of greater accuracy in identifying which murders are and which are not connected to the same perpetrator. Instead, the one tragedy that has occurred is a decreased interest in and concern for the victims. With the serial killer as media star, the victims become merely players, and minor ones at that.

CHAPTER 5

HOW TO CATCH A SERIAL KILLER

The Federal Bureau of Investigation (FBI) estimates that at any given time there are 200 serial killers active in the United States. This is based on guesswork, not sophisticated analysis of crimes throughout the United States. In fact, there is currently no actively used single recording source for crime reporting and analysis in America. Most states have one or more 'central' reporting areas, none of which is likely to share its information with the others. There is also the FBI's VICAP program which is inherently flawed because of its complexity, as will be explained shortly.

Sometimes the problem is jealousy. The FBI has a history of keeping itself apart from street cops. For many years the attitude of most senior agents was that they wanted local police and sheriff's deputies to supply them with all information desired about a case. However, they would not trust those same law enforcement officers with information the FBI agents had gathered.

The FBI/city police controversy received the most attention, but jealousy and pettiness come in other forms. For example, each county has a sheriff, and many of the sheriffs are elected officials who may not have held any other jobs in law enforcement. An elected sheriff ideally has at least been a police officer or attorney. In practice, an elected sheriff might be someone who has worked in business or as a laborer. Whatever the case, their success is determined by how many arrests and convictions they make within their own county. If the county residents feel protected, the sheriff will likely be re-elected. They are not necessarily interested in a problem that is of limited concern to their constituents. Thus a serial killer of prostitutes, especially one committing crimes in more than one county, is a low priority. The threat is not to the 'decent' people who vote to keep him or her in the job.

Even when the victim is at least marginally a part of middle class society, there may not be a great concern. When Harvey Glatman left one corpse per county, the victims received a slightly lower priority than they might have had anyone known one man was killing again and again. Each department had one murder to solve. No one at the top bothered to see if they might somehow be connected with cases investigated elsewhere.

City police share more information than many county sheriff's departments, though not all that much. Each county may have several different cities within its jurisdiction, and hot pursuit cases often involve two or more adjacent cities. There is also the fact that criminal activity is often mobile, a burglar from the inner city working in the suburbs, or a suburban drug distributor selling street quantities of drugs to inner city dealers. Narcotics and vice task forces routinely involve police from two or more cities. Yet the competitive attitude of the generally aggressive men and women in law enforcement ensures that most will take pride in solving their own cases. Cooperation with another department may be seen by them as a sign of personal weakness.

Murder is another situation. The less desirable the victim (homeless transient, prostitute, petty criminal), the more common the method of death (simple stabbing, strangulation, shooting), the less likely that homicide units will share the information. The case is considered less important than those involving socially or politically connected victims. A serial killer of prostitutes who does not kill in an unusual manner, does not do anything to the body that would cause special attention to be drawn to it, and who dumps each corpse in a different county is likely to be caught only by chance.

There is much talk about profiling serial killers, about going to a crime scene and gaining valuable information about the person who committed the murder. As with any crime scene, much can be learned about each specific murder based on general knowledge of homicide.

The information provided in Chapter 4 concerning occult related crime scenes is typical of what might be considered consistent knowledge from scene to scene. If the evidence found matches what is routinely left behind with Traditional occult practices, then one aspect of the criminal is known.

Likewise, homicide detectives have long known that certain details at a murder may provide information about the killer. Was the victim bound? Investigators will be concerned with not only how the body was restrained but will also study the exact type of knot used. People in professions such as surgery and dock working are so accustomed to making knots unique to their work that they may use the same knots when killing. The same is true for people with knot-making hobbies that occupy much of their time, such as sailing. Thus the knot can help identify the killer.

The type of rope used can also be a clue since certain types of rope are either less available in some areas than others, or they have specialized uses again unique to professions or hobbies.

The form of violence may be a clue. A stabbing victim's wounds can narrow the suspects. A heterosexual man typically stabs only once or twice, and rarely any more than necessary to take the life. A woman routinely stabs several times, the knife wounds usually amounting to what might be called overkill. Likewise a homosexual killing that is a crime of passion often has far more wounds present than necessary. The reasons why might be complex, but when a naked male corpse is found with thirty or forty stab wounds, the police tend to place women and homosexual males connected with the victim high on their list of possible killers.

Serial murder is also known to be a younger man's obsession. Most serial killers start acting out violently in their late teens and early twenties. They may not kill then, but they may rape or otherwise engage in very violent activity. This also means that older men with no previous crime record can often be ruled out as serial killer suspects.

The type of gun used and where the person is killed can be helpful. Professional killers using handguns frequently stay close to their victims and use lower caliber weapons than are shown in their motion picture fantasy portrayals. For example, hit men often use a .22-caliber revolver or automatic. The guns are small and the bullets are deadly at close range. And if the bullet has a soft nose or has been slightly altered to increase shrapnel, the breaking apart of the metal in the body as the bullet ricochets off bone and skull will lacerate and puncture. This means that even if a vital organ isn't destroyed, it may still be severely nicked by the bullet. Unstoppable, rapid internal bleeding will take the person's life.

Professionals often fire multiple .22-caliber rounds into the base of their victims' skulls. Higher powered weapons might pass through the skull. The .22 will enter, and if it doesn't destroy the brain, it may ricochet about the skull, sending pieces of metal everywhere.

A hanging corpse may be mistaken for a suicide. If the cause of death is the hanging, the cord will leave an inverted V mark in the neck. Strangulation will leave a straight line bruise around the neck. Someone with a straight line bruise found hanging has probably been hung either after death.

There are other patterns as well. One serial killer who worked in a hospital tended to murder most of his elderly victims in one room. The deaths all looked normal at first. The victims were of an age and in such ill health that they easily could have been terminal. But statistically there were too many, and when it was found that the majority of them had been in one room when the seriously ill elderly population of the hospital were spread among several rooms, an obvious pattern emerged.

Ken Bianchi had his favorite strangulation technique and would not have used a gun or knife on his victims except to subdue them. And bodies consistently dumped at night within a few miles of a truck stop indicate a trucker whose route takes him to that stop on a regular basis. It also means he drives by night, a personal choice that narrows the field of suspects as well.

This is not to say that serial killers are consistent. The most clever and elusive of them will change their patterns to the point where they may all be different or there may be clusters. Some victims may be shot, others strangled, others stabbed, and still others poisoned. Some may be bound with a consistent type of cord, others handcuffed, and still others taped to restrain them. There might be several 20-year-old redheaded women, several married brunettes in their forties, and a few elderly grandmothers.

The corpses may provide clues during autopsy. Do all of them have evidence of heavy drinking prior to death? What about drug use, and if so, what types of drugs? If rape or voluntary sexual intercourse was involved, and if semen was left, how consistent is the semen? A single semen sample from each victim indicates that the man is working alone. Two different samples consistent from corpse to corpse will indicate that two men are probably operating together.

Likewise, if the stomach contents of the victims are all consistent in terms of type of food left and the amount metabolized, there may be a clue to where the killer takes them before the murder. Evidence of Chinese food or Mexican food, or hamburgers and fries that is consistently metabolized for approximately one hour after eating can reveal a pattern of both the foreplay to death, and how soon after going to a restaurant the women are murdered.

The FBI's Behavioral Sciences Unit's profiling techniques includes a determination at the crime scene of whether the criminal is 'organized,' 'disorganized,' or 'mixed.' The last has characteristics of both the organized and disorganized killer. Such studies, which often require knowledge gained only after an arrest, involve four issues. The first concerns how a crime is committed.

The organized serial killer carefully stalks his victims. He may have certain places he likes to go, such as Ken Bianchi's staying within 15 miles of Glendale, California, for the Los Angeles murders. Or he may have a certain type of victim he seeks, such as nurses, women sitting alone in all night restaurants after midnight, or something similar.

The organized killer's murders involve the acting out of well established fantasies, though in a controlled manner. Harvey Glatman was typical of this. He knew what he wanted to do with his victims and how he intended to murder them. He also knew how he wanted to find them, taking his time to be certain he had the 'right' victim.

Strangers are usually hunted by the organized serial killer. He does not want the woman to be connected to him, so if a business co-worker fits his favorite profile, he will probably pass her by. These men do not plan to be caught for their crimes, so they do not worry about any penalties for their behavior. However, they are aware that others have been caught so they try to plan their attacks in ways which will not link them with the murder.

The organized killer has a strong sense of his victim. He sees her as a unique person and not as a fantasy figure. Some rapists, it has been found, are acting out their aggression on someone in their memory. A few have been talked out of committing the rape when the victim is able to convince him that she is not the person who is the focus for his rage.

The organized killer is also comfortable in adapting to change in his plans. The unexpected return of a victim's roommate, the appearance of a routine police patrol, or some other circumstance can be handled in a calm, seemingly rational manner. One of the most prominent yet fascinating examples is that of Jeffrey Dahmer. A victim was able to flee his apartment, handcuffed and naked. The youth spoke no English and seemed to be hysterical. Yet when the two law enforcement officers who confronted the youth took him back into the apartment to see what was happening, Dahmer appeared to be merely embarrassed. He showed no fear. Instead he 'admitted' that the boy was his 'lover.' They were engaged in voluntary sado-masochistic sex, but they were mutually consenting, and though matters had gotten a little out of hand, nothing serious was happening.

In hindsight it is very easy to condemn the two officers. They not only returned the youth to the apartment where he was subsequently murdered, they made no effort to remove the young man from the scene. At the very least it would have been appropriate for them to obtain an interpreter and make certain the youth's story matched Dahmer's.

Aside from the extremely poor judgment, two

important facts remain. First, Dahmer, a serial killer (see the appendix), was able to calmly handle a situation which could have resulted in his immediately going to jail. He acted so much like an embarrassed lover, almost like a man and woman having sex in a hotel bed when the maid opens the door, that there was no suspicion that he might be a murderer. And second, Dahmer had enough of an understanding of heterosexuals or police officers in general to know that a story about homosexual S&M games would be uncomfortable for them. It was the kind of relationship the police undoubtedly knew happened. It was also the kind of relationship that they did not want detailed for them. He utilized perceived homophobia to get rid of the officers so he could kill the young man.

The organized killer also learns from the past. A rapist/murderer who likes to restrain his victims when he attacks them in their homes may start with items found in those homes. He may ransack drawers and cabinets, using scarves, neckties, rope, adhesive tape, or torn items of clothing. With experience, he is anxious to take control of his victims as quickly as possible. Rather than wasting time searching his victims' homes, he will make himself a murder kit containing his preferred restraints, something he has found effective as a gag, and whatever else he feels he needs, perhaps including gloves, condoms, and a weapon. The kit results in consistent success, as well as leaving behind consistent marks on the victim. However, if the killer keeps changing the location of his violence, moving from city to city, county to county, or even state to state, what would otherwise be an obvious connection among the murders is easily overlooked.

The organized killer may also develop a pattern that differs from the early crimes. For example, a rapist may attack his victim and then decide to kill so there is no one to testify against him. He tries to commit the next crime differently, to ensure that the victim does not remember any details about him. But again something triggers his desire to kill. This time it may be the fact that she is begging and pleading, and he cannot stand to hear a 'whiny woman.' Or she may say nothing, laying still, not speaking, not screaming, and not resisting, this time causing him to think that instead of her being paralyzed by fear and desperate to stay alive, she is being arrogant. 'The bitch thinks she's too good for me. She's letting me have my way because she holds me in disdain,' may be his thought process. And that is when he decides to 'show her' by killing her.

Eventually the man knows he is going to kill his rape victim even before he decides who it will be or knows how she will react. He has created a pattern he is comfortable with, one his first killings may not match.

Eventually the organized serial killer realizes that there can be problems when leaving murder to chance, especially if he kills in a ritual manner. Many gun shops, army surplus stores, uniform stores, and similar locations sell handcuffs. These are also available from some adult sex toy shops, though the ones sold in such stores are often padded to protect the wrists, or otherwise more elaborate. The killer will buy one or more pairs of cuffs, depending upon whether he leaves them on his victims or takes them with him. When he leaves them, he is often careful to not buy more than one or two pairs from any single store since a larger purchase will arouse suspicion.

Other serial killers prefer to use lengths of rope or wide, heavy duty adhesive tape or duct tape if they subdue their victims. The rope is usually precut into lengths with which he likes to bind his victims.

A gag may be a part of the murder kit, or the killer may use something at the scene. Most organized serial killers who either kidnap their victims or hold them for a prolonged period of rape and torture, will try to silence the victim to avoid alerting others. Murder kit gags have included large handkerchiefs and scarves, wide adhesive tape, and even Ace Bandages. Sometimes the choice hints at the killer's identity, such as someone with first aid or medical training using Ace Bandages which can be purchased from drug stores. At other times the killer always relies upon an item of clothing he can anticipate the victim wearing, stuffing her mouth with her own panties, socks, or something similar. The act of silencing her can be part of the torture, and it is not uncommon for a gagged victim to smother or choke to death on the material rammed down her throat. Again, the item of clothing and the violence used when silencing the victim may reveal information about the killer.

Knowing whether or not a killer is organized means little unless he is caught. However, once police are able to search where he lives, the organized killer may leave clues in his home. For example, there may be a length of rope similar to one found on a corpse. When the fibers are compared, it may reveal that they are the same original length of rope, the cut marks matching. This is also true if the killer uses adhesive or duct tape. If the ends of the tape binding the victim can be compared with the end of the tape remaining on the spool in the killer's possession, sometimes tear marks can be matched.

The organized offender is quite aware of the possibility of being caught. This is different from thinking about the consequences of his actions. It is often said that threat of the death penalty or other punishment can stop a serial killer from murdering. The fact that the organized killer deliberately obliterates or avoids leaving evidence implies that he knows there is a penalty. The truth seems to be that the killer does not see himself facing that ultimate penalty. Going to jail for life or facing death are not considerations. He just does not want to stop killing, and getting caught will interrupt his pleasure.

In order to avoid detection, the organized killer leaves as little evidence as possible. He may also try to avoid the discovery of the victim since a lack of identification buys time.

Typically an organized killer will wear gloves or be careful what is touched, removing telltale small objects that were handled or wiping areas as clean as possible. Rape will be committed while wearing a condom that is either flushed down the toilet or discarded away from the crime scene. Sometimes the victim is physically altered, from removing the head and hands for separate burial to the wholesale destruction of the corpse as occurred with Jeffrey Dahmer.

The organized killer will often clean blood from the crime scene. If a prostitute is the victim, anything that indicates her identity will be removed. A kidnapped stranger may have her clothing removed regardless of her profession. Even the car is carefully considered, ranging from a borrowed vehicle to a stolen car, to one that is so similar to others, it does not stand out. In Los Angeles, Ken Bianchi and his cousin used a car that was similar to the Metropolitan Unit police vehicles. It was nondescript for the area and would not receive special notice. And in Bellingham, Washington, Bianchi usually drove a truck, a common sight in that community.

The organized killer is most likely to dump the victim someplace other than where the murder took place. The alternative is to kill the victim far from where she was kidnapped, raped, and/or tortured. Harvey Glatman used his home studio to act out most of his bondage fantasies, then drove the women many miles away before murdering them and leaving their corpses.

Many occult Dabbler murders are done by at least one organized serial killer. This person goes to great lengths to set the scene, though because he has created his own approach to religion, the objects and symbols found are unique to his personal beliefs. Likewise some killers deliberately create the impression of violence that was not part of the murder, nor was it part of a fantasy or obsession. This may include the mutilation of the corpse after death solely to obliterate evidence or delay identification.

Organized offenders delight in the keeping of souvenirs. The problem for investigators is that a souvenir does not have to be a personal item. It can be a photograph such as Glatman enjoyed taking of his victims. The souvenirs are not necessarily kept by the killer. Some suspects are found with rings, earrings, watches, and other jewelry belonging to their victims. Others may take shoes or some other item of clothing. Still others may take something they found at the crime scene, such as a personal photograph from the bedroom, an old doll, or something else that he notices during the murder. But many killers discard these possessions within a couple of hours, and others give the souvenir to a girlfriend or spouse. This is especially true with jewelry or clothing that looks new. Even apparent theft for gain may be souvenir taking, such as when an investigator finds the victim's wallet filled with money but a credit card missing. When there is no attempt by the killer to use the credit card in any way, it is likely to have been that killer's souvenir.

Disorganized serial killers are quite different in their actions. Although they are obsessed with killing to the same degree as the organized killer, they do not make plans for their murders. Coral Eugene Watts led a seemingly normal life until he saw a woman he decided had 'evil in her eyes.' Then he would kill her wherever she was and with whatever was handy. He might try to get rid of the body, but his concern was to kill her, not stalk her, rape her, torture her, or otherwise do those things common to organized killers.

The disorganized serial killer is an opportunist who frequently does not drive a car or does not drive to the murder. If he does, it is a matter of chance, not planning. He will also not worry so much about the crime scene and the victim. His concern is murder. He either does not have a sex drive, and many of the disorganized serial killers never achieve orgasm or try penetration, or sex is not important. He will know nothing about his victim in most cases. He will not stalk her for a prolonged period. He will not observe her lifestyle. He may not know whether or not she lives alone should he choose to enter her home. As a result he may choose an aggressive, athletic victim who will struggle. Sometimes this means that the victim has what are known as defensive wounds on her body. And sometimes this means that the victim escapes or does harm to her attacker.

The disorganized killer seldom keeps souvenirs. The person is not important to him. He kills for reasons he alone understands, and often, like Coral Eugene Watts seeing 'evil in her eyes,' he knows the victims only when he encounters them. There are no connections anyone can see, including himself. He does what he has to do when he feels he has to do it.

There often is little difference between the first murder by an organized and a disorganized serial killer. The crime is one of opportunity and little planning has gone into it. The rare exception was Harvey Glatman who seemed to use planning as foreplay, and when he settled on his first victim, he had developed a mental scenario as detailed as a screenplay to be acted out.

After the first meeting there are some striking differences. The disorganized serial killer tends to both murder and leave the bodies within a relatively short distance from his home. The bodies will be found no further than the person routinely walks, for example, or along a familiar bus route. The problem comes when the murderer is a drifter who travels regularly. There may be many corpses in many different jurisdictions, no discernible pattern linking them together. Yet once the police capture the killer, the corpses form obvious clusters based on where he has lived and worked. There is also more likely to be trace evidence left behind – fingerprints, pubic hairs, semen stains, blood stains, and the like.

The disorganized serial killer is usually a loner with his emotions completely self-contained. He may be seen as slightly mentally ill. He may be viewed as a recluse. Whatever the case, he generally has a poor self-image, is somewhat eccentric, extremely withdrawn, and lives either alone or with a parent. He seems to have no temper, though his victims discover that he can suddenly burst into murderous rage. The disorganized killer is generally hurting emotionally, translating this factor into anger towards the person who will become his victim. Instead of seeking counseling, he would rather suppress and explode, suppress and explode.

The organized killer will act out his anger, and it is intense. However, the organized killer has a specific focus for that anger, and that focus frequently reveals a pattern to his victims. Their age, occupation, physical appearance, lifestyle, and/or some other factor will have a logic to them, even if that logic is only understood after the killer is caught and explains his rage.

There is a frustration with life for the organized killer. He is always being shot down by someone or something. Ken Bianchi was convinced that everyone was keeping him from success in his life. He was the type who might get fired for being late to work on a regular basis, then claim the employer never liked him, refusing to see that he failed to meet his obligation to his boss. Even when he was caught, he felt there would be little penalty for the murders since it was believed that he had a multiple personality. The fact that such a diagnosis was not considered insanity under the laws of the states where he was arrested meant nothing to him. Likewise, the serious nature of his crimes and the attitude society had towards men who murder and rape were outside his comprehension. He felt that all would be forgiven, that he would spend no more than a few months in jail, during which he would have counseling, and then he, his girlfriend, and their son would live happily ever after. The fact that his girlfriend, upon learning what he had done, would neither let him touch her nor bring their child near him only caused him pain. They were a family in his mind. How could a little thing like rape and murder separate them?

Charles Manson was convinced he should be a rock star. He hated everything that stood in his way, his anger fueled by occasional success. After all, if a musician such as Axl Rose will buy his music, then think what he could do on his own if given a chance. The fact that most musicians, far more skilled than he was, never find success was not considered. Likewise, the idea that some musicians are willing to get ahead by taking any opportunity to perform they can find, which he did not, also was never considered. He wasn't what he felt he should be and he blamed others for that fact.

Michigan's Leslie Williams frequently justified his urge to rape and murder based on external events. During the 1992 Memorial Day Weekend, Williams was invited to attend barbecues at the homes of a number of friends. He wanted to go, but he felt he should have a date for the events. The fact that none of his friends cared if he came alone did not matter to him. He was convinced that he needed a woman with him, then was angry that he could not accept any of the cookout invitations because he was alone. It was enough justification for him to stop by Hillview Cemetery in the Redford Township of Detroit, a location where he liked to pursue his rape and murder victims.

The anger that had been festering was reinforced when he perceived himself as being 'rejected' by a woman mourner who was in the cemetery to lay flowers on her mother's grave. The woman, 35 years old, thought she was exchanging meaningless pleasantries with someone else visiting the grave of a loved one. She did not know that he was fantasizing about their relationship, creating a role for her which she failed to fill. Yet like many organized killers (Leslie Alan Williams' murder kit primarily consisted of plastic ties of the type used as supplementary handcuffs by law enforcement officers), his anger was projected into circumstances where she fit his plans and his fantasies. He decided to kidnap and hurt her before killing her.

Fortunately for the woman, she was also the last of Williams's victims. A deputy sheriff found the battered, unconscious woman in Williams's car before he could murder her. Plastic ties around her neck limited the flow of oxygen. Other ties secured her wrists so she could not readily flee if she managed to regain consciousness before he could rape her.

Williams knew that his actions would be seen as him committing a crime. He also had the externalized anger so typical of this type of murderer. The woman was responsible for her battering, and had he completed the violence he planned, she would have been seen as responsible for her own death.

No serial killers can sustain long term relationships. The disorganized are generally loners, men who would not seek intimacy beyond casual sex no matter what their circumstances. The fact that they are almost invariably mentally ill further prevents their developing relationships.

Organized killers can usually sustain relationships for

a period of time. They are sexually active, and they often have had multiple, repeat sex partners over the years. Ken Bianchi was involved with the same woman for more than a year. He was married and truly loved his son. But eventually their relationships fall apart – sometimes for bizarre reasons. Bianchi's first wife divorced him because he was too romantic.

School is usually unimportant for disorganized serial killers because they frequently do not do well. Likewise, they settle upon jobs they can either do with a minimum of human contact, or they drift from menial job to menial job. They feel there is nothing else for them, in contrast to the organized killer's more outgoing personality, strong ego, and more 'normal' lifestyle.

If a killer is truly found to be mentally ill, he is usually disorganized. He acts for reasons that have nothing to do with stress on the job or in the family, specific slights, or anything else that provides an obvious cause and effect. Fortunately, the disorganized killers are in the minority. Most fit the organized label, a fact that has helped law enforcement extensively.

The problem with the information about serial killers is that it does not prevent murders, nor does it stop most killers before they strike again. The FBI has been attempting to create a central information center for homicides that might lead to an earlier identification of the killers. But the forms needed for the system often take an hour or longer to fill out, and most investigators either lack the time or feel that they are too much trouble. Even with the central system, only those killers with past records for crimes involving the same method of operations might be found.

Coral Eugene Watts is typical of the type of serial killer who does not fit the efforts of profilers and behavioral scientists to quickly identify a murderer. In fact, although he is probably the most 'successful' serial killer of the twentieth century, he has never served time for murder. In addition, most of the killings he committed remain officially unsolved because of jealousies among departments, and for political reasons within the communities where they occurred.

It was late 1982 or early 1983, Houston, Texas, Police Department Detective Sergeant Tom Ladd has forgotten which, when he was contacted by officers from Detroit, Michigan. The Detroit police said that a man named Coral Eugene Watts was a suspected serial killer who was relocating to the Houston area. There was no solid evidence of his having murdered anyone. There was as yet no reason to make an arrest. However, the Detroit area police were certain the man was a killer and they had been doing everything they could to upset him. They followed him so openly that he was aware of their presence. They stopped by his job to speak with him. They tried to make him feel as though no matter what he did, no matter where he went, the police would always be present. That way they would either catch him in the act or force him to leave the area.

Coral Watts did not fit any of the profiles. He was a Black man, and most profilers were convinced that only White men became serial killers. He was a diesel mechanic, hard working, and dependable. His mother was a school teacher, respected, and made every effort to be a good parent after she divorced his father. There was little male guidance in his family except for his Uncle Smitty, a man Coral delighted in being around. But Uncle Smitty was killed by his wife, and from around the age of ten, following Uncle Smitty's death, Coral began hating women.

Watts supposedly fit the image of the disorganized killer in that he had no plan, no murder kit. Yet he was highly intelligent and sane by all legal definitions. He had sustaining relationships, and his victims fit no profile. They were White, Black, and Hispanic. They were rich and poor. They were young and old. They were employed in good jobs, in menial labor, or had no jobs at all. He also used any means at hand to kill the women.

At the time I began investigating the background of Watts, he was in prison, considered mentally unstable, and not expected to live his full term. He could not be interviewed. However, attorneys, friends, and police officers involved with the case had extensive records from both the investigations and from talks with Watts while he was still quite 'normal.'

From what can be determined, Watts started killing in Michigan around 1969 and continued undetected for more than a dozen years. He killed each victim in whatever way he had to do it. Some were strangled. Some died from multiple stab wounds. Some were struck with blunt instruments. One victim was hung from a tree. He hit one woman in the throat, crushing her larynx. He drowned another woman. In Galveston, Texas, a judge's daughter was out running for exercise. Watts took out a knife and slashed at her throat as she passed him. She continued running for a moment before collapsing, at which time he inflicted multiple stab wounds on her body.

Coral had only one standard when choosing his victims. Each woman had 'evil in her eyes.' No one ever knew how he determined this fact, not even Coral. And the discovery of that evil never changed. A woman he felt did not have evil today would never be seen as a potential victim. The women who had to die were clearly defined and known exclusively by Coral. It was only this fact that led one female attorney to agree to act as co-defense counsel after his arrest. She asked him specifically if she had evil in her eyes. When he said that she did not, she agreed to work with him. However, she could never learn what, if any, standards determined such a designation.

While the Michigan authorities thought they were

harassing him, he privately told Houston police that he was relishing the game. He liked knowing he was being followed, finding ways to elude the surveillance in order to kill the first women he saw with evil in her eyes, then let the surveillance teams find him again. This was also a situation that occurred in Texas.

Watts understood the surveillance methods, no matter which methods were used. He would frequently chase after some of the cars or walk up to a parked officer and ask him to get coffee. In Michigan, during the time he was under surveillance, it was believed that Watts murdered as many as 22 of his victims. He also got satisfaction from detecting electronic surveillance devices, then either destroying or outwitting them.

The problem with the Watts murders was that he did not fit the profiles. Police in Michigan, Texas, and surrounding states knew that they had so many unsolved murders, a serial killer had to be involved. However, they identified the victims by profiles that were inaccurate. One series in Michigan 'proved' that the killer only went after White women whom he killed at night using blunt instruments. Yet the truth was far more shocking.

Coral Eugene Watts lived six months in Houston before he was originally believed to have started killing. He had been watched because of the Michigan alert, but he committed no crimes of which anyone was aware. Then, around 2:30 or 3:00 a.m. he was passing an apartment complex when he saw Lori Lister coming home. Coral decided that she had evil in her eyes, so he went up to her, punched her, took her into her apartment, secured her hands with a wire coat hanger, and placed her in the bathtub. He turned on the water, planning to drown her, when her roommate, Melinda Aguilar, also returned home.

Coral had never experienced such a problem. He knew how to kill, but not how to control two victims.

He forced Aguilar into the bedroom, tied her hands behind her back, telling her that if she did not move, she would not get hurt. Then he returned to the bathroom and the woman he wanted to drown.

It was approximately 6 a.m. when Aguilar, in the bedroom, got to her feet, went to the balcony, and managed to leap over the side. She landed in the bushes, screaming hysterically.

Coral fled the apartment, as Lister, unconscious in the bathtub, began slowly suffocating under the water. She would fortunately be found quickly enough to be saved through mouth-to-mouth resuscitation.

Meanwhile, two police officers, D.R. Schmidt and L.W. Domain, saw Coral coming from the apartment. They approached him, their weapons still holstered because he seemed too calm to be the cause of the telephone call alerting them to screaming at the apartment. He talked with them calmly, lying about his presence. Then, when the officers were off guard, he took off running, his powerful body easily outdistancing the police. The only mistake he made was turning left into walls creating an impregnable barrier to fast escape instead of right, as planned, which would have taken him to the parking lot.

The Houston Police Department was faced with a serious dilemma. They had a probable killer caught in a series of criminal acts that included attempted murder. However, this was not a man with a need to confess. After extensively interrogating Coral Eugene Watts, it became evident that he was not going to talk about the crimes. He also understood the police methods, feeling both superior to them and a little insulted that they were being used with him. After one officer was brought in to play 'hard ass' with Coral, he looked at the detective and told him not to make the partner the 'good guy.' He understood that they were using the standard interrogation trick of alternating between one tough, angry officer and one soft, friendly one, hoping he would talk to the one being pleasant to him.

Watts also had a habit of lying to the psychologist brought in to evaluate him. He was not trying to avoid responsibility. He simply had no intention of telling anyone about himself and his crimes – except his attorneys. Watts felt that he always had to tell the attorneys the truth. He always had to answer their questions accurately and honestly. He would tell his attorney every detail of every murder he ever committed if the attorney would but ask.

Suddenly everyone in the legal system was in a bind. Even today, many years after Watts was sent to prison in 1983, the men and women directly involved with the case would speak freely only off the record. The case had too many complications for them to want the public aware of exactly what deals were made.

The basic case against Coral Eugene Watts was a simple one. He was charged with two counts of criminal attempted murder. There were two living complainants. He was caught in the act. Conviction for those crimes would be a simple matter.

The problem came with the knowledge of how dangerous Coral had been and would continue to be. A number of lawyers were brought in, including those assisting Detective Tom Ladd. Then Coral talked with his attorneys, telling exactly what he had done over the years.

The result of the extensive confession was shock and horror for everyone. The lawyers had represented criminals before, and they had played the game of helping their clients protest their innocence when they knew they were guilty. Sometimes the prosecutor was less prepared or less effective in court than should have been the case, so their guilty clients were acquitted. Usually a guilty client receiving a fair trial was found guilty and sent to jail. When that occurred, the attorneys felt that their success had been relected in the sentence, the less time served, the better for the client. Never mind whether or not the person might commit another crime when released. That was not the concern.

Coral's case was no game. He was a known serial killer who had committed perfect crimes. Without his own statements against himself, there was no way to stop him.

The early background investigation into Coral Watts did not indicate a man with such extreme psychopathic tendencies. He was born in Fort Hood, Texas, then moved to Michigan where he was raised. His mother was from Inkster, and he eventually attended Western Michigan University in Kalamazoo for two semesters in 1974. That same year he was accused of choking and beating a woman in her apartment. He was eventually convicted on December 4, 1975, and served a year in the Kalamazoo County Jail. During this period he was questioned about the fatal stabbing of a 19-year-old Kalamazoo woman, Gloria Steele, whose murder occurred on October 30, 1974. He denied the charge and there was no evidence linking him with the case.

It was on August 17, 1979, that Watts married Valeria Estelle Goodwill. However, the marriage lasted only through December 30 of that year, during which time he lived in the Ann Arbor area and was suspected of three more murders.

Eventually Watts went to work in the Houston area. He had been employed by the Metropolitan Transit Authority as a mechanic while in Michigan, and his record was good enough so that he knew he could be hired elsewhere with little difficulty. He held jobs with Coastal Transport, and later, for two months, with Welltech, Inc., of Columbus, Texas, 75 miles to the south of Houston. He also joined the St Paul Temple

Church of God and Christ, a small Pentecostal Church run by the Reverend Paul Ellis. He was not active, neither singing with the others nor moved to speak in tongues, a major part of their belief. But he did seem to otherwise fit in, the congregation accepting him as a new member.

Detective Ladd figured that perhaps he had killed three or four people at the most in Houston. Then Coral talked about the short time he had been in the city and 13 of the people he had killed there.

A check with the records showed that the police knew only about nine of the murders. The tenth person to whose murder he confessed was officially listed as missing. And three of the murders were unreported at the time of the confession.

The police were suspicious. They had encountered confessors before, men and women who would confess to any crime. Sometimes the confessors were people who wanted attention any way they could get it. At other times they were severely emotionally disturbed, filled with self-hate, and determined to be punished for anything, including something they did not do. Criminals could be confessors as well, exaggerating their killings as would prove to be the case with a man named Henry Lee Lucas. But Coral was different. Coral did not lie.

Sometimes the stories were shocking in their callous brutality, yet the details matched the known facts. For example, a girl walking her dog was spotted by Coral. He decided that she had evil in her eyes, took a long knife, ran it through her heart, and walked away. Coral saw another woman while driving. She was in a nearby car and she, too, had evil in her eyes. He followed her to Austin, Texas, and there saw a woman by her swimming pool. That woman also had evil in her eyes, according to Coral, so he stopped and drowned her before going on. The murder was believed an accidental

226

could look 'tough on crime,' bragging that they had put a notorious murderer behind bars. They knew that there was inadequate evidence to connect Coral with the murders in any other way. But only police and prosecutors in Houston and a few surrounding areas were willing to admit the truth. The man who was probably the deadliest and most efficient serial killer in the United States in the last half of the twentieth century had committed perfect crimes. Even knowing what he had done, unless he confessed, which he refused to do in court or in any deposition that could be used against him, there was no evidence that would convict him. He kept no souvenirs for more than a few hours. He had no direct connection with the victims, all of whom were randomly selected strangers. He had no favorite method for killing, nor did he carry a special murder kit. There were no witnesses who could connect him with the deaths. It was certain that he had gotten away with murder well over a hundred times. But based on what Watts said about his teenaged years when he first started killing people, there was a good chance that he had committed several hundred murders in all.

Proving the accuracy of Coral's statements was both easier and more shocking than anyone imagined. He had to show the officers where he had buried the first body in the Houston area, a woman not officially known dead. She was only listed as missing because no corpse had been found, and thus there was no proof of her death. If Watts could unearth that body, the rest of his statements became far more credible, even if he could not supply details beyond what appeared in the newspapers.

Coral took the investigators to a spot approximately a hundred yards from the woman's apartment. The ground had settled since the murder. There was no sign that anyone had been digging, no mound to act as a marker. But Watts was adamant about the spot, even after digging two feet down revealed nothing out of the ordinary.

Detective Ladd was angry. He told Coral that he thought his information was 'bullshit.' He began to suspect that the man was either not a murderer or was exaggerating his activities. But Watts was adamant and there had always been something about the man that made the police feel he was genuine in his confession. They kept digging.

Suddenly the dirt gave way, revealing a cavern like opening in which a mummified corpse was buried. The cavern itself had been created by escaping body gasses. Most important, it was a body no one but the killer even knew existed.

At first Watts felt comfortable talking freely with the police. He had told the attorneys everything they wanted to know, and they had helped make the plea bargain that would keep him from the death penalty. But he did not want to talk with anyone other than his lawyers, and when he realized that the police knew less than he thought, he became quiet. Inside sources indicate that while he admitted to the 13 murders in Houston, the actual number of cases during the few short weeks he lived in the city was probably double that figure. He attacked more than one woman a night, and it did not matter whether someone was around as a possible witness. A woman with 'evil in her eyes' would die. He never thought about the consequences, only his 'mission.'

Houston is an unusual city in many ways. There is a flamboyance to the community, and an arrogance. Unlike much of the rest of the state which still celebrates its old west and Mexican heritage, Houston looks upon history as something that happened the previous year. Historic buildings are more likely to be torn down, regardless of how well built they remain, than to be retained. And while parts of Texas glorify the nine-

230

teenth century, Houston expresses hostility to projects dating back to the middle of the twentieth century.

The Houston Police often willingly tell of the latest scandal in Dallas, a city which also has the distinction of being known for the Kennedy assassination, strip clubs, and a history of Mafia business influences. They appreciate getting credit for their work in almost the same way as one of the local self-made business wonders. Yet with Coral, there was an intriguing lack of information.

The Houston Police were dealing with a serious problem when it came to Coral Eugene Watts. First there was the issue of how many killings he had done. They knew that they would never be able to close all the murders in all the states, but they wanted to keep him talking as much as possible. They needed the cooperation of authorities in other cities and other states where Watts had killed. And they needed to avoid the type of circus atmosphere that occurs when members of the press decide to make their reputation through writing and broadcasting often exploitive serial killer stories. After all, this was only two years after the media circus that surrounded Los Angeles' fascination with the Hillside Strangler, Ken Bianchi.

Perhaps the most unusual request for downplaying the story came from Watts himself. He did not want his mother to know what he had been doing. She was a school teacher beloved by her past students and neighbors, and he saw himself as a monster when he murdered. He wanted her to remember him as a skilled diesel mechanic, as respectful to others, as being gentle to his girlfriend.

In addition to all this, Coral was Black. He was probably the first identified Black serial killer in the United States. Yet the Houston newspapers complied. The *Houston Chronicle*'s coverage began in August of 1982, and it was low key, detailing what had been learned about the cases on which Watts was cooperating. Some of the Michigan authorities agreed to let him confess in order to clear their records, though other cases remained open. The cases that could be confirmed were discussed.

Today the vast majority of Watts's murders remain officially unsolved because of the reluctance of prosecutors in several cities to make agreements with Watts. They have no case against him, though it is now known that he gave full details concerning the killing of a minimum of 40 people in Michigan over three or four years. He had barely started his confessions when he realized that he had to protect himself through silence to all but his lawyers.

Among the known murder victims were three in Ann Arbor previously attributed to a man nicknamed 'the Sunday Slasher' because their corpses were found on Sunday. In addition, there were:

- *Suzanne Searles*, a 25-year-old customer service representative and production artist for a typography company.
- *Carrie Mae Jefferson*, a 32-year-old postal service employee.
- *Yolanda Garcia*, 21, an employee of Gordon's Jewelers in down town Houston. She was stabbed on her front lawn after getting off the bus.
- *Michele Marie Maday*, who was found strangled in a dry bathtub, though surrounded by wet towels.
- *Elena Semander*, a 20-year-old University of Houston student, whose corpse was discovered in a dumpster.
- *Margaret Everson Fossi*, 25, a fifth year architecture student at Rice University. She was killed by a blow to the throat.
- *Elizabeth Montgomery*, 25, who was stabbed while walking her dog.

- *Susan Marin Wolf*, 21, who was repeatedly stabbed while taking grocery bags from her car and carrying them to her home.
- *Phyllis Ellen Tamm*, 27, an advertising agency art director, who was found hanging from a tree near Rice University.
- *Elizabeth Montgomery*, 25.
- *Susan Wolf*, 21, killed in Houston though originally from Bay City, Michigan.
- *Emily Elizabeth LaQua*, 14, a runaway from Seattle, who was found off Interstate 10 in Houston.
- *Patty Johnson*, 19, of Galveston whose throat was slashed. A man named Howard Mosley was originally charged and convicted of the crime. However, he had been at home with his fiancee, Linda Sanchez, when the murder was committed. He eventually married Sanchez in jail and had his innocence proved when Watts confessed.
- *Jeanne Clyne*, a resident of Grosse Point Farms in Michigan who was stabbed 11 times with a woodworking tool on Halloween night in 1979. She was a *Detroit News* reporter whom Watts spotted while out driving. He followed her, parked his car, stabbed her and left. He then bought potato chips because he was hungry from the exertion. (Ten years earlier he had attacked and choked a woman on *Detroit Free Press* – the rival publication – paper route. She survived, identified the teenaged Watts, and he was sent to a psychiatric facility).
- *Gloria Steele* of Kalamazoo, a student at Western Michigan University who was stabbed 33 times and had her larynx crushed.

The list was seemingly endless. Sometimes there were suspects in the killings, such as with victim Suzanne Searles. There were two or three men the police thought might have been involved, including one with whom she had been arguing. Yet Watts had no connection with the victim and no reason to kill her other than the evil in her eyes.

Because Coral was always so calm, whenever there were witnesses to the immediate aftermath of the murders, no one thought him to be acting suspiciously. He killed when he decided murder was necessary, then buried the bodies conveniently. If he had to transport them, he always used the victim's own car. He gave no thought to being captured, no thought to the fact that there was a penalty for what he was doing. Women with evil in their eyes had to be killed. He expended no more emotion on the matter than he would have done killing a mosquito that had landed on his arm.

Often the witnesses had no idea what they were seeing. There were cases to which Watts confessed in great detail, where his guilt was unquestioned, and yet where witnesses said he was a White man. He was sometimes reported as being short or tall, Black or White, thin or fat. He was a man who never called attention of himself because he had no fear. Later, when asked about what seemed this unusual situation, he commented, 'People see what they want to see.'

There were many questions remaining after Watts admitted many of his murders. There may have been reasons for the variations in how the victims were killed, but if they existed, he told the police he did not want to tell them what they were. All that was known was that when he took souvenirs, he got rid of them quickly so the victims would not be related back to him. He also buried some victims and not others. He drowned some or left them under water, but he did not do that to the others. He frequently wore gloves, and he also often wore a hooded sweatshirt. Watts also refused to talk about murders that involved minors or the elderly, as though he was not comfortable with those types of murders.

I Confess. I didn't do it

While Houston was handling a genuine serial killer, police in Dallas, Jacksonville, Florida, Conroe, Texas, and cities in a total of 26 states were relieved by the arrest of Henry Lucas, a man they considered the most notorious serial killer known. He initially confessed to more than 200 cases, all while being videotaped. Later there would be more, almost all of them nonsense.

Sometimes Henry claimed to have killed with a friend, Ottis Toole, who did have a violent history in his own right. Usually he claimed to have killed alone. Each confession was believed to be genuine, the full scope of the problem not evident until as many as 600 cases in five foreign countries were supposed to have been the work of Lucas.

Lucas was probably one of the best manipulators of law enforcement of any criminal in recent years. Just as reporters will use any ruse to get an interview, so Lucas was willing to confess to anything in order to be allowed off death row long enough to travel the country on a vacation paid for by law enforcement.

This is not to say that Lucas was innocent of any crimes. He definitely committed three murders. In 1960, he murdered his mother, Viola Lucas. Then, 22 years later, he murdered his friend Ottis Toole's niece, Frieda 'Becky' Powell, and Kate Rich of Ringgold, Texas. These were crimes that earned him a cell on death row in the state's maximum security penitentiary. That was why he decided to make confessing a way of staying alive and getting to travel.

The Henry Lee Lucas story reveals more about law enforcement's attitudes towards clearing cases than it does about the killers. Certain types of cases become high profile in a community. Certainly the more prominent the victim, the more pressure there is to solve a case. Murder the White mayor's daughter as part of a crime spree and the attention given the case by police and the news media will be far greater than the death of the same age daughter of Black welfare recipients who have had to periodically live in homeless shelters.

Serial killings also are high profile cases, though the pressures for solving them vary with the victims. Washington state has been plagued by a serial killer known as the Green River Slayer. There have been numerous articles and books written about the case, yet community pressure has been limited because the victims have all been prostitutes. While the police want to get a murderer off the streets, the movers and shakers in the area are less concerned because their lives will not be touched by the killer's violence. So long as their daughters are not prostitutes, they are not at risk. A burglar working their neighborhood who never carries a weapon and never enters any houses that are not empty during the crime will lead to more pressure for an arrest than a serial killer of 'whores.'

But when the victims are consistently prominent, or the victims are a mix of people from all walks of life, there is pressure. The sooner a case is solved, the better a mayor and police chief believe they look to the public. The longer a case goes on, and the longer the media coverage is intense, the better a detective breaking the case looks to supervisors. Thus careers can be made by resolving murders quickly. And when a serial killer is arrested and has spent time in a city with unsolved murders, everyone hopes he is the guilty person.

It was for this reason that law enforcement officers in every area where Lucas was known to have been decided to see if he was the guilty man. They took case notes, photos of the victims, and other details, then carried them to question Lucas in his cell in Georgetown, Texas. Occasionally they also went to see his friend, convicted murderer Ottis Toole, who was on death row for murder in Jacksonville, Florida. But it was Lucas who made the confessions, Toole sometimes admitting to murders beyond the one for which he would be executed, though never claiming to have killed with Lucas.

An interesting aspect of Henry Lee Lucas was the fact that he was given the death sentence in April, 1984, based on his confession of murder. He said that he was responsible for the Halloween night, 1979, slaying of an unidentified woman hitchhiker in her early twenties. That body, naked except for a pair of orange socks, had been dumped along Interstate 35 near Georgetown, Texas. The corpse was in a drainage ditch.

The investigation into Lucas as the murderer began when he was legitimately in jail on charges of murdering Kate Rich, a woman with whom he lived briefly. He murdered her, stuffed the corpse in a culvert, then set it on fire to try and destroy the evidence. The arrest resulted in his being placed in the Montague County jail where he decided to prove to law enforcement that they were stupid. He took Sheriff W.F. Conway aside and told him he had committed a hundred murders.

Conway acted properly as Lucas began boasting. The one certainty of every experienced law enforcement officer is that anyone, regardless of background, education, income, or social prominence, might commit any crime. Coral Eugene Watts was a skilled diesel mechanic, son of a school teacher, and regular church-goer. Murderers have been doctors, lawyers, and major celebrities, as well as psychopathic, disheveled, obviously insane drifters. The sheriff felt he had Lucas dead to rights for the Rich murder and assumed he might have committed others. Since he knew of a murder in Williamson County that seemed similar to the Rich case, he called Sheriff Jim Boutwell to tell him of Lucas.

It was Boutwell who was investigating the unsolved murder case that came to be known as 'Orange Socks.' The case was a good one to investigate because of the facts and the volume of trace evidence at the scene. The victim, a woman, had been strangled to death, though there were few other marks on her body. She had a severe case of venereal disease which would have been passed on to anyone having sex with her. There was a weathered matchbook cover at the scene which advertised a motel in Oklahoma and was believed to belong to the killer. There was also a bloodstained handkerchief. Thus, though Orange Socks was found in an open drainage ditch, not stuffed inside a culvert and not burned, there was a chance Lucas might be connected.

The sheriff brought the medical examiner's report with him, placing it unintentionally where Lucas was able to read the top sheet. He learned the victim's height and weight (5 feet 7 inches to 5 feet 9 inches and 140 pounds), and he already knew the county where she died and the year she was murdered from the information provided when the sheriff made a request to see him.

Lucas told Boutwell that he had picked up the hitchhiker in Oklahoma, killing her on the way to Texas. He said he dropped her in the San Antonio area, adding, 'If anybody's ever found her, she would have been sexually assaulted. She would have several stab wounds, probably some through her breasts, probably, and some through her chest cavity.' There was no question that Lucas' confession was incorrect. Boutwell returned home, then made a decision to return.

What happened next should never have occurred, yet there is no way to lay the blame when a known murderer decides to put himself on death row through confession. If Lucas had killed many people, as he claimed, then Boutwell would be remiss in not questioning him further. He might have confused some murders. For every Coral Eugene Watts who never forgot one of the women with 'evil in her eyes,' there are dozens of multiple murderers who notice as little about their victims as a butcher remembers about the cows he dismembers in preparation for sending their meat to market.

On the second visit, Lucas said he picked up Orange Socks along I-35. The sheriff pointed out the contradiction, Lucas blaming the many states and roads he had traveled for his confusion. When Boutwell reminded him he had originally said 'Oklahoma City,' Lucas was quick to agree.

Next came a controversial action used regularly around the country. Lucas was shown crime scene photos to refresh his memory.

Normally a crime scene photo helps. The criminal remembers details about the murder that are so specific that it is obvious he is guilty. Or the criminal remembers nothing, the crime scene being all wrong in his mind. He may have been guilty of murder, he realizes, but not the murder shown there. But Lucas used every bit of information he could obtain in order to make himself sound more and more guilty.

Lucas discussed the fact that he had sex with the victim voluntarily, then had to fight her when she refused his demand for a second time. He also said that he spotted the culvert while driving, a physical impossibility from the side of the road on which he was traveling. And the crime, according to Lucas, was in mid-afternoon.

The sheriff pointed out that dumping a corpse at mid-day on a busy road would be risky, at which time Lucas said he waited to dump her until dark. Likewise, Lucas went from claiming to never having had venereal disease to having to be treated for it several months after the murder.

Lucas eventually implicated his friend Ottis Toole who did travel the countryside with Lucas for a while. Both of them were working for the Southeast Color Coat roofing company at the time. Work records indicated that they were on the job at the Jacksonville Naval Air Station when the murder was committed, not traveling the highways of Texas.

Everything was soon explained. The foreman was willing to pay 'ghost' employees. He would clock you in and out as though you were on the job. Then, when you got your paycheck, you would kick-back a portion to the foreman for his trouble. Both of you got unearned money, and because the only record was the time card, no one would be wiser.

The idea was plausible. Construction sites are notorious for corruption. The idea of a project with a large number of workers having some ghost employees is not unusual. However, what did not make sense was how the arrangement was made.

Lucas was vague about who was involved with the ghost employee scheme, though he did claim that it was the foreman on duty on October 31, a man whose name was Mac Caulder. He also said that Toole's mother was the one who cashed the paycheck, signing both Lucas's name and her own.

Mac Caulder was an experienced foreman who worked for the various roofing company projects wherever he was needed. Before being employed in Jacksonville, he had been in Tallahassee where neither Lucas nor Toole ever claimed to have met him. His first day on the job in Jacksonville was October 31, and he was not in town prior to that. It would have been impossible for Lucas or Toole to have bribed him. In addition, the paycheck for that period was endorsed by Lucas only. It was cashed on November 1 when Lucas claimed to have still been a thousand miles away.

A later background check on Caulder's work revealed even less reason for him to cooperate. His pay was determined, in part, by the speed with which a job was completed. He made more money by working honestly and effectively.

Eventually, when Lucas's confessions began to unfold as false, lawyers obtained copies of the 43 pay checks he earned from February 11, 1979 through March 19, 1980. They were proof of his being on the job, even though he had confessed to 37 murders in much the same manner as the Orange Socks case. The murders took place in Alabama, Arkansas, Colorado, Florida, Louisiana, Mississippi, Nebraska, New York, Oklahoma, Texas, Utah, and Virginia.

It is difficult to understand the feeding frenzy of law enforcement in early 1985 when anything Lucas claimed was believed. Some law enforcement officers tried to truly track Lucas's past, setting up a chronology of where he seemed to have physically been living or working at the same time as he confessed to a murder. If there wasn't a match, they were skeptical at least. However, there was little utilization of the information.

For example, the Texas Rangers showed that on October 1, 1982, he was in the city of Decatur, Illinois, seeking food stamps or unemployment benefits. Yet a task force trying to prove Lucas's guilt credited him with murdering a woman in Conroe, Texas, almost a thousand miles away. Naturally Lucas said he had committed the murder. And as with Orange Socks, he simply played off information provided to him, often speaking vaguely enough so the interrogators gave him the clues he needed. The various law enforcement officers trying to clear cases by blaming Lucas also allowed for his vagueness by saying that he killed so many people, he could not avoid blending times, dates, and details to some degree.

The saddest case from the standpoint of the victim's family was a Lubbock, Texas, murder that occurred some time between 9 p.m. and midnight on August 24, 1975. The victim was 18-year-old Deborah Sue Williamson, and for several months after her murder, her mother and stepfather, Bob and Joyce Lemons, were harassed. They endured several burglaries, and there were anonymous telephone calls threatening their other two daughters. Eventually they moved to Gainesville, Texas, after both the police and the school where their girls attended said that they could not protect them. Lubbock is a small town where most people are at least familiar with one another, yet there was no obvious link between the harassment and either the murder or people known to dislike the Lemons family.

The possible involvement of Lucas should not have been considered at all. He was in a Jackson, Michigan, prison until August 22. He was known to be in Avondale, Pennsylvania, on August 25. And Lucas claimed, with some supporting testimony, that he was in Baltimore and Perryville, Maryland, along the way to Avondale. He was driving a car, so he theoretically could have detoured, driving straight to Lubbock and back. But that detour would have taken a minimum of 30 hours and lasted 1,500 miles.

Realizing that some of the logistics seemed impossible for one man, Lucas said that he traveled with his friend, Ottis Toole. The trouble was that the police, had already established that Lucas and Toole did not meet until around February of 1979, more than three years after the murder.

But the greatest pain came for the Lemons family when they were given the opportunity to listen to Lucas's confession. A tape was made, along with a partial transcript. As had been his style, he confessed because the case was brought to him, but even a limited amount of research would have saved the family the heartache of listening to the comments.

Deborah was murdered under the carport, but Lucas talked of chasing her through her parents' house, raping, then killing her in a bedroom. Yet there were no bloodstains anywhere and little evidence of theft. Only a wedding picture album was taken, not the jew-

242

elry claimed by Lucas. Lucas clearly remembered the 'white' house that was actually olive green. And he recalled entering through the patio door which was both sealed and not broken after the murder.

Further evidence of the inadequacies of his confessions followed the murders of Rich and Powell. The only time Henry Lee Lucas was able to lead the authorities to where he had disposed of the bodies was with those two cases. In all others he was taken to the locations after being shown photographs and told where they were. Then he simply had to confirm what he was told by law enforcement officers.

The Lucas stories become more outrageous. Although cult experts never heard of a group called 'The Hands Of Death,' Lucas told of 500 members who traveled in the United States, France, Japan, Mexico, and Switzerland. They would kill for hire. They would sacrifice humans, then eat their flesh. But when not getting together for rituals and murder, they lived separate lives in different parts of the United States and Canada. When asked how the members kept in touch with one another in order to know when to gather for murder for hire or some other rite, he said: 'We'd send each other postcards.' Yet no one saw the outrageous nature of his comments.

Don Higgenbotham, the court appointed attorney for Henry Lee Lucas, was told the truth about his client. He recognized that no one wanted to arrange for Lucas to take a polygraph test or use one of the chemically induced methods for determining truth during an interrogation. He knew that the police and sheriffs' departments were too eager to accept anything Lucas said, no matter how outrageous. And he knew his client was living better while traveling the country, staying in county jails whenever he was not in the field, agreeing to murders he was asked if he committed. As he later commented to reporters Hugh Aynesworth and

Jim Henderson of the *Dallas Times Herald* (Sunday, April 14, 1985):

'There is a synergistic relationship between Lucas and the cops. Both are getting what they want.'

He added, 'And the public is getting what it wants. Nobody wants to believe there are that many bad people out there. If they can believe there is just one, they are more comfortable.'

Eventually Lucas admitted to trusted reporters and attorneys that he became scared by what he was doing, yet he felt himself unable to stop. He knew that so many reputations had been made by spending money to take him to murder sites where he 'cleared' back cases that the law enforcement officers could not admit mistakes. It would be easier to murder him, he believed, whether by his 'trying to escape' during transport from one city to another or when confined to death row in the Texas state penitentiary in Huntsville.

But despite the efforts of several reporters to debunk the Lucas claims (the *Dallas Times Herald* devoted a portion of its April 14, 1985, coverage to showing the murders to which he confessed and the actual locations where Lucas had been on those days, and despite the fact that ultimately his confessions did not hold up in court cases, Lucas remained somewhat of a cult figure to writers. In fact, in 1991 a book about Lucas was published and included a cassette tape of Lucas 'confessing' to many of his crimes. He remains a legend in the minds of those who investigated the cases, as well as a symbol of the problems that arise when law enforcement officers fail to retain a healthy skepticism about the suspects they arrest.

Mike Berens finds a serial killer

As much as the media sometimes errs in its actions in regard to serial killers, there are times when the prodding of a reporter can reveal a genuine serial killer. Such was the situation for Mike Berens, a highly respected project reporter for the Columbus, Ohio, *Dispatch*.

It was the fall of 1990 when Berens began looking for a project that might lead to a story for the newspaper. Unlike general assignment reporters, his job was to find a project that could lead to a major story or series of stories of strong local or regional interest. Once he had one, he would be allowed to take as long as necessary to complete it.

Berens was strongly aware of the publicity for the then new movie *Silence of the Lambs* which told of a serial killer and the FBI special agent in training who had to find him. He also had a friend in the FBI who commented that prostitutes are the victims of choice for serial killers due to their lifestyles. 'They have one of the only professions – if you can call them that – that willingly get in cars with strangers. They're often not reported as being missing for days, weeks, even a year if they're reported at all. They're the perfect victim for the guy that wants to kill and kill a lot,' Berens explained.

During this same period, Berens encountered an FBI statistic that indicated that, at any given time, approximately 200 people are on the loose who have killed three or more people over time. He figured that if the statistic was accurate, there was probably at least one such individual killing people within the state of Ohio. Since he is an expert at doing research by computer, he decided to see what he could find.

Berens began exploring a computer data base of newspaper clippings. Although there has been much talk about the 'information highway,' the truth about most computer research is that it is usually handled in one of two ways. Either the computer becomes much like a telephone, though with the user typing a message to whoever he is trying to reach rather than telephoning. Leaving electronic mail (E-mail) is a faster, often cheaper method of leaving a message on an answering machine.

The second use is to obtain what amounts to a giant electronic library. By knowing what key words to use when searching available files, extensive information from a wide variety of sources can be obtained. The search Berens made provided him with information on every woman killed in Ohio who was a known or suspected prostitute. Then he expanded his search to the Midwest, and finally he did it nationwide. Ultimately he created a spreadsheet file that had time of death, the victim's name, on what road were they found, and similar details available from the news stories.

'Pretty soon I had about 300 deaths in my computer, and these were all unsolved killings that I was looking for.' The effort lasted about a month, after which he began looking for a pattern. That was when he found six unsolved killings in Ohio involving women who were suspected prostitutes, and each of the six women were either being bludgeoned (beaten about the face) or strangled. None were shot, and none were stabbed.

'The other interesting aspect of the six Ohio women is that they were all dumped on the road or within inches of the road. None were found 25 yards off the road. None were found behind a tree. Right on the road.' There was no attempt at concealment. 'In fact, there was some blatant "here it is. Come and see." '

While the incidents were curious, Berens found the news stories limited. He also would later learn that some of the forensic details were wrong as well. Sometimes information was withheld, and in at least once incident, false information was deliberately provided.

Berens was later troubled by some of the police actions, a not uncommon problem in certain communities. Information is routinely withheld from the press and the public when it might be used to reveal the killer. For example, if someone always leaves a coin on a corpse's tongue, then closes the mouth so it is only found during the autopsy, this might help flush out the killer. Likewise, if a victim is always restrained with toy handcuffs, that fact might not be given out, though handcuffs in general might be mentioned. But in one of the cases Berens studied, the victim was not identified by police. She was a young woman who had tattoos on each breast. One breast had a rose, the other a unicorn. They were distinctive, and it could be presumed that some of her customers would remember seeing them. Likewise, if the tattoos were put on in Ohio, the police mention might have been seen by the person who made them for her. She could have been identified because of those marks, and that identification would in no way affect the capture of the killer. What it might have done was provide leads to people who knew her, one of whom could have been the person they were seeking.'

Once Berens began finding a few similar cases, he called the police departments in whose jurisdiction the bodies had been found. The cases were mostly older ones, some going back several years. Yet he found that in almost every instance the officers involved with the initial investigation were extremely frustrated. They had been pulled off the cases because of what were deemed more pressing matters. But the detectives wanted to stop the killers, and they were frustrated by the fact that the victims' lack of social prominence or respect resulted in their being given a low priority. It was further proof of the reasons why serial killers often choose prostitutes.

Berens began visiting the law enforcement agencies in the locations where the unsolved, seemingly similar murders had been committed. He was given access to more detailed evidence, such as how the body was positioned – right side or left side? On stomach? On back? Was there blood at the scene indicating she had been killed where found, or was the area clean, indicating the corpse had been moved? Was there any sense as to which direction the killer was going? Were there semen samples which could be used for later DNA testing.

'The primary similarities we found were, to begin, all the women were beaten, strangled, or suffocated.' The latter was a single instance where a scarf had been shoved down a victim's throat. The victims were all found on the road or within inches of the road. They were all known or suspected truck stop prostitutes which is different from city prostitutes.

'Truck stop prostitutes barter for sex over CB radio at truck stops exclusively. They don't work in the city. They actually have a circuit nationwide where they go from truck stop to truck stop looking for the trade.'

Berens found that there were loosely organized rings of prostitutes, much like a gypsy band, which traveled a circuit of truck stops usually in a multi-state region. They would work one area until they felt business might be better somewhere else or to avoid a law enforcement crackdown. Sometimes the women used pimps. Sometimes the women were married and their husbands traveled with them. And sometimes they worked alone, though traveling with other women.

'What makes them unique is they work the truck stops, and they barter over the CB radio.' The channels they use vary from state to state. At the time of Berens', investigation, Ohio prostitutes were using Channel 13, though they sometimes changed. They would make contact on one channel, then switch channels while getting details of where the 'trick' was parked. Most of them used false names – 'CB handles' – as did the truckers. In addition, the truckers sometimes used different names in different parts of the country.

248

One of the girls who was killed used the CB handle 'Tongue Teaser.' Another girl's was 'Sleeping Beauty.'

Berens went to the Austintown truck stop near Youngstown, Ohio, because three of the six linked victims were known to have been abducted from that stop. The first of the Austintown victims was found on June 12, 1985. Her name was Marcia Mathews, 25, and a known prostitute. She was believed to be the first of the linked killings, and her beaten body was found on I-71 near Mansfield, Ohio. She was not quite dead, though she never recovered from her injuries and was dead in the hospital two hours after being found. All together it was believed that she lived no more than three hours after being dumped on the busy interstate, though early enough in the morning so traffic was still sparse and she was not spotted right away. Her torso was straddling the inside southbound lane and berm. She had been battered with a blunt object.

Mathews worked in Newark, Ohio, and often turned tricks at the Union 76 truck stop north of Mansfield. A trucker found her body at 5:30 in the morning.

The lives of the truckers meant that investigating them proved difficult. Every state had laws regulating how long truckers could drive each day. Some liked to drive at night, others drove by day. But the nature of the work was such that they almost all put in far more hours than the law allowed.

Truckers were required to keep logs of their travels which could be checked by regulatory agencies and, in this case, investigating officers. But most of the truckers doctored their logs. They made certain the logs reflected times and locations which would match the legal travel schedule. However, they were frequently elsewhere, often hundreds of miles from where they claimed to be. This made everything more difficult for the investigators.

Fortunately for law enforcement officers, many of the

truckers used credit cards. Their receipts were traceable and made tracking the trips more reliable. Distances between charges could be calculated with accuracy.

Mathews was originally from Akron, Ohio. She was 5 feet 7 inches tall and weighed 135 pounds. She was fully clothed, though there was semen present in her vagina. However, if she was sexually assaulted, there were no marks indicating a struggle so the nature of the crime could not be determined. The man may have picked her up and killed her after she had sex with another trucker. Or he may have hired her for sex, had intercourse with her, then killed her as payment.

The fact that Mathews was fully clothed and apparently had nothing missing caused Berens, and later the police, to suspect that she was the first victim. Generally the earliest death is atypical because it is not planned. Murders such as Harvey Glatman committed followed well developed fantasies. Most serial killers, such as Jeffrey Dahmer, blunder into their first murder, then refine their actions with each succeeding death.

The second death linked to the same man by Berens was July 20, 1986. This time the victim's body was dumped at I-71 near a closed public rest stop near the I-76 Interchange. The corpse was found by a trucker who pulled off the road to urinate.

The victim was 23-year-old Shirley Dean Taylor. She was wearing only a black camisole, and her body was dumped by a three foot concrete traffic barrier that had been placed across the westbound exit ramp into the closed stop. Again she was beaten by a blunt object, and there were thin ligature marks around her neck. She had been strangled before the beating, and at 5 feet 6 inches tall and 125 pounds, she was of similar size as the other victim. She was also last seen at the Union 76 Truck Stop in Austintown.

Berens interviewed prostitutes at the truck stop who knew Taylor. They said that she had been soliciting the day she disappeared, and the last known trick was a trucker who used the handle 'Dr No.' Since the arrangements were made by CB radio, no further information was available. Even worse, 'Dr No,' 'Stargazer,' and 'Dragon,' were all handles that were widely used and could not be linked to any one particular man.

December 4, 1986, was the next known murder. A trucker pulling into a rest stop on I-71 three miles north of Route 30 in Ashland County, Ohio, found the corpse of 18-year-old April Barnett. She had been strangled in a grassy area, and was also a prostitute who had been working at the Union 76 truck stop in Austintown.

Barnett, who used the handle 'Tongue Teaser' when calling the truckers, was naked. However, this time her killer left a trail for the police. For 70 miles down the road towards Columbus, he tossed her clothing out onto the center of the highway, one piece every few miles.

These three formed the first connection. They all were murdered in a 50-mile strip of I-71, and two were known to have been last seen at the same Union 76 truck stop in Austintown. All were killed in a similar manner. Two were Black and one was White. All three were similar builds, but there seemed no obvious connections other than the location from which they were taken, the method for murder, and how they were dumped from the truck. It seemed that the trucker stopped along the road, opened the door, tossed them out, and continued on his way. However, because he dumped each body in a different county, there was no pooling of information among the county sheriff's offices investigating the cases. Because sheriff's offices are political operations, they had no interest in linking the murders.

On December 4, 1986, there was a murder outside of Ohio. Jill Allen was found in Madison County, Illinois. She was a new face at Illinois truck stops on *I-70* which ran east and west. *I-71 ran north and south.* Thus there was an important connection that now brought together different sheriff's offices in the investigation.

Allen was 28 years old. She had been strangled by a thin ligature, and had been working relatively briefly as a prostitute. She was probably found within minutes of being dumped, though she had been dead a few hours.

Anna Marie Patterson was found in Warren County, Ohio, near the city of Cincinnati on March 23, 1987. She was a prostitute who had also worked at Austintown at the Union 76 truck stop.

'There is an Austintown police detective that knew that some women were disappearing from the truck stop up there. He worked special duty at that truck stop, and so he knew Anna Marie personally since she was a prostitute who also worked at Austintown – she's the third one now who also worked at the truck stop.

'He approached Anna Marie and said, look, you know, I think we got a problem here. We got some prostitutes who are missing, and they're ending up being killed. He asked Anna Marie to keep her eyes open and see if she knew anything about any trucker who appeared to be weird. She told this officer that she feared for her life about this so she would check into it. She disappeared the next day after she talked to this officer.'

Berens said that the officer told him that Anna Marie thought she had a lead to the man. She was scared, said she would check into it, then disappeared the next day. She never gave him a name or any information he could follow before she was murdered.

The corpse, wearing a pullover shirt, maroon panties, and panty hose, was found more than 250 miles from Austintown. She was also found on I-71 north of Cincinnati. She was found off the freeway on a dirt ramp where there were tractor trailer marks, made by a semi-rig, 40 days after she was reported missing. She was 5 feet 5 inches tall, weighed 130 pounds, and used the CB handle 'Sleeping Beauty.' There were massive blows to her head, making her face unrecognizable, and she was partially wrapped in a sleeping bag. Because it was February when she disappeared, and because the weather had been cold, her body was partially preserved. However, there was no blood, indicating that she had undoubtedly been killed elsewhere.

There were some differences in this case, though not meaningful ones. She was found to be six months pregnant, and her husband had been her pimp, another odd detail of the life. Unfortunately, because the body had been kept cold by the weather, once she was taken to the morgue, the change of temperature caused very rapid deterioration that may have hidden some of the evidence.

Among the truck stop prostitutes who used pimps, a number of them worked with their husbands. That was the case with Patterson whose husband dropped her off for a few days of work, then returned to pick her up to take her to another location. He was planning to move her to a truck stop in Pennsylvania when he discovered her missing, calling the police on February 14.

The important point about the Austintown truck stop murders, along with those that seemed to be connected to the same killer, was the fact that they were transported from the site. Prostitutes working truck stops always feel themselves as safe as prostitutes working on call to hotels. A woman picked up on the streets always runs a risk of being kidnapped. Even if she has sex in the car, it will not be at the corner where she meets the man. She will always drive somewhere else, and that fact always makes her vulnerable.

Truck stop prostitutes get into the parked cabs of the trucks. The cabs have a sleeping area that usually contains a mattress. Whatever they do with the man, from oral sex to full intercourse, is limited by the space.

Since there are always other truckers all around, they feel as though they can get help if the 'John' tries to hurt them. It was believed that the women were strangled or struck unconscious, and perhaps killed, right in the cab by the murderer. Then he would pull out of the lot and transport them wherever he dumped them. The cab was probably the scene of the crime, the place where the bloodstains would be found.

On August 10, 1987, there was a 'Jane Doe' discovered wearing blue jeans and pale blue panties. The corpse was found near a Dayton truck stop in Montgomery County. She had been strangled with a thin ligature, and she was found to have old needle marks. Her body again was similar to the others at 5 feet 5 inches tall. She was found on a grassy area by the ramp to I-70 near Hoke Road. She was wearing jewelry that had not been touched. She was also the victim with the tattoo of the rose on her right breast and the tattoo of a unicorn on her left breast. The abrasions in the grass indicated that she had been dumped from the cab of a semi.

Lamonica Cole was the next victim connected with the cases. She was 19, with a 9-month-old daughter, from Akron, Ohio, and her body was found in Bedford, Pennsylvania, on December 22, 1987. She was a prostitute who worked for a pimp specializing in teenaged girls, and had previously been a girl scout. She was also known to be part of a circuit that traveled throughout Pennsylvania, Ohio, Florida, Mississippi, North Carolina, and other areas with large truck stops. She moved whenever either the money seemed to slow in one location or whenever there were regular police raids interfering with their ability to work.

She had been working at the Breezewood truck stop at the junction of I-76 and I-70. According to the other prostitutes who were monitoring the calls the night she disappeared, she was last seen going to the rig of a trucker using the handle 'Dragon.'

The world of the truck stop was like a closed society, a fact that made the location ideal for criminal activity and almost impossible to police. Off duty police officers hired as security personnel, law enforcement assigned to the truck stop as part of their jurisdiction, and private security guards might work at some of the larger locations. But as Berens learned during his investigation, many factors ensured that a serial killer could literally get away with murder.

The truck stops themselves share only one factor in common – a parking lot so massive that it can hold from several big rigs to several dozen or several hundred. The smallest of the stops are often just inside a city limits, a mile or two from the highway exit and along a main road. They will combine a motel and restaurant, perhaps having a counter area offering small containers of deodorants, prepackaged toothbrush/toothpaste combinations, mouthwash, and similar items. The men's restroom of the restaurant will usually have a vending machine selling condoms.

The largest truck stops have repair bays, massive tanks of fuel, gift shops, a convenience food type operation, and/or what looks like a general store. The rooms can be luxurious, and the food can be excellent. Typical is the Inn At Little America in Flagstaff, Arizona. It is immediately off the freeway, offers full service to the truckers, and is a luxury motel with conference rooms often used for large meetings in the city. It is the most popular motel in the city for tourists, yet its primary reason for existing is to serve the truckers.

Some of the truckers are family men who want to do their job and go home. Others are couples, often married, and either childless or with children cared for by relatives or a live-in nanny. Husband and wife driving teams will often travel 24 hours a day, trading off the chores, in order to make maximum earnings.

A surprisingly large number of independent truckers do not have a permanent home. They live in their rigs, combining a comfortable mattress with a stereo system, small color television and VCR. When they want to take a few days off, they go to one of the truck stops and stay in a room. The rest of the time they are sleeping in their cabs.

Anything can be bartered at a truck stop. There are drugs, of course, mostly amphetamines meant to help the drivers stay alert over a long haul. They can impair judgment, alter reflexes, and cause personality changes when used to excess, but truckers are in a lonely profession known for its eccentrics. No one can be certain who is over-dosing and who is an eccentric acting normally.

Other things are sold, including handguns, watches, and similar items of value. Truckers have extensive out of pocket expenses when they are on the road. Monitoring a CB, you can frequently hear someone radioing that he is on a layover after delivering a load. This means that he has no money coming in, and if he is hungry, he will offer an item of value for a low enough fee to get some food. The hungrier the man, the more desperate he becomes, the cheaper the item. It is not unusual for a handgun to sell for as little as $15, not because it is cheap but because that is the only price he can get when he needs food.

The prostitutes charge different amounts for different services. At the time Berens was investigating, the truck stop prostitutes along the Eastern portion of the United States were averaging $25 for oral sex and $40 to $50 for intercourse. Frequently there was far more demand than there were women to go around, so waiting lists were created. The men would make radio contact with the prostitutes who usually had their own radios in cars just outside the lot. The man would explain where his rig was parked and what type it was. He would give the row and as much of a description as she would need to locate it. Then he would tell her he was going to sleep, and that she should come to his door and wake him up when it was his turn. Then the woman would service the men in order, usually taking no more than a few minutes with each one.

The men who used the prostitutes both appreciated their services and, to a degree, held them in disdain. Among themselves, the truckers passing through Ohio would call the woman 'Commercial Ladies,' 'Lap Lizards,' and 'Pavement Princesses.'

Some of the truck stops were located near Oriental massage parlors. These were reminiscent of the San Francisco, California, 'cribs' used during the gold rush era in the last half of the nineteenth century. The cribs were like a series of caged rooms, always barred, in which the prostitutes would work. Many were a prisoner of White slavery, and many of the women were just over from Asia where they thought they would find a husband, wealth, and happiness. Since they did not speak English, and since they were usually made addicted to laudanum, an opium compound, they went along with what was demanded of them. The life was hard and they were often dead within 18 months to two years of being forced into the cribs.

The Oriental massage parlors had Asian women who lived and worked in a building that was high security. There were bars on the windows, and limited access, that prevented anyone unauthorized from entering or leaving. The lobby was also barred, and there the women would await their customers, usually wearing minimal clothing. They also slept in the building on mattresses placed on the floor, and they were expected to be on call 24 hours a day, resting only when there was no business for them.

The most popular activity for a man was receiving a body shampoo. This cost $50 and was purchased by bored truckers who wanted to be entertained without risking bringing home a disease to their spouses or lovers. The body shampoo was like getting an erotic cleaning. It ended with the prostitute using her hand to bring the customer to orgasm.

The truckers' cabs were high enough so that everyone coming into the lot on foot or in cars could be easily observed. In addition, many of the truckers had CBs equipped with devices that told them the relative signal strength of people broadcasting. It was possible to pinpoint approximately how far away a broadcast signal was coming to them. Reporters, police, and curiosity seekers trying to penetrate the world of the truckers were always noticed. In addition, when there was a crackdown on some illegal activity, the truckers would often protect each other and the criminals, if they felt they should be left alone.

For example, during a crackdown on prostitutes, police monitoring the CB would learn where the girls were going, then move out on foot to arrest them. As they moved through the lot, truckers would 'accidentally' open their doors, striking the detectives in the face. There was never any way to prove the action was deliberate. The truckers were never arrested for obstructing justice. And the prostitutes usually were able to get away.

Given such a subculture, everyone can remain anonymous. So long as the serial killer is careful to not call attention to himself, he can murder without anyone other than prostitutes experiencing fear. And so long as the prostitutes routinely travel among the truck stops, unless someone reports the person missing, or unless a corpse is found, the disappearance does not seem unusual. The woman is presumed to have moved to a more lucrative territory.

Police academies teach new police officers that the vast majority of crimes are solved in the first five minutes of an investigation. This does not mean that the criminal is caught. It just means that the evidence found at the scene, testimony of a witness, or some other aspect of the case will ultimately prove critical to the conviction. Even cases that may drag on for years before an arrest is made often rely for conviction on evidence stored as a result of being discovered during those first five minutes.

The murders Michael Berens was uncovering had no known crime scene that could be checked. Information about the murderer could be determined by the pattern used for killing the prostitutes. But that information was like most profiling, usable only after the arrest to confirm what was suspected but not known. The bodies were dumped away from where the deaths took place. There was no trace evidence unique to a specific crime scene. And the suspects included every man who routinely followed certain trucking routes, narrowing the suspect list to hundreds of men with alibis that could neither be proved nor shaken in most cases.

Even worse was the fact that there was a frequent lack of coordination among the various law enforcement agencies. For example, there was an accident near Mansfield, Ohio, in which a trucker crashed into a bridge abutment. It was a one vehicle crash that overturned his truck. Inside the cab the police and emergency rescue personnel found approximately a hundred pieces of women's clothing in all different sizes. The clothing appeared to be used rather than new, and the fact that the sizes varied indicated that the man was not a cross-dresser.

In addition to the clothing were dozens of devices used for sado-masochism. These included leather restraints, handcuffs, and numerous other items in addition to pornographic magazines.

The man was taken to the hospital where he stayed for a month. There were no forensic tests conducted on the clothing or the restraints. No effort was made to interview the man. There was no computer check which might have revealed more about him and his background. When the Ohio Highway Patrol tried to get county sheriff's offices, police officers, and others in law enforcement to look at what was found as possible forensic evidence relative to murders, rapes, or some other violent crime, no one would do it.

There was also defensiveness and denial on the part of some law enforcement officers. Most were anxious to end the killings, but Berens found one police chief to be in total public denial of what was taking place. Berens felt the man was uncooperative to the point of dishonesty when it came to discussing murders that took place at a truck stop within his department's jurisdiction. For example, at one point the chief informed the reporter that one of the victims who was known to have disappeared from the truck stop had to have been somewhere else. He refused to admit that she was taken from his jurisdiction. Yet on the wall directly behind him was a poster with the woman's picture on it. The poster clearly stated that she was last seen in the truck stop.

All together there would be a minimum of nine murders that could, with almost total certainty, be linked to the same killer. Terry Roarke was found murdered in Saratoga County, New York, on March 29, 1988. She was 31 years old, a prostitute who worked several states, going as far southwest as Texas, and as far northeast as New Jersey and New York. She frequently hitchhiked from truck stop to truck stop, so she was fairly well known.

In what appears in hindsight to be a misguided effort to hide clues from the public, the cause of death was said to have been a fall or push from a truck. The official report to the public originally claimed that the woman was going over a bridge on 1–87 when she was thrown down onto the bridge or jumped from the cab. Yet the truth was that she had been dead for hours before hitting the pavement.

More important than the cause of death and way in which the corpse was left was the way her clothing was handled. She was wearing only her left shoe, the rest of her clothes tossed onto the next ten miles of highway, one piece at a time.

April 19, 1990, was when an unidentified corpse was found in Licking County, East of Columbus, near the Pilot Travel Center truck stop off 1–70. The woman had been beaten with a blunt object and was only wearing her panties. Her physical size was proportionate to the other victims at 5 feet 3 inches and 115 pounds. She was in her twenties or early thirties, and she had given birth to at least one child. Again she had been killed somewhere other than where she had been found, and again she was the perfect victim. There were no known missing person reports anywhere in the country that matched her description.

As of this writing, the story of Michael Berens's work has no ending. The killer has not been caught. There are no suspects, though the fact that each body was placed in a different county implies that the murderer might have law enforcement experience. The variation in routes also indicates that he may have changed jobs or where he had to work. There is also a possibility that he drives a refrigerated truck. Yet knowing these possibilities, knowing how he kills, and knowing where he dumps most of his victims means nothing when trying to catch him.

There is now a task force comprised of law enforcement officers from several departments, each having experienced one of the murders. But shared information is of little value if the details needed for conviction are missing.

What matters is the fact that the serial killer was discovered because of the curiosity of a reporter, not because of law enforcement teamwork. The cases were old ones. The victims were 'nobodies,' prostitutes being looked upon as somehow low priority. High officials generally wanted to forget about the cases, never closing the books on them, yet rarely looking back. By contrast, many of the field investigators were much more concerned with stopping the killer without regard to the social status of the victim.

Yet because there is not yet an actively used, national center for information, it took a curious reporter to uncover the existence of a serial killer who may still be both alive and continuing to take lives. By picking victims who were 'nobodies,' and dumping the bodies where politics, jealousies, and/or indifference prevent the active sharing of information, this latest serial killer is 'getting away with murder.'

CHAPTER 6

THE FREEDOM TO KILL

'Donald Chapman, age 37, was released from the Adult Diagnostic and Treatment Center at Avenel on November 17, 1992. He had been incarcerated for eleven years having been convicted of Kidnapping (2C:13–1b1) and Aggravated Sexual Assault (2C:14–2a6). He was sentenced to 20 years at Avenel with a mandatory 10-year period of ineligibility.' So began the rather stilted material released from the office of John J. Fahy, Prosecutor for Bergen County, in Hackensack, New Jersey. The information, provided to the press, was a graphic example of one of the greatest problems facing law enforcement officers fighting serial killers. This is the issue of whether or not Americans should have the freedom to kill.

'On July 12, 1990 Chapman was driving his 1976 Ford Pickup truck when he first saw the victim, a 23-year-old woman, riding on Clinton Road in West Milford, New Jersey at about 5:30 in the afternoon. (The defendant later said he thought the victim was only 16 years of age.) Chapman, who was carrying a brown vinyl bag, asked the victim if she could help him and then told her to come with him. The victim resisted and Chapman put his hands over her mouth and dragged her into the woods. The victim screamed. Chapman threatened to hurt her and then put a gag in her mouth and tied her hands. He then put her into the back of his truck, covered her with canvas and drove her to a secluded place five miles away in a wooded area.

'Once in the woods, Chapman left the victim tied to a tree, still gagged, while he retrieved her bicycle and went to his home in Wyckoff to retrieve bondage equipment. Once home, he retrieved a shovel, pick axe, two fire extinguishers, a vibrator, hypodermic needle, B-B gun, several scalpels, lighter fluid, rubber hoses, black and red ink, gunpowder, firecrackers, black spray paint, two canisters of extra BBs, scissors, razors, shaving cream, soap, gauze pads, various straps and ropes. In his later confession to police, Chapman said he was planning to use the fire extinguisher to torture the victim by forcing the nozzle into her vagina and spraying the CO_2 into her. He said that this would freeze her and burn until she was dead. The pick ax and shovel, he indicated, were intended to dig her grave as his intent from the beginning had been to torture her to death.

'When Chapman returned to the victim in the woods, he untied her, tied her hands behind her back and walked her down to a nearby lake. It was now 9:00 p.m. and dark outside. He tied the victim to two trees and told her that he wanted her body. He took off her pants and panties and inserted a vibrator into her vagina; she screamed. He then penetrated her vagina with his penis. The victim after repeatedly saying no, was forced to fellate Chapman; she then began to choke on his penis. Chapman then withdrew his penis and ordered the victim onto her back whereupon he forced a dildo into her vagina. He then inserted his own penis into her vagina again, made her roll over and inserted the vibrator in her rectum. She screamed again. The victim's rectum bled.

'Chapman stopped. He untied the victim, asked her to get dressed and threw all of the items from his bag into the lake. He asked the victim if she knew where he could get help and he told her he was sorry. He took her back to the truck and gave her his knife, telling her not to be afraid to use it on him. Then he handed her a can of mace as protection for the future. This is not his first conviction.'

This was not Donald Chapman's first assault against women. The prosecutor released his entire history in order to show a 20-year pattern of violence. He was concerned with letting the public know the danger this man posed. The report released to the press stated:

'In 1973 Chapman was convicted of three counts of abduction (*N.J.S.* 2A:86–2) and three counts of impairing the morals of a child (*N.J.S.* 2A:96–3). He was sentenced to an indeterminate term at the Youth Correctional Facility not to exceed eight years. The facts of that matter were as follows:

'On October 20, 1973, three young girls (nine and ten years of age) two of whom were sisters, were in the Campgaw ski area in Mahwah when they noticed Donald Chapman following them. Chapman asked if they were going up the slope and told them there was a nice trail with wildlife; they followed his directions and he followed them. After walking for several minutes the girls got tired and decided to walk back. Chapman held a knife to one girl's throat and led the girls down the trail away from the ski center and off the path. He tied up two of the girls to a tree and took the third further into the woods, out of sight of the other two. Chapman asked her to take her pants down. She said no. Chapman then walked her back to where the other two girls had been left tied to a tree. The girls had freed themselves and ran to a nearby home where they had called the police. Chapman told the third girl to give him a 'five minute head start' and he ran. He was arrested and confessed to this offense.

'He was also convicted of drunk and disorderly conduct involving a fight with a police officer in 1973, an incident in which he tried to seize the arresting officer's gun. He was sentenced to six months in the Bergen County Jail and three years probation. In 1978 he was convicted of possession of a switchblade (he received a suspended sentence) and possession of a Billy Club in 1979. He stated that he likes to catch and trap animals and "play" with them.'

No one, including Donald Chapman and his immediate family, questioned the fact that he was an ongoing violent man. He was a sexual sadist driven to do harm to girls and young women. He had been sentenced to the Adult Diagnostic and Treatment Center at Avenel, New Jersey, following his last assault, and the professionals at the institution agreed that he was dangerously violent. But more important, they determined that, despite their best efforts, he was as dangerous when he finished his time served – November 17, 1992 – as he had been when he entered. Dr Kay E. Jackson, Ph.D., a Clinical Psychologist on the staff, gave a report that he posed a 'clear and present danger to others' when, by law, he had to be released because he had served his full sentence. The statement was so serious that three other psychiatrists were asked to examine him and all of them agreed. However, under the laws of the state of New Jersey, so long as Chapman was not 'experiencing psychosis, as evidenced by overt thought disorder, or hallucinations,' he could not be committed civilly. He had to be allowed back into society.

According to the report to the prosecutor from Dr. Jackson, Chapman 'had related to her threats to commit the same kind of crimes he had committed in the past, but would kill his victims this time. He says he will not be caught as he has learned how to avoid detection by the police. Chapman continues to harbor strong negative feelings toward his ex-girlfriend for "abandoning" him and in Dr. Jackson's opinion, "will probably kill her." Chapman further related that he considered himself a "failed rapist" because his victims were alive. He said he would not fail in the future.'

Equally chilling was the doctor's opinion that the preferred victims would be eight to ten years old.

The prosecutor's statement to the press further stated:

'Chapman admitted to assaults in Mahwah, Franklin Lakes, Midland Park and Rockland County; assaults for which he was never arrested. He is a "stalker" and diagnosed as a sociopathic personality, and he currently has a "concrete grasp of reality." He is preoccupied with sexual sadism and although he respects police authority, this will not, again, in Dr. Jackson's opinion, deter his future criminal activity.'

'ADULT DIAGNOSTIC & TREATMENT CENTER AVENEL, NEW JERSEY INTEROFFICE COMMUNICATIONS

To: Ike Gauzy, Assistant Prosecutor, Bergen County
From: Kay E. Jackson, Ph.D., Staff Clinical Psychologist
Date: November 18, 1992
Re: See Below

This is to give you a brief report on my assessment of Donald Chapman. Mr. Chapman is currently denying either homicidal or suicidal ideation. He is not at present experiencing psychosis, as evidenced by overt thought disorder, or hallucinations. However, he is in my opinion represents [sic] a clear and present danger to others, because of his sexualized rage, deep-seated feelings of low self-esteem and resentment and fears of others. Mr. Chapman is able to recognize the rather obvious fact that he would be confined should he acknowledge his homicidal ideation to authority figures capable of confining him. He was, for example, able to convince three psychiatrists here that a publicly stated threat to commit [sic] a similar crime, culminating in a murder, was merely an expression of his fear about release. Specifically he claimed that he was so afraid of being released that he was trying to force the ADTC staff to confine him for additional time due to probable dangerousness. He claimed that he would have been willing to be confined here on a voluntary basis, but because this is a correctional facility, it was not possible to hold him beyond the max date of 11/17/92.

I have spoken with Mr. Rizzo at your request, and he is concurring with the previous psychiatric opinions about confinement. We have discussed the possibility of my contacting his parents, and obtaining permission for the Bergen County Screening unit to come to their home to arrange mental health services for Donald Chapman. On Friday, 11/13/92 in a meeting with his parents, he confirmed his interest in identifying out-patient services for the purposes of continuing his psycho-tropic medication as well as for outpatient services.

I must reiterate that in my opinion, Mr. Chapman remains a clear danger to others; no psychiatrist has disputed that opinion, though they all concur that he is not at present involuntarily confinable.'

Donald Chapman had no illusions about his condition or his desires. During the meetings with his parents and the therapist prior to his release, he talked freely about the sexual arousal he felt whenever he thought about raping, torturing, and mutilating women. His favorite fantasy was kidnapping a woman, taking her to the woods, tying her to trees, then sexually assaulting and torturing her. He also thought killing might be a good idea.

Prior to his release, the editor of a weekly newspaper

that served his home community interviewed him about his life, his plans, and his fantasies. He made clear to the editor that he realized his mistake when raping was in not killing the women as well. Had he killed them, he would not have been locked away. He explained that he would not make that mistake again.

Donald Chapman, like Leslie Williams and others, was a serial rapist. He was also a serial killer waiting to happen. But Chapman had served the years required by law for the crimes he committed. He had not murdered. He had not raped since he was placed in a locked psychiatric facility. He was an innocent man whose fantasies were no more illegal than those of a happily married couple thinking about playing voluntary light bondage games during intercourse they both desire. Yet if the couple acted out their bondage fantasies, no one would be hurt and each would be trying to give pleasure to the other. If Chapman acted out his fantasies, women would suffer the horrors of the damned.

The Donald Chapman case was one of three cases that typify the problems that arise with serial killers. American domestic law enforcement is mandated to be reactive. This means that a crime has to be committed before anyone can act.

The idea of a reactive force allows some flexibility, though. It is legal to set up circumstances where a person desiring to commit a crime can do so more easily because an undercover police operation is in place. For example, the police might arrest several women working as prostitutes on a downtown street. Then the women are replaced by undercover women police officers who dress and act in the same manner as the prostitutes. They may walk back and forth, smiling at passing men, perhaps standing so that they seem available for sexual activity. Naturally, when approached by a man, they will become extremely friendly. However, no arrest is considered until the man offers them money for a sex act. Then the circumstances, the exact language used by both parties, and ideally corroboration by a witness will determine if the arrest will hold up in court.

Likewise there are undercover sting operations. The police may set up a pawn shop, for example, offering to buy 'anything.' They are provided with a large sum of money, a warehouse or office equipped with tape recorders, video camcorders, and similar equipment needed to prove what has taken place. Then they will make purchases of whatever is brought to them, making clear that they ask no questions. Sometimes the items sold to them are legitimately owned. At other times they are stolen. Eventually the undercover operation has to be ended. The men and women who sold the stolen items are arrested, and the recorded tapes were used to help convict them. The only problem that would arise would be if a car thief, for example, said to an undercover police officer, 'Would you like me to steal you a blue Lincoln Continental?' The officer agrees, and then tries to convict him. That would be considered entrapment since the officer encouraged the crime knowing he would arrest him at the end.

Donald Chapman had to be watched when he was released. He could not be arrested for a crime he talked about. He had to act out, and that meant that someone might be raped or murdered.

To try and protect the community, several actions were taken. First, Chapman was placed under surveillance and efforts were made to deny him access to weapons. It was learned that his father, Richard, owned a shotgun, two rifles, and two pistols. Since Donald would be staying with his parents until such time as an alternative was found for him, Richard Chapman agreed to voluntarily give them to the police to hold. However, he requested the return of a shotgun and pistol to use while hunting, and the request had to be granted. Richard Chapman had done nothing wrong. Donald Chapman had served his time and could legally live in a place where weapons were available.

A continuous surveillance was also maintained at first. This is an extremely expensive and difficult task, much different from the television image. It is hard to follow someone inconspicuously, and while the police wanted their presence known as a deterrent, one person following another is easily eluded. At the very least, a small community force would have to designate one man per shift, three shifts per day, seven days a week. Ideally there would be several plain clothes officers used each shift, especially for following a car. Real rolling surveillance involves several cars, including one or more that may lead the one being followed, other cars traveling on parallel streets, waiting for the chased vehicle to turn off. The cost is horrendous, the return often minimal. In the case of Chapman, he held the officers in disdain, justifiably bragging about his ability to elude them. He also looked upon them as knowledgeable, helpful friends:

'On December 1, 1992, Donald Chapman told a member of the surveillance team that he still loves his ex-girlfriend and can't get her out of his mind.' He indicated that he was trying to locate her. He had been making several trips to a local fast food establishment where he said he was looking for a young girl as young girls 'understand him better.' He also wanted to know if he could buy a bow, as he knew a gun was out of the question. At the restaurant, Donald Chapman was involved in two separate incidents that concerned management; he blocked the door to the ladies room on one occasion and on another he spoke to a couple that he did not know, telling them that they had a beautiful young daughter and should be proud. As of December 11, 1992 Donald Chapman has been barred from the restaurant by their management.' (From report by Ike

R. Gauzy, Assistant Prosecutor, Bergen County, New Jersey.)

Chapman's parents also wanted him to be able to lead a normal life after his release from jail. 'On December 4, 1992, with his parents' assistance and knowledge Donald Chapman hid in the back of his parents' car when the family went out to dinner. He hid himself under a tarpaulin to avoid detection and on several other occasions attempted to elude surveillance teams in the wooded ravine behind his home.'

When the Bergen County Prosecutor's Office began researching possible placement for Chapman after his release, they found that his personal history made such placement impossible. The Rescue Mission program in Syracuse would not take someone with so violent a past. Others said that since his violence involved sexual assaults, he was too great a risk. All of them said that they would need locked in-treatment areas, and none of them maintained such facilities.

The closest available facility was the Moderate Security Unit of Princeton run by the New Jersey Division of Development Disabilities for ex-offenders. They did have a locked area. They could handle someone whose past was as violent as Chapman's. But they were not able to take anyone who was not severely retarded. The maximum IQ among the in-patients was 65.

The situation was somewhat similar to that of Richard Chase, the 'Vampire' of Sacramento, California. Chase was an extremely disturbed man who believed his mother had fed him laundry detergent, turning his heart to stone, then reversing it in his body. He was always irate when, after going to hospital emergency rooms for treatment, he was briefly locked away in their psychiatric wards.

Chase was eventually placed in a hospital that truly could help him, at least to the degree that his psychotic mind could be treated by anyone. However, believing that fresh blood would keep him alive, each time he was walking on the hospital grounds, he would catch birds. Then he would bite the heads off the living birds and quickly try to drink their blood. The sight so sickened staff members that they released him despite the fact that he was severely disturbed. Chase quickly turned to people, killing six, mixing their blood and organs with cola, placing it in a blender, then consuming it. Had the hospital staff not released him because they did not wish to handle so disgusting a case, Chase would not have murdered.

Bergen County was facing something similar, though in this case Chapman had served his maximum time. He was no longer legally responsible for his past crimes. Yet because of the crimes, because he was considered potentially sexually violent and in no way changed from the man who so brutally raped, no one wanted to accept him. There was an out-patient program at Avenel, but it was voluntary and Chapman refused to attend. He wanted to be free to live his own life his own way.

Ultimately the county officials contacted the Safer Society Program of Orwell, Vermont. This is a national clearing house for information on all the facilities available for sex offenders. They were told that there are no in-patient treatment facilities anywhere in the United States for men or women who are previously convicted rapists.

The situation became critical on November 25, 1992. Investigators from the County Prosecutor's office went to Chapman's home to see if he would cooperate in the effort to find a way to get him ongoing treatment. He was both helpful and arrogant, bragging about his having beaten the surveillance in the past, and how he just might commit a crime, then use the surveillance team to 'prove' he never left a house they were watching. In the end he made a comment that he would not elaborate on, yet which hinted that matters had reached the level everyone feared. He said, 'I don't want to kill again.'

Chapman's neighbors were not particularly worried about the man living in their midst. The editor of a local weekly newspaper interviewed both Chapman and nearby residents. Chapman again indicated that he did not plan to repeat the mistakes of his past by letting future rape victims live. The neighbors, who rarely saw the man, were not worried about his living in their midst. Yet matters seemed to be getting worse, Donald becoming increasingly angry with what was happening. Even his parents admitted that they feared his potential for violence as his anger increased.

At this writing, the Bergen County authorities are using every legal means possible to keep Donald Chapman in short term treatment programs. However, while everyone agrees he is dangerous, including Chapman, he is also a citizen who has paid his debt to society. As a result, there is a chance that there will come a day when nothing further can be done, no money is available for additional surveillance, and Chapman is allowed to live a free man. Again, at this writing, the violent sexual fantasies have not stopped, the desire to act out those fantasies continues to occupy his mind, and someone may be raped, tortured, and killed before he can be locked away for life. He is a known serial killer waiting to happen, and in a free society, he has the right to murder before being stopped.

No one except his defenders wants to go on record talking about their feelings for Dr Jack Kevorkian, the retired pathologist who is the Renaissance man of death. He is a skilled artist whose paintings haunt the viewer, often for years after seeing them. I first viewed his work during an exhibition at Michigan State University, Oakland, in Rochester, Michigan, in 1963. One of them was a painting of a recently hung corpse from the perspective possible only if you were laying on your back below the trap, looking up at his bare feet. The subject and the angle of view were chillingly unforgettable.

Kevorkian is also a writer and a man who enjoys playing the organ for relaxation. At one point, during the early 1970s, he moved briefly to California when his interest turned to film. It was right after a series of still unsolved child murders in Oakland County, Michigan, where Kevorkian had been living and working. But while that fact intrigues his enemies, there have been no connections made between the murders and Kevorkian other than that he, like thousands of other men, was in the area at the time.

Kevorkian is a pathologist, a doctor whose 'patients' are all dead. He has also been an experimenter with various aspects of death, including the use of blood transfusions from fresh corpses. Such transfusions, though sounding odd, have their primary benefit in wartime where they, in theory, could save lives during battlefield procedures.

In Kevorkian's book *Prescription Medicide*, he talked of creating a machine for death that could be used with death row inmates. He explained that when a man had to die, instead of killing him in the electric chair, the gas chamber, by lethal injection, or the other methods mandated by the various state laws, he could be rendered unconscious. Then either his organs could be taken for transplanting into others in need, or medical experimentation could be conducted on his still living body. The experimentation would be of a type where, when it was over, the person could be allowed to die. Since he would be unconscious the entire time, there would be no pain. And since death would follow without the person being brought back to consciousness, the judgment of the court would be carried out.

Organ transplantation is a major aspect of Kevorkian's justification for alternative means of death. But his first love, at least as evidenced by his work (Kevorkian sent a note refusing to be interviewed on advice of counsel because of legal trials he was facing), was a method for allowing individuals to commit suicide.

Kevorkian long dreamed of building a death machine that would be used by the patient. The individual wishing to commit suicide had to trigger the device to prevent the person assisting, preferably a doctor, from being charged with manslaughter. Kevorkian also wanted the method chosen to be 'rapid, serene, and sure.'

The original idea was to perform a venipuncture, then start an intravenous (IV) drip of normal saline solution, a harmless liquid used in all hospitals. There would also be an electrocardiogram (ECG) monitoring the patient's heart. Then, with the drip in place, the patient would press a hair-trigger device that would release a second liquid, this time thiopental, into the person's body. The release would both stop the first IV and start a timer. Sixty seconds later, potassium chloride solution would begin to flow as well. The thiopental would induce coma, and the potassium chloride would paralyze the heart muscle. This meant that the patient/suicide would be in a deep sleep when his or her heart stopped, a seemingly painless process taking no more than six minutes. The death would be confirmed by the ECG.

The original device was named the 'Mercitron' and was made from a variety of parts found wherever he could. He used a clock motor, switch, and solenoid he obtained at a local flea market (cost: $3). The cover was made from scrap aluminum. Eventually the triggering device, stand for the IV, and other items cost a total of approximately $30, Kevorkian wrote.

What is interesting about the ever contradictory Kevorkian is that, though he began his career with a device using the IV, he eventually switched to carbon monoxide. While discussing why he settled on the combination of thiopental and potassium chloride for assisted suicide, he mentioned other forms of chemistry. One of these was cyanide which he dismissed because, though it acts rapidly, it causes suffocation.

The rejection of cyanide for someone trying to kill peacefully made sense. Cyanide prevents the absorption of oxygen into the lungs. The person who is given cyanide breathes normally in that air is taken into the lungs which expand, then contract. But because the lungs cannot absorb the oxygen, the person begins struggling, often violently. He or she essentially suffocates, much like someone who has tied a plastic bag over their head.

Carbon monoxide poisoning is viewed by the general public as a peaceful way to die. Many a suicide has occurred in a closed garage, the person inside a car, the motor running, and a hose running from the exhaust pipe into the passenger compartment. Oxygen is replaced by the carbon monoxide, and the suicide drifts off to sleep, the sleep ending in death.

In truth, as every pathologist is likely to know, carbon monoxide poisoning is not a quiet way to die. According to Keith D. Wilson, MD, physician/author of *Cause of Death*, the carbon monoxide, like the cyanide, prevents the absorption of oxygen. At best, the person will develop a headache, then a feeling of exhaustion, often followed by nausea and vomiting before collapse, coma, and death. If the poisoning occurs very slowly, the symptoms may include problems with memory, hallucinations, and slowed movement. But breathing carbon monoxide through a mask, as Kevorkian would later utilize for his assisted suicides, does not ensure a gentle death. Certainly it does not predictably meet the criterion of 'serene' that Kevorkian claimed to be trying to achieve.

Kevorkian's first recorded assisted suicide was also one of his most questionable cases. Janet Adkins, a woman in her late forties, was diagnosed as having Alzheimer's disease. She was an active outdoorsperson, a musician, a teacher, mountain climber, mother, and grandmother. She was also too young to be diagnosed with absolute certainty.

Doctors have found that Alzheimer's disease is not easy to diagnose, and the younger the sufferer, the more difficult it is to diagnose with accuracy. A dangerous brain biopsy can be used. Or an autopsy can be performed after death. Other than that, doctors follow a test that was first published in the journal *Neurology* back in 1984. A series of questions had to be addressed, including such concerns as skilled motor actions, language skills, orientation to time and place, and related matters. Memory loss was an issue, but not a critical one. There are many illnesses that can cause memory loss, both temporarily and for the long term. In fact, nursing homes offering diets high in sugar have occasionally had patients exhibiting signs of what was believed to be Alzheimer's, in some instances, and senile dementia in others, when they actually had severe hypoglycemia or undiagnosed diabetes. When their diets were changed, sometimes supplemented with B-complex and other vitamins, all symptoms disappeared. The people became mentally alert and active, belying the earlier diagnosis.

In April, 1990, after Janet Adkins, suffering drug side effects, had been dropped from an experimental therapy program at the University of Washington in Seattle, Kevorkian was contacted. Janet was determined to end her life, though her own physician was opposed. As Kevorkian wrote in *Prescription: Medicide*: 'Even though from a physical standpoint Janet was not imminently terminal, there seemed little doubt that mentally she was – and, after all, it is one's mental status that determines the essence of one's existence.' Later, in response to the Janet's doctor's concerns, Kevorkian added: ' . . . from Ron's narrative I concluded that her doctor's opinion was wrong and that time was of the essence.'

Detractors wonder about the statement. Janet Adkins was to be the first person Kevorkian would help die at the person's request. He did not want anything to get in the way, whether that meant a change in her mental condition or restrictions against assisting with suicide in churches, funeral homes, and other locations he considered in Michigan. Since Janet would be coming to Kevorkian's home state, a place where assisted suicide was not illegal, he felt that he should find a clinical or home-like setting. However, ultimately he utilized his 1968 camper, a vehicle that was rusted on the outside, clean on the inside, and could be set up at a campsite where there would be electricity to run his machine. He used a public campsite since the commercial site nearest him refused to allow such use.

It is important to note that there are several issues that arose at this time. Allegations made against Kevorkian as time passed and the assisted suicide body count rose to 10, and then 20 were not yet important. Instead, the issue at the moment was an individual's right to die in the manner he or she desired.

Healthy individuals are often more in favor of suicide than those who are terminally ill. Many people develop a zest for life that belies their disabilities, illnesses, and other problems. Interviews with hospice workers and others who deal with the terminally ill talk about how they embrace life instead of passively waiting for death. And interviews with the severely disabled reveal a desire to be productive, to gain access to offices, recreational facilities, and other places that will make them feel a part of mainstream society. It is the exception who wishes to take his or her own life, and among those are some who are depressed because of circumstances other than their medical condition.

For example, often severe depression can be caused by a lack of full spectrum light – either daylight or daylight fluorescent bulbs frequently used for indoor gardening. Severe depression can be caused by a high sugar diet, especially if the person is a hypoglycemic. Allergies, including to household dust, will cause depression, as will a lack of exercise. This knowledge has changed the way many illnesses are treated and has prolonged the quality and, presumably, the quantity of life. Where once someone with a heart attack was told to stay home and take life easy, today every effort is made to get the person up, outside, and walking. Retirement is not encouraged, and if a job is too strenuous, then a different occupation is recommended. The old style treatment merely created what came to be known as cardiac cripples, and they had far earlier deaths than their conditions warranted.

Yet Dr Kevorkian has not been known to counsel would-be suicides other than to make certain they are comfortable with suicide. He does not help them seek out pain management experts. He does not help them find a way to treat their depression on the chance that its cause is quite different from an unchanging will to die. And because of this, he has been severely criticized by those who feel that there are circumstances where a person who is both terminally ill and helpless should have a right to die with whatever assistance is necessary. They feel that his actions endanger all assisted deaths because they create too broad a range of approved suicides.

Ultimately most of the critics who favor discussion of a person's right to die with medical assistance have come to question Kevorkian's methods while admiring the way he has brought the issue to public attention. They feel that the idea that there should be special practitioners of death goes against the idea of medicine as a healing art. The Oath of Hippocrates states that a doctor should first do the patient no harm. The idea that a doctor might regularly be available to take a life goes against American medicine. Spiritually there may be healing in death, but those who feel that way also trust in God to decide when that death should occur.

The second concern about Kevorkian's methods is the way a patient is counseled by the doctor. They feel that professionals from different disciplines – pain management, psychology, religion, and so forth – should meet with the patient. While the men and women doing the counseling must be accepting of the idea of suicide, they must also present valid alternatives and help the patient explore life as a choice.

But there is another question which has risen in all this, one that many in law enforcement feel is the primary issue. This is the question of whether or not Dr Kevorkian might be the most ingenious organized serial killer in history. Certainly his use of carbon monoxide belies his earlier statements about making transplant organs available. Even if he was allowed to go into a prison and work with inmates who give their consent, the suicide machine that presently exists kills in a way that destroys the organ's usefulness.

The doctor has assisted in the deaths of 20 people with his machines (at this writing), and indicates that he will continue with what he considers humanitarian efforts. All his victims have asked to die. All family members who could readily intervene have accepted their loved ones' decisions. Yet no one other than a serial killer has ever taken so many lives in so methodical a manner. He has his death kit. He has souvenirs, if only in the form of paperwork and, when the press is around, pictures. Everything about him fits the profile of an organized serial killer except for the fact that his victims have asked for his help.

The problem everyone faces is that if Kevorkian is a serial killer, by letting his victims do the work themselves, he has not committed a felony. Laws are being passed to stop assisted suicide, but these are not the same as laws against murder. In a sense, Kevorkian is little more at fault than the arms dealer who sells someone a shotgun the buyer then uses to blow off his own head.

Kevorkian, like Chapman, presents a moral dilemma. Chapman is currently an innocent man who has made his intentions of violence quite clear to anyone who will ask. Kevorkian has been present for 20 deaths and is seeking more individuals who can use his services. But where Chapman's victims want to flee, Kevorkian's assist in their own deaths. And neither can be stopped under the American system of justice.

282

CHAPTER 7

EPILOGUE

In the end, serial killing is about choice. That is not a popular opinion, nor is it meant to challenge the very genuine concerns about the abusive childhood most serial killers have endured.

Dr Ronald Markman, the psychiatrist/attorney who has been involved with such high profile cases as the Hillside Strangler and Sirhan Sirhan's assassination of Senator Robert Kennedy, points out three basic facts about serial killers. All of them have childhoods where they wet their beds later in life than most children, played with matches, and tortured or abused animals. Yet Markman also points out that many children have the same three traits, then grow up to be mentally healthy, loving and productive citizens.

Leslie Williams's case is a perfect example of the issue of choice. He and his sister both endured a miserable and wicked childhood, and they both paid a severe emotional price. Yet she is a loving wife and mother, a productive citizen who has overcome self-destructive tendencies to be an asset to society. He will die in jail for his series of rape/murders.

Jeffrey Dahmer, perhaps the most extreme example of a serial killer today because of his habit of devouring parts of his victims, sought refuge in the church. However, he simply used the ritual of attending Sunday services, there was no willingness to reach out to clergy or therapists. And when prayer and acting the role of the 'good boy' did not work, he chose to kill repeatedly, not ask for help.

This is not to say that serial killers are normal people. They are driven by internal pressures the rest of us do not face. They derive pleasure from actions that ultimately take the lives of some of the people they encounter. Yet they are rarely out of control. They are almost certainly not devil possessed. And for the most part, they are not insane under the laws of the particular state in which they commit crimes.

Some serial killers are arrogantly pursuing power over others. Donald Harvey, a man who worked in support capacities – nurse's aid, orderly, etc. – in hospitals in Cincinnati, Ohio, and in Frankfurt, Kentucky – later told interviewers that he liked proving himself smarter than the doctors. He wanted the power of life or death over his victims, and the fact that he murdered 34 people with cyanide, arsenic, or cleaning fluid and was only caught by chance was something he relished. No one detected what he was doing despite his murders taking place in the midst of medical professionals. Later, after being jailed, he denounced another Ohio born serial killer, Jeffrey Dahmer, for being so crude and disgusting in his handling of his victims' bodies.

It is this arrogance, including the beliefs of some serial killers that they will be released quickly because they are smarter than the courts, which causes a few professionals to consider them insane. Yet there are few madmen among them. That is both the horror of serial killers and the reality that the justice system has to face.

Is there anything that can be done? Obviously early intervention with troubled youths is critical. Frequently there are stories of parents who took their children to doctors who noticed that at least one of the parents and the child were both disturbed. They duly noted their observations in the medical records, then filed away that record until the next visit. The pattern was always clear, yet no one wanted to act.

There have been families active in their churches who were known to be troubled yet no one tried to help them. Instead, the minister or priest might make a half-hearted suggestion that he was available for counseling if it was ever needed. And other parishioners might ask if anything was wrong. But beyond that, little or nothing was done. The family was active in church, after all, so certainly God would provide whatever was needed.

Sometimes the problem was within the school that ignored the child abuse. There have been killers with childhood school pictures showing black eyes and bruises which were never investigated. Or a trouble-maker was expelled at an early age because expulsion took less effort than learning the cause of the problem.

And there are neighborhoods where, for one reason or another, no supervised recreation is available. Yet there have been children with similar backgrounds as serial killers who claim to have been turned around through youth clubs, an adult supervising a basketball game, or some similar, caring contact.

Such thinking is the ideal. There is also the question of whether or not the men and occasional women involved with serial murder have a severe character flaw which means they would not choose to get help. They may be ones who would choose to act out aggressively regardless of circumstances in their early lives.

Some of the Vietnam veterans' groups have looked at the ex-servicemen who so thoroughly fell apart following their war experience that they have never been able to function. They cannot commit to a relationship. They cannot hold a job. They are frequently homeless or living in substandard conditions. And they are always blaming the events of the war, one shared by thousands of other men who, though traumatized, have recovered and live whole, productive lives. It is the belief of some of those who handled the studies that many, if not most, of the men who have not functioned since the war could not have functioned anyway. Had they not gone into the military, they might have fallen apart because of something else in their lives. Trouble on a job, trouble with a woman, perhaps even the experience of leaving home for the first time might have caused the same dysfunctional status. In essence, these are perceived as emotional 'losers,' somehow weaker than the majority of men and women who shared similar backgrounds.

Whatever the case, these are not obvious monsters in our midst. These are our neighbors, the adults we may have played with as children, a co-worker in an office, a factory, or in government service. They are sometimes loners, though not neurotically so. They are sometimes outgoing and friendly. And when the serial killer is discovered, when we learn the identity of the 'devil' we have been reading about in the press, whose crimes have been reported with appropriate horror on television news shows, he is invariably a surprise. As one friend said about Ken Bianchi after his arrest on suspicion of committing as many as 17 murders, 'but he was so nice.'

APPENDIX

On August 2, 1991, a report was filed concerning the murder of Oliver Lacy on July 23, 1991, by Jeffrey Dahmer. At that time, the investigating officers filed the following report concerning Dahmer's murders. It reads:

'Below is a list of the Homicides Victims that Jeffrey DAHMER has confessed to and he states this is the order in which he had killed each individual. Included in this list is his description of the subjects, the approximate time when he killed them, and how he had lured these individuals to his residence, also the identity of each one if they had been identified and what part of the body he kept of the individuals, if any.

1. White male, 25 yoa, 5'6, 130 pds, fair complected, smooth skin, blond shoulder length straight hair. He states he met him approximately 1 week before Thanksgiving, in November, 1987. He states he met him around the 219 Club on 2nd St., and he offered this individual money for sex. He states when he got him to the Ambassador Hotel, where he rented a room, he gave him a drink mixture of rum & coke with approximately 5-7 crushed sleeping pills [illegible]. He states they both went to bed in the nude and when he awoke he observed this individual to have a black & blue chest and blood coming from his mouth. Dahmer also states

that his forearms were black & blue, therefore he figured he had killed him by beating him. He then kept the room for another night, proceeded to the Grand Avenue Mall where he purchased a large suitcase at Woolworth's, returned to the Ambassador, placed the victim in the suitcase and took a cab to his grandmother's residence at 2357 S. 57th St., where he was living. He dismembered the victim in the basement, placed him in various garbage bags and threw them in the garbage. He did not keep any remains. As of this time this victim has not been identified.

2. Hispanic male, 16–18 yoa, 6'0, 150 pds, slim build, dark complected, regular cut hair, clean shaven, lives in the vicinity of 10th 7 National. He states he met this individual in front of the 219 Club on 2nd St., around 1:00 a.m., and the individual was waiting for a bus. He stated he offered him money for sex, he accepted, and they took the bus to his grandmother's house at 2357 S. 57th St. He stated they had light sex, kissing, body rubbing and masturbation. He states he gave him the drink mixture of rum & coke with approximately 5–7 crushed sleeping pills [illegible]. He states that after the victim fell asleep he strangled him, dismembered him, smashed the bones with his sledge-hammer and disposed of the bones inside garbage bags and into the trash. He viewed a photo array and tentatively picked out I.D. [illegible] which is the photo of *DOXTATOR, James E.* Indian male, 03–01–73, [illegible], reported missing on 01–16–88 and the report came in on 01–18-88. DAHMER states he met this individual in approximately January, 1988. There were also no remains of this victim.

3. Hispanic male, 19–21 yoa, 5'8–5'10, slim build, light complected, short straight black hair, wearing a long knee length coat. DAHMER states he met him in

March, 1988, in a bar called the Phoenix, in the doorway, offered him money for sex, at which time they took a taxi to his grandmother's house at 2357 S. 57th St. While there, he gave him the drink mixture of rum & coke and sleeping pills, they had oral sex, the victim fell asleep, he strangled him, dismembered him, broke up the bones, threw them in garbage bags and into the garbage. He did not keep anything on this victim. This victim was subsequently identified by DAHMER, as GUERRERO, Richard Hispanic male, 12–12–65, [illegible]. GUERRERO was missing since 03–29–88.

4. Black male, 21–22 yoa, 5′9, 150 pds, slim build, light complected, short curly hair with a small ponytail, with a rubber band on it. He stated he met this individual the night before Easter, at closing time at the LeCage, on 03–25–89. He states that a friend of this individual, a white female drove them and dropped them off near a tavern by his grandmother's house, the Mai Khi Tavern (phonetic). He states they walked to his grandmother's house, he gave him the drink, and the reason he got him there was money for sex. He states they had sex, he fell asleep, and he killed him. He dismembered him on Easter Sunday, but kept his scalp, genitals, and skull. He subsequently painted the skull and genital area and preserved the scalp. This victim has been identified through photo by the suspect and also through dental records, as last name SEARS, Anthony L. black male, 01–26–65, [illegible]. Reported missing 03–25–89.

5. Black male, 22 yoa, 5′8–5′9, 140 pds, curly black hair, slight mustache. He states he met this individual in May, 1990. He offered him money for sex and for posing for him and watching videos. He states he met him in the area of the 219 Club, about 2 months after he had been released from the House of Correction.

DAHMER states they took a cab from the 219 Club to his apartment. He gave him the drinking potion, and took pictures. After he died, he had oral sex with the victim, took photographs of him, dismembered him and subsequently kept his scalp and painted it. This victim was also identified by the suspect, as *SMITH Raymond L.* black male, 08–10–57, a/k/a BEEKS Rickey Lee, black male, 08–10–57, with a nickname of *"Dash D"*. This individual had not been reported missing.

6. Black male, 24 yoa, 6'2, 170 pds, medium build, dark skin, prematurely bald, close cut hair, clean shaven, and he used to dance with the Milwaukee Ballet. He states this victim wore a headband like a Arab. He states he offered this individual money for sex and posing and that he had met him approximately in July, 1990. He states he met him at the Phoenix Bar, they took a cab to his apartment, had oral sex, gave him the drink mixture of rum & coke [sic] or coffee, and sleeping pills, strangled him, dismembered him and also took 4 or 5 photos of him, and disposed of the body by placing it in garbage bags and putting it in the trash. He states he also disposed of the pictures of this victim. This victim was identified by the suspect, to I.D. Photo [illegible] that being a *SMITH Edward W.* black male, 08–02–62, [illegible] reported missing on 06–23–90.

7. Black male, 24 yoa, 6'0, 160 pds, medium build, medium complexion, chin whiskers, short black hair. He states he met this individual around September, 1990, in the 800 block of N. 27th St., in front of the bookstore. He states he offered him money for sex and for posing. This individual agreed and they proceeded to his residence where he gave him the drink mixture, had sex, and then when he fell asleep he cut his throat. He photographed the body, cut it up, and kept this

individual's skull, his biceps and heart. He states he painted the skull and kept his biceps and heart to eat. He also kept the entire skeleton and bleached it down. He also took numerous photographs of this individual. This individual was identified by the suspect, and through dental records as MILLER *Ernest,* black male, 05–05–67, of Chicago, Il. He had been missing since 09–03–90.

8. Black male, 25 yoa, 150 pds, slim build, medium to dark complexion, short dark hair. He states he met this individual around October, 1990, on 2nd & Wisconsin, and they walked to his residence. He states he offered him money for sex, to pose for him, and view videos. When he got to his apartment he gave him the mixed drink with the sleeping pills in it, they talked, didn't have sex, because he wasn't his type. He states after the individual fell asleep, he killed him because he had already given him the potion and thought when he woke up he would be "pissed off". He states he took two pictures of this individual, he didn't keep anything because he wasn't his type. The suspect, DAHMER, viewed a photograph of the victim and identified him to this photograph. This victim was subsequently identified by relatives, through photographs. He has been identified as THOMAS *David C.* black male, 12–21–67, [illegible] and has been missing since 09–24–90, I.D. [illegible]

9. Black male, 18 yoa, 6'0, 140 pds, slim build, medium complexion, three inch perm, mustache. He states he met this individual approximately February, 1991. He offered him money for posing, sex, and videos, while this individual was waiting for a bus near Marquette. He states they proceeded to his residence, where he gave him the drink mixture containing the sleeping pills. They had oral sex, the victim fell asleep, and then

he killed him and photographed him. He then cut him up, kept his skull, hands, and genitals. He states he used a strap to strangle this victim. He also stated this victim was wearing an earring, but he disposed of it. This victim was subsequently identified by the suspect, and by dental records, as *STRAUGHTER* Curtis, black male, 04–16–73, [illegible] and he has been missing since 02–18–91. He states that he disposed of this individual in two barrels, one for bones and one for flesh and used acid to melt down the bones and flesh. He did take pictures of this victim also.

10. Black male, 20 yoa, 5′9–5′10, 150 pds, short black hair, medium build, medium complexion. He states he met this individual approximately March, 1991, on the corner of 27th & Kilbourn. He states he offered this individual money for posing, and to view videos. He states when they got to his residence, he gave him the drink mixture with the sleeping pills, and when he fell asleep he strangled him, had oral sex after death on the victim, took pictures of him, dismembered him and saved his skull. He also disposed of this individual by putting the bones and the flesh in the two barrels with the acid. This individual was subsequently identified by the suspect, and with dental charts, as being *LINDSEY Earl*, black male, 03–03–72, [illegible].

11. Black male, 26 yoa, 6′0, 150 pds, and a deaf mute. He states he met him approximately early May, 1991, in front of the 219 Bar on 2nd St. He states the victim was with friends who were also deaf mutes, and these friends drove them to 23rd & Wells, where they got out and subsequently walked to his apartment. He states he had them drop him off there, so they would not know where he lived. He states he communicated with this victim by writing notes to him and that he offered him $50.00 for sex. He states he does not remember

whether or not they had sex, but upon going to his apartment, he gave him the drinking potion and the victim subsequently passed out and so did the suspect. Suspect states when he woke up this victim was dead. He states he dismembered him and kept his head. He states he disposed of the body and flesh in the two barrels of acid. He did not take any photos of this individual. The victim was identified by the suspect, and through dental records, as *HUGHES Tony Anthony*, black male, 08–26–59, reported missing in Madison, WI., on 05–31–91, and last seen on 05–24–91.

12. Asian male, 18–19 yoa, 5'5, 120 pds, slim build, black hair. He states he met him in late May, 1991, in the Grand Avenue Mall. He states he offered money to take pictures of him and to view videos, but not for sex. He was hoping it would lead to sex. He states they took the bus back to the apartment and the individual posed for two photos while he was alive. He states he gave him the drink mixture and the victim passed out. Suspect states he then had oral sex on him, after he passed out and finished watching a video and then he ran out of beer. He then went to the Care Bear Tavern, in the 900 black of N. 27th St., drank beer until around closing and returned to the apartment. As he was returning to the apartment he saw the victim sitting on the curb at 25th & State in the nude. He was taking him back to the apartment when the Police and Fire Dept., showed up. Someone put a yellow blanket around the victim and he told the Police that the victim always acted like this when he got drunk and that the victim could not speak English, because the victim was not speaking English. Police questioned him, subsequently escorted him back to the apartment, at which time he convinced the Police it was his homosexual lover, the Police left, and later on he subsequently strangled the victim, had oral and anal sex with the victim

after death, took numerous photos of the victim, dismembered him and kept his head. He put the bones and the flesh of the victims in the acid barrel. This victim was subsequently identified through photos and dental charts as *SINTHASOMPHONE Konerak*, Asian male, 12–02–76, [illegible] and he had been reported missing on 05–26–91.

13. Black male, 22 yoa, 5'8", 140 pds, medium build, dark complexion, having a high top fade to the left side. He states he met this individual on June 30th, after the Gay Pride Parade, at the Chicago Bus Station. He states he offered him money for sex, posing, and to view videos. This individual accompanied him back to Milwaukee on the Grayhound [sic] Bus and then took a cab to his apartment, namely a City Vet Cab. He states he then gave him the drinking potion and they were nude and playing with each other. He states this victim fell asleep, so he strangled him, possibly with a strap, and did not have sex with him. He then took photos, dismembered him, and kept his head in the freezer and the body in the blue 57 gallon barrel which he had purchased a short while before this. The victim was identified by the suspect, through a photo from Chicago. He was also identified by friends from Chicago. This individual has been identified as *Turner Matt*, black male, 07–03–70, a/k/a *Donal MONTRELL*. DAHMER states that he disposed of this individual's flesh in the trash.

14. Puerto Rican male, part Jewish, 23–24, 5'10, 140 pds, slim build, light complexion, short black hair, thin mustache. He states he met this individual around July 6th, at Carol's in Chicago (gay bar). He states they left about 4:00 a.m., returned to Milwaukee with the victim, via the Grayhound [sic], and took a cab to his apartment. He states they spent two days together. He states

they had oral sex the first day and on the second day the victim wanted to leave, so the suspect killed him, by giving him the drink mixture with the sleeping pills and when he fell asleep he strangled him, took photos, dismembered him, put his head in the freezer and his body in the 57 gallon barrel. This subject was identified by the suspect, through pictures, as *WEINBERGER Jerimiah*, Puerto Rican male, 09–26–67, 3404 N. Halstead, Chicago, Il., 929–2478. DAHMER states that he threw the victim's flesh out in the barrel.

15. Black male, 24 yoa, 5'9, 160 pds, muscular build, short hair. He states he met this individual on 27th St., between State & Kilbourn, which would be the 900 black. He states he met this individual about the 2nd week in July. He states that he offered him money to pose for pictures and watch videos with him and have a drink. He states the victim proceeded with him to his apartment, he gave him the drink mixture, they did some body rubbing, the victim fell asleep, and he killed him. He states he had anal sex after death. He then took photos, kept the victim's I.D., and two other personal photos, because he wanted more pictures of him. He dismembered this individual, placed his head in the bottom of the refrigerator in a box, kept his heart in the freezer to eat later and ate his right bicep. He also put his body in the freezer. He states the victim was wearing a white shirt and bluejeans [sic] at the time he met him and that the victim told him he was a Weight Lifter and a Model. The suspect identified the victim to his I.D., which was found in his wallet and he was also identified through dental records and prints, as *LACY Oliver*, black male, 06–23–67, [illegible]. The suspect stated that he disposed of the victim's flesh in the trash, but that he kept his head, body, heart, and took photos, and he also ate the bicep. This victim was reported missing on 07–15–91, last seen on 07–12–91.

16. White male, early 20s, 5'9, 140–150 pds, brownish blond hair, short mustache. He states he met this individual approximately 07–19–91, at around Wisconsin Ave., near the Marquette University. This victim was waiting for a bus, with a "6 pack" in his arms. He states he offered this individual money to pose for pictures and to view videos. He agreed and they took a bus to his apartment. He gave this individual the drink mixture, had oral sex before he fell asleep. When he fell asleep he strangled him with a strap, dismembered him, put his head in the freezer, and placed the body in the 57 gallon barrel. He states he disposed of the flesh in the trash. He identified this victim from a photo in his apartment, as *BRADEHOFT Joseph*, white male, 01–24–66, [illegible].

17. White male, 18–19, 6'0, 150 pds., light hair. This victim was killed in June, 1978. After further questioning he identified him as wearing a necklace with braces on. He states this individual did not have a shirt, but had jeans and shoes. He states he met him hitchhiking on Cleveland Massing (phonetic) Rd., in Ohio, picked him up, took him to his home to drink beer. Once they got there they were drinking beer in his bedroom when the victim wanted to leave. He states he hit him in the head with a barbell and then strangled him with the barbell. He states he did not have sex with the victim. He states he then put him under the crawl space under the house. He subsequently dismembered him, put him in three garbage bags. Two weeks later he broke up the bones and threw them in the woods behind his house. He disposed of the knife he used to dismember him and the victim's necklace in the river. The victim was identified by the suspect, through a photo, and by the suspect recalling his last name, that being *Hicks Steve M*, white male, 06–22–59, (illegible). He stated he

recalls the name HICKS, because he states "you don't forget your first one."

DAHMER states he gave the drinking potion to most of his victims, therefore being easier to control them and he could kill them without having them fight with them. He stated the reason he killed them, because there was excitement and gratification in it and he wanted to keep the victims.

Further investigation pending.

Report dictated by: *Detective Dennis MURPHY*

M: hvs 08–02–91.'